Chino

THE ASIAN AMERICAN EXPERIENCE

Series Editors
Eiichiro Azuma
Jigna Desai
Martin F. Manalansan IV
Lisa Sun-Hee Park
David K. Yoo

Roger Daniels, Founding Series Editor

A list of books in the series appears at the end of this book.

Chino

Anti-Chinese Racism in Mexico, 1880–1940

JASON OLIVER CHANG

UNIVERSITY OF ILLINOIS PRESS
Urbana, Chicago, and Springfield

Publication of this book was supported by funding
from the University of Connecticut Humanities
Institute CLAS Book Support Committee.

Library of Congress Control Number: 2016961495
ISBN 978-0-252-04086-3 (hardcover)
ISBN 978-0-252-08234-4 (paperback)
ISBN 978-0-252-09935-9 (e-book)

To
Julie Choffel

Contents

List of Illustrations

Figures

Maps

Tables

Acknowledgments

I remember my mom and dad telling me that to do something great, you must work with other people. If I have done anything well with this book, it is because of all the wonderful help I had along the way. I first acknowledge my friend and Prescott College mentor, Bernardo Aguilar, who facilitated my political awakening in Latin America and my enthrallment with Mexico, which has gripped me ever since.

My research was nurtured by the faculty in the Department of Ethnic Studies, University of California, Berkeley. My mentors Catherine Ceniza Choy and David Montejano taught me how to think about methodology, writing, and making intellectual contributions. Laura Perez, Sau-Ling Wong, Katharya Um, Tom Biolsi, Michael Omi, Jose David Saldívar, Ramon Grosfoguel, Beatriz Manz, Nelson Maldonado-Torres, Jon Gjerde, Margaret Chowning, and Ronald Takaki all challenged me to critically engage with the central problems in the fields of comparative ethnic studies and Mexican history. Thank you to Thomas Swenson, Juan Herrera, and Dalida Maria Benfield for your friendship and scholarship—I'm still learning from you. Cal was also where I met Falguni Sheth; thank you for your insights, friendship, and intellectual sharpness. I thank Chase Smith for his friendship and accompanying me to archives and letting me crash with him in San Diego; he is the best research partner and border-crossing buddy anyone could ask for.

Thank you to the Chinese community of Mexicali, Mexico, for their hospitality and generosity.

Austin, Texas, is a second home to me, and the Institute for Historical Studies (IHS) at the University of Texas at Austin was a nurturing environment for my intellectual development. Julie Hardwick, former IHS director, and Seth W. Garfield, IHS director, welcomed me into their community of scholars, where I met Ellen Wu, Jason McGraw, José Moreno, Ben Flores, Nancy Applebaum, Erica Bsumek, Eiichiro Azuma, and Mitch Aso. Madeline Hsu's mentorship and counsel have been invaluable in and out of Texas. UT's Center for Asian American Studies provided vital space to connect with Eric Tang, Nhi Liu, Snehal Shingavi, Julia Lee, Naomi Paik, Lok Siu, Sharmila Rudrappa, and Sam Vong.

My colleagues at the University of Connecticut, Storrs, especially, were the critical infrastructure for me to conduct new research, write, revise, and rethink everything. To my mentor Cathy J. Schlund-Vials, director of the Asian and Asian American Studies Institute (AAASI), who has always given me sage advice and encouragement, thank you for your support, friendship, and all the hilariousness. I thank other AAASI faculty, Margo Machida, Fred Lee, Victor Zatsepin, and Peter Zarrow, for their generosity and friendship. Institute staff members Fe de los Santos and Maxine Smestad-Haines helped keep me afloat innumerable times. I am deeply indebted to the institute's sponsorship of a manuscript review with Jeff Leser, who pushed me to make important changes at an early stage. Thank you, Mark Overmyer-Velasquez, director of El Instituto: Institute of Latina/o, Caribbean, and Latin American Studies, for the constant support, encouragement, and all the marathon playdates to make sure we raise our niños well; and, also at El Instituto, thank you, Mark Healey, Melina Pappademos, Guillermo Izzary, Blanca Silvestre, and Anne Gebelein. When I joined UConn, I had no idea how lucky I was, surrounded with such generous, brilliant, and supportive colleagues: Sylvia Schaffer, Brendan Kane, Alexis Dudden, Nina Dayton, Nancy Shoemaker, Fiona Vernal, Frank Castigglio, Chris Clark, Shirley Roe, Chris Vials, Elizabeth Mahan, and Ed Canedo, who kept me on my feet, read drafts of chapters, encouraged me, and accompanied me through ups and downs. I thank Anne Eller for her friendship and brilliance. A key companion in life and the development of this manuscript was Lucho van Ischott, whose friendship and careful reading of early drafts kept me grounded and helped me understand my own thoughts.

I made invaluable progress on this book during my two visits to the University of Washington at Seattle by invitation from the bighearted Tony Lucero under the Mellon-Sawyer seminar B/Ordering Violence: Boundaries, Indigeneity, and Gender in the Americas. The workshop on chapter 2 and the disarticulating-mestizaje seminar allowed me to work with and benefit from

Maria Elena Garcia, Simon Trujillo, Ileana Rodriguez-Silva, R. Allen Baros, and Rachel Albarran, as well as Ileana Rodriguez, Alicia Arrizón, and Kathy Lopez.

I feel immense gratitude for other friends and colleagues that helped me along the way through reading drafts of chapters, workshopping writing in development, presenting together at conferences, hosting me to deliver a lecture, and just being all-around great friends: Mohan Ambikaipaker, José Angel Hernández, Aimee Bahng, Lisa Lowe, Erika Lee, Lisa Yun, Ana Maria Candela, Robert Ku, Min Song, Joseph Jeon, Fredy Gonzalez, Aja Martinez, Robert Chao Romero, Grace Peña Delgado, Moon-Ho Jung, Martin Manalansan, Rudy Guevarra, Elliott Young, Evelyn Hu-DeHart, Zelideth Rivas, Camilla Fojas, Ana Paulina Lee, John Cheng, Shinpei Takeda, Julia María Schiavone Camacho, Roberto Tejada, and Tanya Hernandez. Thanks to Franklin Odo, Konrad Ng, and Lawrence Minh-Bui, among others, at the Smithsonian Institution for the stimulating environment to think through Asian and Latino intersections. I specially thank the AAASI junior-faculty retreat in 2015 for the chance to work with Natasha Sharma, Tina Chen, Kevin Escudero, Jan Padios, Julian Lim, and Melissa Borja, who helped sharpen my writing.

The Asia and Pacific section, as well as the Ethnicity, Race, and Indigenous Peoples sections, of the Latin American Studies Association also proved to be important spaces for my intellectual development, thanks to the generosity of Christina Sue, Monica Moreno Figueroa, Edward Telley, Emiko Saldivar, Monica DeHart, Kathy Lopez, and Junyong Véronica Kim.

Research in more than a dozen locations means that I have relied upon the expertise and patience of many librarians and archivists. First and foremost, I thank Tracey Goode, a consummate professional, for help in investigating Mexico City archives. I also benefited from the generosity and patience of Christine Hernandez at Tulane's Howard-Tilton Library. Thank you to the library staffs of the Huntington Library, University of California, Berkeley; Benson Library, University of Texas at Austin; and Babbidge Library, University of Connecticut; and the archivists at several National Archives and Records Administration offices. In particular, I owe enormous gratitude to Katharine Johnson of the University of Connecticut's Mapping and Geographic Information Center for working with me to produce this book's beautiful maps.

I also worked with several editorial voices that strengthened and elevated my writing. Thank you to the six anonymous reviewers, who helped shape and sharpen the book; Dawn Duarte at the University of Illinois Press has been an excellent shepherd and a key source of support; and Michael Needham of Humanities First, who did skillful, detailed, and insightful copyediting of the manuscript. Also thank you to my undergraduate students who gave important feedback.

Several institutions financially supported the research and writing of this book: the UC Center for Race and Gender, Chiang Ching-Kuo Foundation, Huntington Library, and University of Connecticut's Fund for Innovation in Research Endeavors; publication is supported by the University of Connecticut Humanities Institute CLAS Book Support Committee.

Thanks to Barbara, Harriett, and Ken for letting me take over your kitchen tables to write while visiting.

I thank my parents, LeRoy and Elise, for their tireless cheerleading and support and who gave me the values of compassion and respect that I returned to throughout the research and writing. Thank you to my sister, Jennifer.

Julie Choffel, I can never thank you enough for your love and support. At times the work on this book took over both of our lives, but you were always the reason for pushing on and moving forward. Our family life with Cora, Omi, and Leo has given the work immense value for me.

Any omissions and oversights are completely my own, and I hope those whom I have not mentioned see their influence on the following pages.

Maps were redrawn from the following sources:

Data and Maps for ArcGIS. ESRI. Redlands, CA: DeLorme, 2014.

Great Britain. Naval Intelligence Division. *A Handbook of Mexico*. London: H. M. Stationery Office, 1920. Perry-Castañeda Library Map Collection, University of Texas at Austin. http://www.lib.utexas.edu/maps/historical/mexico_handbook_1919.html.

Instituto Nacional de Estadística y Geografía (INEGI). "Shapefiles from the 2015 Population Survey." Cartografía Geoestadística Urbana y Rural Aman-zanada. Cierre de la Encuesta Intercensal, 2015. 24 March 2016. https://blog.diegovalle.net/2016/01/encuesta-intercensal-2015-shapefiles.html.

Villegas, Daniel Cosío. *Historia Moderna de Mexico*. Mexico City: Editorial Hermes, 1965.

Chino

Introduction

Finding Mexico's Chinese, Encountering the Mestizo State

In 2009 I visited the regional museum run by the Centro de Estudios Culturales de la Universidad Autonoma de Baja California, in Mexicali, Baja California, Mexico, to see an exhibit that featured representations of the state's ethnic diversity. The curated assemblage of material culture, presented with textual explanations, invited visitors to interpret Baja California's past. Surprising, representations of individuals of Chinese origin were the most prominent and detailed of any ethnic group. Visitors first encountered Chinese people through a panel with six photographs, a map backdrop, and a showcase of objects from Chinese immigrants (figure 1). The photographs' labels indicated that the images depicted Chinese workers, a building used by a Chinese association, a Chinese boat, a Chinese cotton farmer, a Chinese family, and a family with a Chinese father and a Mexican mother. The map illustrated the various migration routes that people of Chinese origin took on their way to Mexicali, showing routes via Canada and the United States and throughout Mexico. The map also served as a narrative device to illustrate how Mexico's Chinese population has been consolidated in Mexicali, a process that took place in the 1920s and 1930s. The showcase of objects included iconic symbols of material Chinese culture, including a fan, a plate with decorative embellishments, and an abacus.

The second element of the exhibit was a life-size model of a Chinese worker picking cotton in an empty, open cotton field (figure 2). A brief text explained how British, Japanese, and German steamships brought Chinese immigrants

FIGURE 1. Photographs and objects from Chinese immigrants. Chinese exhibit, Regional Museum of the State of Baja California, Mexicali. Photo by the author.

FIGURE 2. A life-size photograph of a Chinese worker picking cotton. Photo by the author.

to Latin America to replace enslaved African workers and told the reader that Chinese immigrant networks allowed them to expand their work on farms and ranches by sending for their countrymen. The text also stated that between 1923 and 1930 the Chinese began to diversify their businesses in downtown Mexicali, opening hotels, laundries, small workshops, bars, and restaurants. Finally, the text explained the prejudice of anti-Chinese campaigns through worker discontent during the Great Depression and that racism decreased when the majority of Chinese immigrants chose to voluntarily cross the border to the United States.

The third element was a showcase with two opium pipes and a scale next to a picture of a Chinese man, who, we are told, is smoking opium (figure 3). This montage was supplemented with an original document from 1915 describing the regulations for importing, purifying, selling, and taxing opium in Mexicali.

FIGURE 3. Opium paraphernalia and information. Photo by the author.

The panel does little to prevent the viewer from drawing strong associations between the Chinese people and drug addiction and trafficking. No background or context was provided to explain how the British forced opium into Chinese markets in the middle of the nineteenth century or how Mexican and American people aided the trafficking of opium into the United States, where white consumer demand increased the value of such contraband. Nothing in the display told the museum visitor that the governor of Baja California in 1912 legalized opium in order to bolster tax revenues, build roads, open new schools, and pay his soldiers.

The fourth element of the exhibit was a mock grocery store (figure 4). It was set into what appears to have been a small closet. Foreshortened images and floor-to-ceiling enlargements of photographs of an actual store provide

FIGURE 4. A mock Chinese-owned grocery store. Photo by the author.

the impression that the doorway is a real entrance that opens into a large store stocked with merchandise. The doorway was surrounded by photographs labeled as street scenes in Mexicali and by signage denoting a Chinese-owned store. Again, no explanation is provided. This composition showed casual relations between Chinese proprietors and Mexican customers.

With these four elements taken together, the exhibit hides more than it reveals, and it conforms to dominant stereotypes of Mexicali's Chinese people as drug addicts or traffickers or self-interested petit bourgeois proprietors and who are disinterested in settling or—more explicitly—resistant to becoming Mexican. This image invokes the stereotype, familiar in the United States, of Asians being a "perpetual foreigner" to the national community.[1] The generalization achieved by the text removes the agency of Chinese immigrants as both migrants and businesspeople, masking the influence that Mexican colonization policies and the U.S. and Chinese exclusion acts had on shaping patterns of migration. The text's characterization of foreign-owned steamships as the primary driver of Chinese migration to Mexico made immigrants appear to be the negative side effect of foreign-led industrialization. The characterization of the transformation of Chinese businesses from agriculture to urban service industries as merely "diversification" hid the ways that Mexican people, through formal segregation, prohibitions, popular violence, and boycotts, shaped the types of business opportunities that were available to Chinese people.

The contrast of Chinese absence and marginalization in Mexican historiography with the Chinese people's prominence in the exhibit illustrated the importance of racial narratives in Mexican national culture and the symbolic instability of a nationalism that centered *mestizos* (persons of mixed-race character with Indian and European heritage). The significance of the Chinese portion was intertwined with the overall composite of the exhibit. The freestanding displays in the center of the exhibition room were devoted to a national racial ideology of *mestizaje*, or race mixing, that idealized the combination of indigenous peoples with Spanish settlers as a distinctive national mestizo race. Mexican nationality is a complex and shifting identity, but since the 1910 revolution, it has been structured by nationalist ideologies of Indian incorporation, racial improvement, and mestizaje. The museum's inclusion of the Chinese people related them to mestizo ideology by defining their difference. The depictions of Chinese people crafted a racial narrative of alterity and, thus, helped defined what it meant to be Mexican in Baja California.

In particular, the narrative that the Chinese community dissolved voluntarily was an important falsification that supported a popular mythology of the peninsula's integration with the revolutionary state. The exhibit's representation of the event known as El Asalto a las Tierras (Raid on the Land) symbolized the single most-important feature of state's political and symbolic integration with the rest of the nation. The exhibit's text explained that Chinese people came to Mexicali from many different places to escape the devastation of the economy during the 1910 revolution and 1930s' Great Depression. The text explained that the Mexican people from other states experienced Baja California as "foreigners" because it had not yet undergone the process of Mexicanization and was still under the control of unnamed foreigners. It then described El Asalto as a peasant uprising against American landowners, which forced the federal government to enact agrarian reforms. The exhibit symbolically referred to the fact that the *ejidos* (tracts of government-owned land with collective rights) in the Mexicali valley are all named after the other states of the republic to connote a thorough Mexicanization of the region. This exhibit presents a convenient narrative of the political and economic consolidation of the revolutionary state's power without any reference to the ways that Baja California agrarian discontent, mobilized by government officials and anti-Chinese organizations, was directed at Chinese farmers. This altered narrative appropriated the political mobilizations of popular anti-Chinese politics to signify for museum visitors national camaraderie and patriotic agrarianism. The museum's story about the Chinese people explained the good intentions of the government and the natural collectivity of Mexican society.

The exhibit created a racialized profile of the Chinese people. The visual composition combined with the impersonal characterization of larger economic forces restricts the viewer's attention to a crafted nationalist narrative. The racialized narratives of the Chinese people masked the exercise of state power and the authoritarian methods of mass political domination. By relating Mexican revolutionary nationalism to the undoing of Mexicali's Chinese community, the museum simultaneously asked and answered the question, Who are we? Our understanding of the Chinese people in Mexico has yet to confront the revolutionary government's creation of a racial state—a hobbling and incomplete bureaucracy that, nevertheless, shaped the destinies of Chinese Mexican people as well as those of millions of others who became its mestizo citizen-subjects.

Chinese Racial Form and Maintenance of the Mexican State

Late nineteenth- and early twentieth-century Chinese migrants in Mexico made substantial contributions to Mexican society. Yet, their importance exceeds the labor they provided, the businesses they established, the families

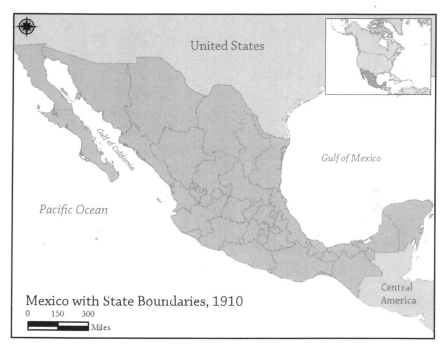

United States

Gulf of California

Gulf of Mexico

Pacific Ocean

Central America

Mexico with State Boundaries, 1910

0   150   300

Miles

MAP 1. Mexico with state boundaries, 1910

they formed, and the cultural practices they performed. To understand the significance of the Chinese in Mexico, *Chino: Anti-Chinese Racism in Mexico, 1880–1940* uses an Asian Americanist lens to examine the discursive and ideological construction of the Chinese racial figure in Mexican culture and politics. From 1880 to 1940, the figure of the Chinese people underwent significant changes, reflecting the increasingly integral role that race played in governmental reconstruction after the 1910 revolution. As the country burst into revolt in 1910, anti-Chinese politics became intertwined with the articulation of a state-sponsored brand of racial nationalism centered on an abstract racial figure, the mestizo. The racial transformation of the Chinese people identifies mechanisms of oppression upon Chinese individuals and reveals how such practices contributed to the revolutionary state's efforts to dominate the broader social life of the country. This book is the first to examine the intimate bonds between Mexican anti-Chinese politics, or *antichinismo*, and the romantic nationalist ideology of Indian redemption and modernization, *indigenismo*.

In the last decade of the nineteenth century, diasporic Chinese men from different social classes began migrating in the thousands each year to Mexico.

Responding to the national colonization policies of the Porfirio Díaz government, every month hundreds of poor workers disembarked at Mexico's Pacific and Caribbean ports as contracted laborers to work on plantations, railroads, and mining operations, continuing the traffic in Chinese coolie labor. Officials hoped that the Chinese men would leave the country when the work was completed. The Mexican ruling class referred to these coolies as *motores de sangre* (engines of blood, which draft animals were called), which reflected their exploitation as subhuman, disposable labor. Many arrived in Mexico voluntarily; however, even after the turn of the century when the abusive coolie trade system was closed, Mexico remained a destination for coerced and destitute Chinese men because of the national colonization policy and intentionally gray legal conditions. The perception that Chinese motores de sangre were necessary to Mexican modernization reflected a racialized image of the Chinese as a nonsettler population. It also reflected the *criollo* (Mexican-born Spaniards) ideology that stated that the majority Indian populations were unreliable agents of industrial capitalism, or worse, the key obstacle to national modernity, both ideas the legacy of centuries of Spanish colonial rule. However, by the turn of the century, *antichinistas* (those who espoused antichinismo) began to advocate for Chinese expulsion in order to realize self-colonization, a plan to directly incorporate peasants and other indigenous republics into the central government's modernization policies. In this period, anti-Chinese attitudes favored Indians as acceptable agents of capitalism, if not potentially patriotic citizens. This association would continue to develop and evolve for the next three decades.

In 1910 a widespread rebellion led to the collapse of the Porfirian government and the reconstruction of a new revolutionary state. In November 1916, during that war, rebel leader Francisco "Pancho" Villa ordered his troops to kill sixty apprehended Chinese residents of Parral, Chihuahua, by throwing them down a mineshaft to their deaths.[2] Later that day, six other Chinese residents were executed in city streets.[3] Other foreigners suffered death by the hands of Villa's soldiers at Parral that day; however, no other ethnic group in early-twentieth-century Mexico received the same level of vicious and systematic violence. During the revolution, the racialized figure of the Chinese people shifted from motores de sangre to corpses, or killable subjects of discontent. During the revolution, Villa regularly ordered his troops to kill any Chinese person encountered across northern Mexico. Yet, Villa was not alone in his predilection for killing Chinese residents. Revolutionaries killed nearly a thousand civilian Chinese immigrants in the first decade of fighting, more than seven hundred in the first two years alone. Massacres, assassinations, and routine looting and harassment of Chinese people were distinctive, yet overlooked, features of this well-known revolution.

Revolutionary cries for peasants to close ranks as mestizos and support insurgency against the Díaz government were commonly heard together with "Down with the Chinese!" Women, farmers, soldiers, and politicians big and small gave life to these associations through their writings, speech, and deeds. Throughout this period, anti-Chinese vitriol was part and parcel with the mestizo rapture of revolutionary leaders. The mestizo collective imagined by leaders was underwritten by the revolutionary call to attend to the good of the Indian. At the outset of the revolution, these calls were greeted with skepticism: "When politicians call for the 'the social good' these are the signs of power."[4] By the 1920s a growing group of state legislators began to push mestizo racial nationalism through an anti-Chinese polemic. Plagued by rivalry, economic contraction, weak governance, and reluctant reforms, the revolutionary state struggled to govern and extinguish challenges to its professed sovereignty. Senators, congressmen, and presidents became architects of a national anti-Chinese organization called Liga Mexicana Antichina (Mexican anti-Chinese league). Their slogan, "United we will eliminate the Chinese from Mexico," was used to advocate for a wide spectrum of policy reforms that used Chinese expulsion to facilitate the articulation of a national mestizo race and state benevolence.[5]

The interwoven racial formations of Chinese immigrants with that of indigenous and other de-Indianized peasants in Mexican culture reveal how ideas about the Chinese population shaped notions of a racialized mestizo public good and helped define what ethical, or truly revolutionary, governance looked like. Mexico's Chinese people continued to experience violence, although their image changed from killable subjects to pernicious defilers. As a profane race, they were subjected to forced expropriations, discriminatory taxes, segregation, antimiscegenation laws, mobs, riots, and state-led deportations, as well as popular expulsions, all for the purported good of women, children, and Indians. The gendered and sexualized image of the Chinese race from the 1920s to 1940 shaped local politics, infiltrated state legislatures, inspired numerous debates in the federal congress, and continuously occupied the concern of the most successful political party in modern Mexican history, the Partido Nacional Revolucionario (National Revolutionary Party) (PNR) formed in 1929. The PNR, later the Partido Revolucionario Institucional (Revolutionary Institutional Party) (PRI) in 1946, held power until 2000.

The ideology of antichinismo both racialized the Chinese people and imagined new relationships among Mexican people. Other studies of Mexico's anti-Chinese politics have established a solid foundation of research on the statutory content of discriminatory legislation and key moments of popular discontent. The current volume expands upon these works through an Asian Americanist critique that locates the inquiry in the larger context of the reconstruction of the revolutionary government with a theoretical framework of racial states. By following expressions of antichinismo from the streets to the meeting halls to legislatures and national-party convention floors, this book reveals the ways that anti-Chinese publics contributed to rewriting the relationship between the government and the governed.

While violence was a common experience for the Chinese people in Mexico, they also found many non-Chinese allies, friends, business partners, and spouses. Not all Mexican people engaged in violent expressions of antichinismo; for many, the hate was merely abstract. It was common to decry the health standards of the Chinese and then buy groceries from them. Alternatively, government officials could publically condemn Chinese greed while protecting Chinese businesses through policy. Chinese Mexican people made their lives within the space of these contradictions. Hidden in the structure of these contradictions are the everyday means by which Mexican actors used anti-Chinese politics to alter the meaning of revolutionary rule. The influence of antichinismo on Mexican society has been hidden in plain sight, and the absence of its recognition points to a pervasive ethos of racial innocence in Mexican society.

In Mexico, Chinese populations—in fact, all Asians—are known as *los chinos*. This term is commonly heard across Latin America in reference to all Asians as a racial category carried over from the colonial era. Like all racial labels, it hides more than it reveals. In modern Mexico, the Chinese people have played an important but overlooked role in the reconstruction of the revolutionary state's racial governance. Over the course of sixty years, from 1880 to 1940, thinking of the Chinese as disposable laborers, killable subjects, and pernicious defilers has helped Mexico change the meaning of race and revolution. Changes in the Chinese racial form, directed at tens of thousands of Chinese people, facilitated broader racial constructions of millions of Mexican Indian people and peasants from objects of extermination to subjects of improvement. The core claim I make here is that the tropological changes to the Chinese racial form actually indicate changes in the social structural mechanisms by which those discursive forms acquired material significance. In other words, the path of antichinismo indicates the degree to which revolutionary governance depended upon the social and political effects of a racial state. These changes involved more than words and thoughts; they impacted the manner that such ideas penetrated politics and institutions. By examining the transformation of the Chinese racial form, this book builds an appreciation for how racialized Chinese-ness changed and became instrumental to various racial projects, from winning the revolutionary war to building state power to clenching national hegemony in order to dominate and rule the majority nonwhite population with varying degrees of indigenous association. The Chinese people were made to suffer not only because they were vulnerable but also because anti-Chinese publics created indispensable political resources for nation building and statecraft.

Save for a handful of scholars, generations of historians have either ignored the Chinese presence in Mexico or characterized their troubling treatment as an unfortunate side effect of revolutionary passions. Disavowing the Chinese past has helped sustain convenient nationalist narratives of collective action and state benevolence. This book argues that centering the Chinese people in Mexican history is not simply a forgotten chapter on a marginalized ethnic group. It opens up a larger story about how antichinismo was deeply embedded within both the revolutionary national state and a state-sponsored mestizo identity and sheds light on the history and practice of racial domination in Mexico.

Before a discussion of the historiographical and theoretical interventions made in this book, some historical context may be useful. Chinese migrants were the second-largest immigrant group in revolutionary Mexico, totaling more than twenty thousand residents in the 1930s. Official numbers are unreliable because many Chinese people migrated through clandestine channels, and some regularly hid from authorities during the violent era of reconstruction. The precarious position of the Chinese population in Mexico was a part of their mode of integration. The highest concentrations of Chinese people in Mexico were in regions of hostile indigenous resistance to national incorporation, where the Chinese people made important contributions to the construction of railroads and irrigation infrastructure as well as fomenting domestic and international commerce. Mexico became an important destination for Chinese migrants in the 1880s because of immigration restrictions in the United States and land reforms in Mexico. In 1882 the United States passed the Chinese Exclusion Act, barring Chinese immigration for ten years. This act made the Chinese people, and eventually all Asian people, racially ineligible for naturalization in the United States. While the gates of immigration were closing in the United States, they were being thrown open in Mexico as the government began aggressive new colonization policies. In 1883 President Díaz issued an executive decree reforming national colonization policy. This

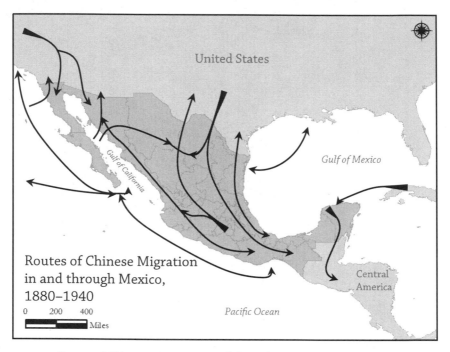

MAP 2. Routes of Chinese migration in and through Mexico, 1880–1940

transformation of land policy initiated rapid economic change. U.S. restriction combined with Mexican colonization laws caused individual streams of several hundred Chinese immigrants, swelling to thousands each year after 1882 (map 2).

The rapid transformation of Mexican society during the Díaz administration sowed the seeds for widespread revolt in 1910. His policies fostered capitalist intensification and exacerbated inequalities that led to riots when famines struck the countryside in 1907. Meanwhile, a new class of aspirational industrialists became frustrated by Díaz's thirty-year reign and began to contest his power. The 1910 revolt spawned numerous factions and counterfactions, killing more than a million Mexican people. The Chinese immigrants were noncombatants but became enveloped in the revolution. In the most infamous event of anti-Chinese violence in the hemisphere, 303 Chinese people were massacred in Torreón, Coahuila, in 1911 as rebels sacked an important federalist position. Despite the racialized violence, the number of Chinese immigrants actually grew during the 1920s. The republic that Díaz once governed had collapsed, but Chinese immigrants continued to expand agricultural enterprises and increase retail and grocery establishments amid increased urbanization and expanded irrigation into arid hinterlands.

National census figures from 1895 to 1940 show important regions of Chinese population growth (in the Pacific northwest, the Texas-Caribbean corridor, and the Yucatán peninsula) as well as population drops due to mass removal (in the northern Pacific coast) (table 1). Simultaneously, Mexicans were fleeing to the United States in droves to escape the violence and economic depression. In 1931 and 1932 the states of Sonora and Sinaloa expelled thousands of Chinese people and their Mexican families. In 1936 thousands of Chinese farmers were evicted from land in Baja California. These expulsions also coincided with massive repatriations of Mexican people back to Mexico. Tracing the shifting demography of the Chinese population in Mexico attests to their social presence but also reflects the power of the state to give racial

TABLE 1. Mexican census by state for Chinese nationals, 1895–1940

State	1895	1900	1910	1921	1930	1940
Aguascalientes	8	12	21	14	47	14
Baja California North	71	138	851	2,806	2,982	738
Baja California South	—	50	—	165	206	50
Campeche	3	5	70	61	113	36
Chiapas	13	16	478	645	1,095	347
Chihuahua	63	330	1,325	533	1,127	29
Coahuila	59	202	759	523	765	318
Colima	—	5	80	32	38	726
Distrito Federal	43	117	1,482	607	886	104
Durango	23	148	242	46	229	853
Guanajuato	2	11	102	21	37	16
Guerrero	—	3	27	3	10	13
Hidalgo	—	—	38	50	70	59
Jalisco	—	20	69	53	151	107
Mexico	3	15	57	24	57	17
Michoacan	1	4	26	5	12	18
Morelos	—	5	18	3	3	5
Nayarit (Tepic)	1	29	173	152	170	86
Nuevo Laredo	34	90	221	68	167	110
Oaxaca	13	81	259	158	158	54
Puebla	1	11	29	17	44	29
Querétaro	—	1	5	1	2	1
Quintana Roo	—	—	3	3	10	8
San Luis Potosi	12	32	109	111	291	136
Sinaloa	182	234	663	1,040	2,123	283
Sonora	310	859	4,449	3,639	3,571	155
Tamaulipas	8	38	211	2,005	2,117	951
Tlaxcala	—	—	—	—	—	—
Tobasco	4	2	35	48	64	17
Veracruz	11	116	433	847	2,314	707
Yucatan	47	153	875	773	972	485
Zacatecas	4	19	41	19	142	89
Totals	916	2,746	13,151	14,472	19,973	6,561

Source: Dambourges, *Anti-Chinese Campaigns.*

ideology a spatial and lived reality. These issues raise a set of questions about the roles of racism, violence, and state power in the practice of mestizo nationalism. To explore these questions, we must know more about the relationship between Indians and the Mexican state.

The biggest obstacle to the security of the Mexican state has predominantly been the consent or subjugation of the majority peasant and indigenous inhabitants, Mexico's so-called Indian problem. The issue of immigration in Mexico has been largely and intimately tied to the colonial imperative to settle indigenous land and expand industrial capitalism. Mexican immigration policy in the nineteenth century was shaped by the criollo belief that Mexican natural resources had the potential to make the country wealthy but that the domestic and native populations were insufficient in number and "racial quality" to realize that wealth.[6] Since national independence from Spain in 1821, criollo administrators thought immigration was the only solution to increase the overall population and improve (basically, to whiteness, to not be brown) the racial attributes of the workforce, a process called *blanqueamiento*, or whitening.[7] Historian José Angel Hernández contends that Mexican colonization policy never explicitly gave racial preference to white foreigners and emphasizes the recruitment of Mexicans immigrants in the United States to return home to participate in national colonization. However, the history of measures to regulate the Chinese population, explored in the following chapters, demonstrates that even raceless statutes were executed with explicit racial preferences.[8] The government's inability to court large numbers of Europeans led key officials reluctantly to a policy to import nonsettler laborers (mostly Chinese but also some black African people). Simultaneously, some government officials reevaluated the peasant population, reversing long-held criollo opinions that Indians were unruly, incapable, or uninterested in modernization. Porfirian national-colonization policies became the inexorable context that encompassed the coupled racialization of Chinese and Indian populations in mestizo nationalism. An analysis of antichinismo without an examination of the peasant and indigenous populations misses a significant effect of antichinismo—the racial transformation of Indians into mestizos in one generation.

Mestizo national identity remains an important part of understanding twentieth-century Mexican history because this identity is a contested field that people struggle with to define their relationship to each other and the revolutionary national state. Although the significance and impact of the 1910 revolution remain vibrant sources of debate, one of the most profound changes it inaugurated was a revision to the social contract between the revolutionary government and the citizens. When revolutionary leaders rewrote the republic's constitution in 1917, they guaranteed the social rights of the indigenous peasant majority of the country. This new kind of legal document based the revolutionary state's sovereignty upon an invented mandate to care for the interests of its people—a race of people that the state defined as mestizo.[9] Antichinismo was one way that Mexican people responded to the collapse of the Porfirian state and the struggle to build a new political culture. By the 1930s antichinismo provided useful political and cultural resources for every strata of the country for the necessities of constructing a discourse of the common good and the legitimacy of the revolutionary state.

Antichinismo could not have had power in the Porfiriato (or Díaz's reign) to modify the category *mestizo* in the same way it did in the postrevolutionary era. The invention of the public good through the 1917 constitutional mandate changed the political meaning of *Mexicanidad* (the core quality of this Mexican nationality). Before the revolution, the political circle drawn around legitimate citizens was so exclusive that anti-Chinese politics would not have justified attention. Before the revolution, local and regional complaints about the Chinese population rarely led to meaningful government attention. Local complaints or protests against the Chinese people during the Porfiriato were politically discounted in light of the perceived benefits derived from their exploitation in colonization projects. As chapter 2 illustrates, even after a presidential commission to study the influence of the Chinese people and the outbreak of plague, which was erroneously attributed to the Chinese people, the government remained committed to a strategic use of Chinese labor and capital in areas of Indian rebellion.

Anti-Indian thought permeated Mexican ideologies of nation and modernity, but such ideas were not destroyed by the revolution. These ideas were not simply carried over into the new regime, though. The political exigencies of a decade of civil war and the pursuit of consent to rule by the revolution's victors redefined populist politics. From the late nineteenth century to the early twentieth century, overtly anti-Indian discourse shifted from outright extermination to a pedantic call to bring the indigenous masses into a process of institutionalization designed to discipline and educate them for the tasks of modernity. It was in this transformation that antichinismo began to modify Mexican nationality as racially mestizo. As scholar Claudio Lomnitz-Adler has argued, the process of nation building in revolutionary Mexico is not about forging fraternal bonds; it is about the reworking of rule and consent.[10] Stated more bluntly, hating the Chinese people was good for everyone except the Chinese people.

Before and after the revolution, social, cultural, and political conditions made it impossible to draw fast lines between a collective national identity and a coherent sense of the public good. The mosaic of distinctive indigenous republics was a key feature of the structural complexity of Mexican society. Variation and regionalism reigned, as evidenced by the gradations of political and economic citizenship, interethnic conflict, and regional rivalries. As scholar Nicole Guidotti-Hernández contends, by the end of the nineteenth century a considerable number of Mexican peasants ceased to view themselves as Indians even though they grew up in indigenous communities. This seeming contradiction was a predictable social and political response to the previous century's hostilities and the state's pursuit of national modernity.[11] However, distancing indigeneity did not necessarily bring people closer to the state. I argue that antichinismo helped accomplish another operation: antichinismo emerged as a salient and effective substitute for political discourses of public welfare—as a popular means both to persuade public officials and to signify the generosity of the revolutionary state's expansion of industrial capitalism. Expressions of antichinismo were contingent upon its utility for political actors situated in particular contexts. These same contingencies also marked the decline of antichinismo during the intensification of world war at the end of the 1930s. President Abelardo Rodríguez said in a speech to the nation about World War II, "If the war has been the cause that unites and makes a single unit of the Mexican people, the war is welcome."[12] A devout antichinista and one-time governor of Baja California and president of the republic, Rodríguez saw the coming war as a useful substitute for racial nationalism to propel collective action and consent to the continued expansion of the capitalist state. By the 1940s World War II had created an alternative ideology of racial nationalism to organize the country's capitalist industrialization. As a result, the significance of antichinismo declined, but its legacy has endured.

This book demonstrates the ways that antichinistas became organized and reached the federal legislature and the office of the president with an influential racial polemic. Throughout the early twentieth century, anti-Chinese organizations and antichinista policy makers introduced and popularized a cultural notion of the state as a benevolent guardian of a vulnerable peon populace. Protection from the so-called yellow octopus of Chinese racial degeneracy provided an effective political, social, and economic rationale for consent to the perceived security of centrally organized agricultural capitalism in the ejido system. National colonization in the revolutionary era was thus conceived as a multifarious project to modernize the majority peasant and indigenous populations through education, economic discipline, and eugenics to prepare them for citizenship and industrial modes of production.[13] This idea was succinctly captured by one official in the 1920s: "Perhaps the Indian's love of the land will convert them into settlers and later to become a citizen."[14] In a number of cases, antichinismo became instrumental to agrarian reform because it helped convert disinterested and "unruly" Indians into patriotic, disciplined settlers of their own land. In other words, Chinese death, dispossession, and disavowal produced material effects as well as racialized and gendered discourses that Mexican people used as political capital. Antichinismo helped Mexican people navigate the moral and political conditions of revolutionary rule, as diverse rural and urban poor became subjected to a capitalist program of national racial inclusion.

Mestizo nationalism was not inevitable. The government's brand of mestizo identity had to be fought for among other nationalist visions. Antichinismo was an important, but obfuscated, part of the political contest for racial hegemony. It made the intensification and expansion of the state apparatus popular without democratic reforms. The figure of the Chinese population helped sponsor a racial logic of the revolutionary imperative to reform through authoritarian rule. Discussions in the national congress reasoned that in order to save the mestizo nation from Chinese defilers, the state must dominate social life, expel the Chinese people, and dictate a disciplined mestizaje for eugenic benefits. The culmination of Mexican anxieties regarding the Chinese population became a popular polemic platform, organized by middle-class leaders and state-level legislators who defined and interlinked race, sex, and economy as public priorities for the revolutionary state. My approach focuses on racial discourse as well as on the process whereby racialization is connected to the self-preservation strategies of the state. Put a different way, anti-Chinese and pro-mestizo political discourses argued for the necessity of the state by providing reasons for consent and subjection to ruling institutions.

The Case for an Asian Americanist Critique

The central story found in these chapters is the formation and function of anti-Chinese publics in Mexican national culture. Readers may know that the critical enterprise of investigating the role of racialized Asian-ness in U.S. political culture and the making of white supremacy have been at the core of Asian American studies, but they might not be aware of its application to Mexico. This book expands upon the analytical tradition established by such scholars as Alexander Saxton, Roger Daniels, Sucheng Chan, Lisa Lowe, Kandice Chuh,

Kornell Chang, Colleen Lye, and Moon-Ho Jung, that examines the function of anti-Asian racism as a capitalistic logic of racialized governance.[15]

The analysis and interpretation found in these pages rest on the central tenets of an Asian Americanist critique. Yet, it also heeds the pitfalls of the transnational paradigm. The U.S.-based field of Asian American studies emphasizes gendered and racial formation analysis of Asian people as abstracted subjects of difference among other racialized positions in a white-supremacist social order. Attention to Asian racialization in the United States has shown how ideas of racial difference have permeated the national economy and political state. These are key insights because they show why the construction of racial differences are central to the changing conditions of domination as well as shifting modes of reproducing the state. I make the interpretative shift to Mexico with equal parts of caution and skepticism.

Asian Americanists have long speculated about *hemispheric orientalism*, or the coincidence of anti-Asian–immigration legislation in numerous national states in the western hemisphere. Others, like anthropologist Arjun Appadurai, have asserted the importance of tracing the transnational scope of global connections and local articulations of an "oriental ideoscape." Across transnational space, meanings are widely circulated yet differentially signified.[16] Nevertheless, historians Evelyn Hu-DeHart, Erika Lee, and Elliot Young, along with anthropologist Lok Siu, have argued that the western hemisphere is the appropriate geographic scale for Asian American studies because of the ways that Asian diaspora migration routes crisscrossed the Americas.[17] One of the important aspects of the hemispheric framework is that it has opened up a rich field of inquiry that traces complex migration routes and has recovered the forgotten forms of difference that shaped Asian migrants lives in the Americas. This direction in Asian American studies, as seen in the growth of Asian Canadian studies,[18] seeks to do more than simply pointing out that other national cultures *also* despised Asians. The current volume answers Lee's call for contextualized analysis of the production of Asian racial difference in the Americas but differs from her intent to detail the historical transnational circuitry of Asian diasporas.[19] My goal here is to examine the role of anti-Chinese racism in the transformation of racial rule in Mexican society. I distinguish between Orientalism as the culture of imperialism found in Euro-American empires and the Asian racial form developed in a Latin American context as the domesticating racial populism of revolutionary nationalism.

This book approaches hemispheric Asian American history through an investigation of different Asian racial forms and the contests of state power from which they emerged. The Mexican story is an important node in the greater constellation of sites in a hemispheric Asian America because it helps to tell a larger story about the practice of racial domination in majority non-white postcolonial societies. For example, it is widely believed that Mexican anti-Chinese prejudice was borrowed from the United States, but this premise is unstable. First, Mexican actors used elements of a globally circulated anti-Chinese discourse, including sources other than from the United States, but these appropriations were selective, partial, and utilized by competing interests for different utopian visions.[20] Second, to characterize antichinismo as adopted bias does not give the diverse array of Mexican actors the credit they deserve. They made sense of their political world and invented novel negotiations of state power, even as those responses spilled the blood of Chinese immigrants, deported Chinese Mexican families, and cheered state-sponsored eviction of Chinese farming communities. For these reasons I take a different approach than that Hu-DeHart pioneered that emphasizes the way that class antagonism exacerbated xenophobic revolutionary nationalism.[21] Instead, the following chapters attend to the shifting instrumentalities of popular and state-led racist action.

In recognizing fundamental structural and discursive differences between U.S. and Mexican racial formations, my approach emphasizes the relationship between anti-Chinese racial projects and the maintenance of the post-revolutionary state apparatus as a significant historiographical problem in Mexican history. Even though Mexican antichinismo shares some anxieties with the U.S. anti-Chinese movement, the similarities are limited. To argue that Mexicans appropriated U.S. Orientalism dislodges and isolates the discursive production of racial difference in Mexico from the material, cultural, and historical conditions from which it emerged and blurs the definition of Orientalism.

Four key structural features illustrate the limited effect that U.S. anti-Chinese prejudice had on the character of Mexican antichinismo. Even when Mexican politicians explicitly and blatantly appropriated U.S. anti-Chinese discourse, it differed in fundamental ways due to an alternative cultural lexicon of state authority. As I lay out more fully in chapter 1, the primary structural difference between the United States and Mexico is their relationships to indigenous people. Whereas the United States is a dominant white settler majority, Mexico is composed of an Indian majority with a white criollo ruling class. Associated with this difference between the United States and Mexico are other differences in national ideologies and political legitimacy. Unlike in the United States, Mexican national ideology has always been a state project saddled by its colonial origins, wherein sovereign authority depended upon making the nation relevant to the majority Indian population. Moreover, the incomplete architecture of the state apparatus meant that the Mexican state was incapable of the type of racialized discipline and regulation practiced by the United States at the turn of the twentieth century, especially during the chaotic years of the revolution. Mexico's racial projects were not any less influential or harsh, but Indian-state relations were conditioned by a regional exercise of state power. The fourth is that despite the virulence of antichinismo, Mexico neither completely barred the Chinese people from immigration nor erected racial boundaries to naturalization. Bans in Mexico were partial, temporary, and unevenly implemented.

The field of Asian American studies was founded on the critical project of attending to the silenced and disavowed social history of Asian people in the United States. This political project of telling lost stories did not aim only for recognition and validation; it also aimed to understand why racial domination is the foundation of U.S. society. Asian American studies is important to everyone, not just Asian American people, because it critically engages the manner that racialized Asian-ness functioned in relationship to governance of a racially stratified republic. In other words, Asian American studies matters to everybody because it takes seriously the co-constitutive nature of racial formations and multiple points of contact and intersection with other racialized subjectivities. The inter-racial framework in Asian American studies is key to understanding the relationship between the U.S. empire and its domination over a multi-ethnic, multiply raced populace. This intellectual foundation is the reason why an Asian Americanist analysis of Mexico offers new insights.

This book centers on the role of ideological and structural relationships *between* racial groups as the basis of contests over national identity. This inter-racial nexus is a crucial arena by which people in Mexico encountered the terms of the revolution's racial contract. It is necessary, for instance, to interrogate both Villa's orders to kill Chinese as well as his characteristic use of new terminology such as *hermanos de raza* (race brothers) and *nos mestizos* (we mestizos) in his political speeches, interviews, and rallies.[22] The current volume follows this methodological focus for several different classes of Mexican actors from different regions to explore instances when anti-Chinese vitriol becomes diametrically linked with a mestizo rapture and, thus, to observe how antichinismo ended up helping to rework the terms of rule and consent.

An Asian Americanist critique of Mexican history offers a number of innovative interpretations and revisionist narratives. The following chapters demonstrate the utility of antichinismo by showing how actors used this racial discourse to respond to new ideological constructions of the public good. When they campaigned from state to state in the 1920s to build support for a constitutional amendment to bar and expel the Chinese population, antichinistas fostered a popular imaginary of collective identity. By shifting focus from the Chinese Mexican population to the larger political context of national colonization, the multiple sovereignties of the 1910 revolution, and political consolidation during reconstruction, this book discusses the ways that anti-Chinese politics fostered citizenship among ethnic Mexicans and created new rationales for state authority. Anti-Chinese politics enlivened larger debates in the reconstruction of the Mexican state through the intersecting discourses of race, sex, and economy and shaped the racist character of national policies. Orientalist thought was used to popularize programs designed to instruct, discipline, and improve the majority Indian population.

Diverse Mexican actors conjured the discursive figure of the Chinese as animals, corpses, and defilers for different reasons. The idea of degenerate Chinese people applied continual pressure to the Mexican people to define the powers of the revolutionary state and to determine how best to realize the purported potential of the mestizo nation. From the 1916 mayoral campaigns of José Maria Arana in Magdalena de Kino, Sonora, to the 1924 state negotiations of Tamaulipas governor Emilio Portes Gil to rally labor union support to the nation-wide patriotic athletic parades sponsored by the Partido Nacional Revolucionario in 1932, antichinismo connected common people to the state in novel ways. Antichinismo evolved from popular sentiments of revolt to a polemic cry for racial nationalism to a catalyst for programs of authoritarian national unity. To account for this social process, this book employs a mixed methodology to capture important periods of transition and transformation, shifting the focus from social and economic history to cultural and political history.

Theorizing Antichinismo in a Mestizo Racial State

The meaning of the term *mestizo* and what it signifies in Mexican nationalism continues to be debated. However, few studies have examined the ways that mestizo nationalism functions as a category of whiteness, an abstract ideal used to reward loyalty and punish resistance. George Lipsitz and others have enumerated the ways that whiteness is born from the protection of structural advantages to those with lighter skin and European heritage and the denial of those advantages to those with darker skin from elsewhere in the world. In the Mexican context, I ascribe to the definition of whiteness that Aníbal Quijano developed, defining it as an ideological legacy of colonialism, to discuss the ways that Mexican ideals of normativity are structured by Eurocentrism.[23] This theoretical framework accommodates the ways that antichinismo helped Mexican people use mestizo nationalism to negotiate the inherited anti-Indian ideologies preserved in postrevolutionary reconstruction. This book shows how antichinistas used scientific discourses of a Chinese racial threat to organize a state-endorsed ideology of enhanced mestizos in order to align with Eurocentric aspirations. The historical narrative found here shifts the stakes of the interpretation of race in Mexico away from the discursive politics of inclusion and belonging and toward an understanding of the mestizo nation as subjection to state power. Too often, the question of race in Mexico is framed as a problem of acceptance or prejudice. This characterization limits critique of racial politics to the condemnation of discriminatory legislation or the misguided ways of individuals. Mexico is commonly described as a nonracist country, but Christina A. Sue, among others, has clearly identified the ways that the study of race in Mexico must confront a powerful mythology of racelessness. This national myth is based upon three sources of ideology: The belief that mestizos cannot be racist because they are a people of mixed-race ancestry; the belief that Mexican legal codes have abolished race; and the belief that the absence of Jim Crow–type laws prove a lack of racism.[24] An analysis of discursive and ideological formations must always be grounded in historical and institutional context. Tanya Katerí Hernández traces the articulation of what she calls "racial innocence" in Mexican jurisprudence. This racism functions through the application of race-neutral statutes executed by local actors who apply unwritten racist traditions that define their regional authority.[25] In Mexico, as in other Latin American states, federal authority was translated through local racial ideologies.[26] Mexico's racial mythology can, in part, be traced to the Constitution of 1824, which abolished the Spanish racial caste system—although it left intact the criollo belief that Indians did not possess enlightened rationality and thus were exempt from citizenship. This racial paradigm was gradually transformed from "exclusively white" to "whitening" and then, explicitly, to "mestizo" after the 1910 revolution, but it retained a disdain for Indians, black African people, and Chinese people. Sue contends that Mexico's racial mythology is effective because it relies upon discourses of racial mixing that absolve the state and individuals from accusations of racist particularism. The erasure of antichinismo from the Mexican historical imagination, as seen in Mexicali's museums, is necessary to maintaining this form of racial innocence.

In order to analyze the racial dimensions of Mexican discourses of ethical governance, I attend to the methodologies of comparative racial formations and the framework of racial states. The racial state is a set of governing institutions founded upon the creation of a racial hierarchy and the main-tenance of inequalities.[27] The revolutionary Mexican government is a racial state, transformed from a Spanish colony into a sovereign republic and altered through imperial interventions, civil war, and rebellion. The Mexican racial state was dramatically revised from the revolution through the 1917 constitu-tion and postrevolutionary reconstruction of a new state apparatus. This new state drew its political authority from an emergent nationalistic public sphere and social-rights mandate. The term *public sphere*, coined by Jürgen Habermas, Sara Lennox, and Frank Lennox, emerged in political theory as a framework to understand the multifaceted interface among the governing institutions of the state and the demands, concerns, and needs of the governed in demo-cratic societies. The public sphere was thought of as a special field of social engagement and formal political discourse defined by unrestricted access, the elimination of privilege, and a shared cultural logic.[28] This abstraction of an idealized political process is a complementary concept for thinking about the historical influence of antichinismo because it builds an appreciation for the ways that racial ideology aided the development and fulfillment of the terms of governance. Attention to the public-sphere qualities of antichinismo helps to differentiate between expository, or descriptive, content, such as skin color, behavior, or eye shape, and that which interprets the common good through ideas of racial difference. By this measure, the current volume attends to the ways that antichinismo functioned as an unrestrained forum about the use of state authority for government action in the interest of the public good.[29]

Emphasizing the influence of antichinismo on Mexico's postrevolutionary state draws attention to the reconfiguration of the social contract as a racial contract, a concept of U.S. racism that was famously described by Charles W. Mills. I propose that a similar racial dynamic is at work in Mexico.[30] Mills's seminal book articulated the U.S. racial contract under white supremacy as the consent among whites to exclude nonwhites both politically and cultur-ally in the service of legitimized exploitation of nonwhites. In contrast, the racial contract born out of Mexico's revolution evolved in an ad hoc fash-ion to respond to the republic's diverse and unruly indigenous peasantry. Antichinismo can be added to agrarian concessions, union negotiations, and expansion of the educational system as state responses to popular demands to uphold the social rights of the constitution. The contract set the dubious bargain to trade access to land and institutions for membership in the mestizo nation and an abandonment of indigeneity. The bargain, drawn up by military generals and Porfirian bureaucrats who seized control of the state, assumed that legally defined subject-citizens would relinquish indigeneity and take up defense of the revolutionary state as their patrimony and guarantee to constitutionally defined social rights. Unlike the U.S. racial contract as described by Mills, the Mexican racial contract sought to build consent while deepening subjection to state discipline of a nonwhite majority. Mexican anti-Chinese politics helped construct the state's mestizo ideology and induct the previously marginalized peasantry into the state's care and discipline. Although some of the literature on Mexican anti-Indian prejudice argues that racism serves the ideological function of socially excluding and politically diminishing indigeneity, most assessments fail to engage a legal or institutionalized basis for this ideology in favor of a culturalized hegemony.[31] The concept of the racial contract seeks to ground the documentation of this ideology to inquire about how it functions as both a political strategy of the governed and a rationale for state rule. Sociologist Monica Figueroa has described how contingency, not outright racial statutes like Jim Crow segregation in the United States, structures the terms of racial identification under Mexican mestizo hegemony. She illustrates how racial identity for everyday people in Mexico is unevenly distributed through space, thus drawing attention to the ways that context and gender alter the way one flexes and utilizes a range of mestizo, or mixed-race identities. These performative features of the process of identification differentially assert a whiteness that is socially and materially rewarded and validated by the state. In this way whiteness upholds Eurocentric standards even as nonwhites practice it.[32] Theorizing from the history of the formation and practice of antichinismo, I read racist acts against Chinese immigrants as instrumental to negotiating the terms of racial belonging for millions of Mexican people in the first half of the twentieth century.

This notion of race as a contested field of power helps to explain why antichinismo became an instrumental strategy to gain legitimacy, prestige, and status under unstable conditions.[33] Racial-formation theory corresponds to the idea of the Mexican racial contract in that racial formations are the historical accumulation of contests for the meaning of race, whereas the racial contract represents the implicit agreement that lays out basic rules between the government and the governed. The focus of this book is less that antichinismo in the Mexican racial state was a repressive disciplining force upon Chinese immigrants and their families. Rather, I stress that antichinismo made racial politics important to early twentieth-century discourses of mestizo, nation, and revolution.

The terms *prejudice* and *discrimination* were too blunt to capture the changing cultural and political expression of antichinismo found in the archives.

Putting antichinismo in the context of a mestizo racial state reveals that people became antichinistas for different reasons. Antichinista discourse had the remarkable ability to transform bourgeoisie nativists into revolutionary patriots, peasants into rightful citizens, rebellious Indians into discontented nationalists, agricultural capitalism into national colonization, and state subjection into secular revolutionary nationalism. Racist tirades targeted the Chinese people as the ultimate Other, although the broader effect was the consolidation of state power. Anti-Chinese politics made this phase of reconstructing state power palatable and desirable in certain ways. Thus, antichinismo helped usher in a new regime of state capitalism and the socialization of Indians to institutional subjection as citizens. In other words, the true mark of antichinismo's success is not the expulsion of the Chinese population but the integration of Indians into agrarian capitalism. Other racial discourses may contribute to the maintenance of the revolution's racial contract, but antichinismo was the right kind of racism for the Mexican state to construct a mestizo hegemony.

The point of departure this book emphasizes is that antichinismo engendered particular forms of violence and a process of social transformation across different regions that has gone virtually unnoticed within Mexican history. The focus is on the *invention* of postrevolutionary political belonging, not just Chinese disavowal. The evolution of the Mexican racial state, not just the presence of race politics in postrevolutionary reconstruction, is underscored. The history of the Chinese racial form in Mexico unsettles a field of history that has grown accustomed to a past devoid of Chinese people. The perception of the Chinese as a racial threat not only strengthened the authority of the state but it also strengthened the means with which the state validates antichinismo and contributes to the means of reproducing the state itself. The story of antichinismo is, therefore, necessary to show the Mexican category *mestizo* as an effect of state power.

This book branches out from the tremendous and groundbreaking work of other historians of the Chinese presence in Mexico. I am greatly indebted to the pioneering research of transnational-migration histories by Grace Delgado, Evelyn Hu-DeHart, Elliot Young, and Julia María Schiavone Camacho; the detailed social histories by Roberto Chao Romero, Maricela González Félix, Catalina Velázquez Morales, and José Manuel Puig Casauranc; and the political histories by Raymond B. Craib III, José Jorge Gómez Izquierdo, Moisés González Navarro, and Gerardo Rénique. The current volume draws heavily from this group of historians to expand their analysis.

Organization of the Book

Chapter 1 examines the historical development of the Mexican racial state and the structure of the Chinese diaspora by attending to the two formative state measures that shaped the Chinese presence in Mexico: the U.S. Chinese Exclusion Act of 1882 and the Mexican Colonization and Land Law of 1883. This chapter will provide basic background on the importance of the Mexican context and the social organization of the Chinese diaspora. It describes the establishment of the Mexican racial state through government records regarding land reform and national colonization, and it provides a survey of Mexico's other Others to compare the Chinese to other immigrant groups and the role that they played in national colonization. The history of the Chinese diaspora is used in order to relate coolie and other Chinese migrant streams to the Mexican context. These comparisons examine the precedent for Chinese-immigration restriction in the U.S. Chinese Exclusion Act of 1882 and revisit key structural differences between the United States and Mexico. The impact that U.S. enforcement had on structuring life for the Chinese in Mexico is also explored. Lastly, the chapter pays particular attention to the reign of Porfirio Díaz, a revered military general who inaugurated a wave of modernization through scientific administration, liberal ideology, and brutal repression—an era referred to as the Porfiriato. The culmination of ideas about colonization and immigration in the 1883 law are traced to show how the Chinese people were conceived of as motores de sangre and directed to territories with hostile Indian resistance. This practice created a structural position that shaped the persecution of Chinese at the onset of the revolution in 1910.

Chapter 2 examines the specificity of the late nineteenth-century national colonization schemes that Chinese migrants were strategically positioned in. The chapter explores the records of national colonization policy to detail the ambivalence of Mexican actors in acquiring Chinese laborers. Officials, industry leaders, and politicians produced a discourse of Chinese racial identity as motores de sangre to rationalize the introduction of large numbers of nonwhite nonsettler laborers. Evidence of Chinese participation in projects across the country illustrates the diversity of labor in addition to the multiple, and regionally specific, angles of entry into Mexican colonization. Each site of government-prescribed Chinese employment is followed by an analysis of prevailing Indian-state relations. This approach reveals how the use of Chinese laborers was concentrated in regions with the greatest conflict among indigenous residents and the central Mexican state. The chapter also traces popular, industry, and government concern about the effects of introducing large numbers of Chinese people, with particular focus on the political dynamics evident in two government reports. The reports recommend that Chinese expulsion should be paired with the educational training of the peasant and indigenous population. Lastly, the chapter examines several cases where diasporic Chinese immigrants became indispensable functionaries for national colonization. Immigration documents and business records from the United States trace how industrial expansion in Mexico relied upon the social and economic organizing strategies the diasporic Chinese people practiced. The treatment of the Chinese people as policy instruments allowed them to become a ubiquitous immigrant group.

Chapter 3 shifts the evidentiary focus from documents of Mexican policy and business records to documentation of anti-Chinese violence at the onset of the 1910 revolution and during its subsequent unfurling. This chapter makes extensive use of U.S. consular reports on Mexican anti-Chinese activities. U.S. State Department agents regularly wrote letters and sent telegrams to Washington, D.C., documenting the uncoordinated, synchronous anti-Chinese activities that took place as a part of the revolutionary battlefield. This body of correspondence and other firsthand accounts are combined with the existing scholarly literature on the revolution to describe three types of anti-Chinese violence: mass killing, tactical assassinations, and ritual violence combined with looting. These forms of violence trace the transformation of the Chinese racial form to that of killable subjects—a wretched embodiment of the Porfirian regime.

Various sources on the 1911 massacre of Chinese at Torreón, Couahila, provide evidence of the social conditions that led to that mass killing. The sources paint a picture of ad hoc, unplanned, collective violence against the Chinese population as a rejection of the Porfirian regime rather than an embrace of nationalist solidarity. This chapter traces the social relations that gave rise to cooperative violence in the context of the revolution to describe the emergence of new social ties based upon Porfirian discontent and doing harm to Chinese. Individual cases of tactical assassinations and ritual violence against the bodies of Chinese people further illuminate the absence of mestizo nationalism as motivation. The chapter details reports of ritualized violence that present a battlefield where Chinese immigrants are under constant attack. During these episodes of expropriation and theft, Chinese people suffered innumerable humilies, cruelty, and death. These modes of popular violence against them shifted the political identity of assailants, no matter their allegiance or affiliation, to patriotic revolutionaries. This particular cultural dimension of revolutionary violence provided popular ways of voicing peasant discontent.

In other words, peasants and Indians did not threaten the bourgeois military leaders of the revolution when they expressed antichinismo.

Chapter 4 follows anti-Chinese violence from the streets into the meeting halls. Again, the evidentiary focus shifts, this time to records of anti-Chinese organizations and their dealings with the revolutionary state up to 1928. Tracing the footsteps of these organizations also shows the evolution of their use of racialized discourse to capture the attention of public institutions. Here, the dominant image of the Chinese shifts again, now to that of pernicious defilers. Through their mobilization and consolidation, various classes, regions, and ethnic groups developed antichinismo as a recognizable political identity with clear objectives (segregation, anti-miscegenation, and repeal of the 1899 treaty with China). The propaganda literature and correspondence from antichinista organizations also show the absence of previously revered intellectual architects of mestizo national identity, José Vasconcelos and Manuel Gamio. The chapter attends to the abundance of material from athletics enthusiasts and eugenicists as parallel tracks for the development of mestizo nationalism that both supported and intersected with antichinismo throughout the 1920s and 1930s.

The contours of antichinismo in the first half of the 1920s also reflect the reluctance of the new revolutionary ruling class to expel and eliminate Chinese functionaries from the floundering remnants of the Porfirian economy. Antichinistas challenged the new government's inherited reliance upon Chinese commercial circuits. Correspondences from these organizations with the government show how their national consolidation in 1925 mobilized new strategies to capture public priorities. Antichinista literature and presence in the public record of numerous state legislatures tell the story of a broad, coordinated national campaign to affect state-level policies in the pursuit of constitutional reforms barring Chinese people from the country. The varied experiences across the national campaign ultimately converged in the articulation of Mexican women's concern for the prevention of Chinese sexual relations with Mexican women. Antichinista literature and cartoons depicted Mexican women's sexual reproduction as an evolutionary mechanism for racial betterment and spread a popular discourse of a mestizo national racial future to which the Chinese men were the most significant threat. In doing so, antichinistas constructed a popular discourse of ethical governance that celebrated for the intensification and expansion of authoritarian state power.

Chapter 5 documents the far-reaching consequences of the rise of antichinistas within the revolutionary state as officials and politicians forged a racial logic of revolutionary governmentality. The chapter follows the spread of antichinismo as it coursed through the veins of the revolutionary state from the 1930 census to the famed depression-era Campaña Nacionalista and gave new direction and inspiration to the fledgling PNR. The party's literature, various newspapers, and the public record of congressional debate all illustrate the ascendancy of key antichinistas as well as the broad appeal of antichinismo in various policy areas. It became popular not because it reviled the Chinese people, but because reviling the Chinese altered the interpretation of the state's role in intervening into the social life of the country. From labor unions to health policy and eugenic sex education, antichinismo inspired and motivated individuals and groups to approach the indigenous peasantry as fragile racial subjects in need of protection, guidance, and discipline. The 1929 presidential campaign also made a powerful statement about the roles of race mixing and legitimate authority. The PNR successfully argued in campaign newsletters and other propaganda that true revolutionary action resides in the creation of a racial state, not the populist pandering of an undisciplined mestizaje as had been preached by PNR challenger Vasconcelos. The PNR's articulation of a disciplined mestizo subject would shape revolutionary changes to peasant's agrarian citizenship—more a program of recruitment than of enfranchisement. These attitudes and official positions authorized new waves of local violence and motivated the governors of Sinaloa and Sonora to take matters into their own hands, leading to the expulsion of thousands of Chinese people and their Mexican families in 1931 and 1932.

The last chapter concludes with the lost presidency of Rodríguez as the substitute president in 1932 through 1934. The ways that antichinismo made Rodríguez the most powerful man in the country are traced. He was governor for seven years of Baja California, home to the largest concentration of Chinese people in Mexico by 1930, reaching almost twenty thousand. His anti-Chinese hostilities bolstered his reputation as a patriotic nationalist. Under Rodríguez, antichinismo reached the height of its power. Strengthened by PNR's political discipline, Rodríguez ushered in a rapid transformation of the revolutionary state apparatus from reluctant reforms to aggressive administration. Public records from the national congress and PNR literature document the participation of antichinistas in popularizing a racial logic of the revolution's obligation to protect and provide social guarantees. Antichinistas convinced people that the state must dominate and discipline the peasant population in order to protect it. The path of the postrevolutionary state was paved through the articulation of benevolent concern for the peasantry and the reformulation of self-colonization as revolutionary agrarian reform. These reforms recruited reluctant and desperate peasants into collectivized industrial agriculture, which marginalized indigeneity and severely curtailed the scope of citizen-ship rights. Finally, government sources document a deliberate program to flood Baja California with three Mexican people for every Chinese resident. Predictably, the mix of unemployed agrarians, repatriated workers from the United States, and colonists began to agitate for the expulsion of the Chinese people. Eventually, a popular agrarian movement emerged to run the Chinese people off their lands and claim them as its own. Following the mass displace-ment of thousands of Chinese people, the federal government began to award designated ejidos to different agrarian groups. In Baja California, antichinismo delivered thousands of Mexican people into government programs that further stripped them of indigenous identifications and tied their well-being to the fulfillment of industrial agricultural expectations. It would appear that the Porfirian goal of self-colonization had finally been achieved, thanks to the help of antichinismo. In the 1930s, hating Chinese people facilitated entry into the mestizo nation, particularly, through recruitment into the regulatory institutions and political economy of the revolutionary state.

1

The Politics of Chinese Immigration in the Era of Mexican National Colonization

A Cuban-based Mexican economist and diplomat named Manuel Zapata Vera proclaimed in 1882 to the *El Monitor Republicano*, an ardent liberalist, Mexico City newspaper, of the changing conditions of Chinese immigration and its potential for Mexico: "There is a lot of hope for Chinese immigration." Comparing Cuba's coolies and California's Chinese sojourner population, Vera asked his readers to consider the benefits of Chinese "corporeal faculties" for mass employment in Mexican development. Even after describing California's grievances against Chinese vice and labor competition and after explaining Cuban officials' anxieties about the growth of mixed Chinese African families, Vera pauses to question, "Is this a complete condemnation of Chinese immigration to Mexico?" which he answers with an emphatic "NO!" Vera's essay offered Mexico City readers a view of Chinese immigration as a consummate solution to the perennial frustrations of capitalist development and industrial expansion.[1] One month later, the U.S. Congress seemingly gave the opposite answer to Vera's question when they passed the Chinese Exclusion Act of 1882.

Chinese migration and settlement in Mexico were neither accidents nor mere side effects of U.S. exclusion. This U.S. immigration law paralleled a new wave of Mexican land reforms to facilitate economic expansion. U.S. immigration restrictions made simultaneous Mexican policies more successful by pushing Chinese migrants from the United States south to Mexico as they looked for clandestine entry. The U.S. Chinese Exclusion Act banned Chinese immigration and barred the Chinese people from naturalization as aliens ineligible, based on their race, for citizenship. The law was the result of years of anti-Chinese hostility, white labor-union agitation, and legal arbitration to enact immigration restrictions.[2] *El Monitor Republicano* reporters explained the U.S. law's passage and content to Mexico City readers. While the United States enacted restrictionist measures, Mexican officials attempted to propel national colonization by articulating an aggressive regime of land reform and settler recruitment, for which the Chinese people became the most significant immigrant group. Only immigrants from Spain outnumbered the Chinese immigrants in Mexico, and the Chinese people were the most geographically distributed foreign-born group in the republic. In December 1883, Mexico passed the Colonization Law, also known as the Law of Demarcation and Colonization of Vacant Lands (Ley de deslinde y colonización de terrenos baldíos), which enacted sweeping transformations to legal title that affirmed the rights of some and disavowed the rights of others. Land reform was important because it changed peoples' relationship to territory, which fundamentally altered their political and social identities. Mexican colonization laws introduced a selective bias for which Chinese immigrants were recruited into development projects.

This chapter describes how different streams of Chinese migration intersected with Mexican national colonization policy. To explain some of the ways that Mexican colonization policy shaped the Chinese experience, the chapter offers an overview of the formation of the Mexican racial state and examines the Mexican racial state through its history of Indian relations with national colonization policies and the various racial projects generated. These nineteenth-century projects show how liberal ideology shaped the meaning of race through colonization policy, an area of governance that tied land, Indians, and immigrants together. Mexican colonization policy stratified economic and political rights and led to a graduated citizenship that reflected the aims of modernization. Graduated citizenship was indexed by racial discourses, class structure, and instrumentality to the reproduction of the state apparatus. The Porfirian administration introduced Chinese men as racialized instruments of policy in order to expand and deepen the power of the state through the expansion of infrastructure projects. Although Mexico is not traditionally associated with the nineteenth-century coolie trade, Mexican colonization policy permitted the continuation of these exploitative labor practices while labeling the policy as open immigration and economic development.

This overview also describes several of Mexico's other Others, such as African, Jewish, and Japanese people, because understanding the racial foundations of the Mexican state and the influence of colonization policy is important when framing the influence of anti-Chinese politics in the reconstruction of state power after the revolution. This and the next chapters address a pressing question in Asian American studies: Can we compare Chinese immigration regulation in political contexts other than the United States by describing migration circuits, differences in political context, bureaucratic structure, and statutory content? Scholars David Scott Fitzgerald and David Cook-Martín argue that the diffusion of racist immigration policy originates from states with institutions of democratic input and that open policies are initiated by more-authoritarian states.[3] This chapter shows that the meaning of immigration restriction or openness goes deeper than the size of a nation's welcome mat. A theory of racial states implies that an immigration statute's degree of selection is a poor measure of openness because all states seek immigration policies that reinforce foundational domestic racial inequalities. In Mexico the openness of immigration policies was designed to undermine indigenous resistance to national colonization. These analytical dimensions also illustrate that while both the United States and Mexico racialized their Chinese populations, they did so with different intents and outcomes.

Scholars of immigration have long moved away from a one-way–journey, nation-centric model of immigration in order to represent immigrants' choices and migration patterns by describing the larger transnational factors that push and pull people through migration and integration and remigration.[4] Chinese immigration to Mexico in the second half of the nineteenth century reflected the convergence of new forces that pulled or attracted Chinese immigrants to Mexico and two forces that pushed Chinese migrants into Mexico: the decline of the coolie system and U.S. restriction of Chinese immigration, both of which began in the 1870s. This historical background is useful to illustrate the deep political and structural fissures that determined Chinese experiences and shaped Mexican perceptions of the Chinese people. The forces that pulled Chinese immigrants to Mexico were a mix of regional conditions that included *caudillos* (political strongmen); the degree of hostility, indifference, or cooperation of different and competing Indian populations; tensions between provincial powers and centralized state authority; the legal rights granted to foreigners; and the prevailing policies of colonization. In 1876 Porfirio Díaz became dictator of Mexico, enacting aggressive colonization policies that favored foreigners and intensified suppression of Indian resistance. The Porfiriato resulted in several decades of programs to modernize the country during a period that the Chinese people were rejected from the United States and that colonial officials dismantled the system of Chinese indenture. Porfirian officials and industry leaders intended to redirect these streams of migration to the deserts of Sonora, the coastal plains of Yucatán, the fertile valleys of Coahuila, the mountains of Oaxaca, and the highlands of Chihuahua.

However seductive it may seem to attribute Mexican racism to mimicry of U.S. racial forms, this study stresses the importance of decentering the racial imaginary of U.S. imperialism and the necessity of building an understanding of an autonomous Mexican racial state. I acknowledge that theoretical frameworks of imperialism and empire make it necessary to consider how imperial states shape the conditions of other states, but empire is not everywhere, and it is never complete. I diverge from the majority of scholars who claim that Mexico borrowed anti-Chinese attitudes from the United States. Instead, the focus of this book is on endemic institutions and intellectual thought that organized Mexican perceptions of Chinese racial difference.

Vera saw Mexico positioned between the Cuban and Californian realities of the Chinese diaspora. Both transpacific sojourners and the coolie trade began in the first half of the nineteenth century. Chinese emigration rapidly expanded at midcentury due to the discovery of gold in California and the outbreak of violent conflict between Qing China and European powers, a conflict often called the Opium Wars. The imposition of trade policies that favored European aggressors led to the formation of coastal trading colonies, such as Hong Kong and Shanghai. Gradually, officials and plantation owners turned to indentured Asian workers to fill the labor gap created by the emancipation of enslaved Africans in European colonies around the world. Drawing resources from both British India and the Chinese trade colonies, the English coolie system recruited, entrapped, and kidnapped displaced and desperate people. Mexico would not become integrated into these networks until the system began to decline.

Mexican independence from Spain included the emancipation of slaves and the abolition of chattel slavery. By the dawn of the nineteenth century, a majority of Mexico's African slaves had already been freed, but outlawing slavery itself was a pragmatic proclamation by the constitution's framers to gain the support of African Mexican communities, which was vital to the war for independence.[5] Because of this precedent, Mexican officials abstained from the coolie trade, as an extension of its prohibition on human bondage. However, from 1847 to 1874, more than 220,000 contracted, male, Chinese workers were brought to newly independent Peru and Spanish Cuba. At that time, Liberals in Mexico City viewed slavery as a moral offense and as a sign of economic weakness—a mode of production that would not survive in a market with free labor. The economic rationale followed that free wage earners would work better and harder than either conscripted slaves or contracted coolies.[6] As the attitude in Vera's *Republicano* article attests, Mexican Liberals disdained coolie indenture, calling it slavery by another name. However, the high-minded ideals of Mexico City philosophers did not reflect the actual practices of debt peonage in Yucatán, the trade in indigenous slaves in the north, or the use of recruited work gangs for the republic's infrastructure projects.

In the United States Chinese migrants had flocked to California in response to the gold rush, their numbers expanding from twenty thousand in 1850 to more than fifty thousand in 1870. These migrants spread out through the U.S. west, in mining, agriculture, railroad construction, and manufacturing, and when the economic depression of the 1870s struck the nation, white labor unions responded by condemning the Chinese labor force. Despite being voluntary migrants, Chinese men were perceived by U.S. whites as innately willing to indenture themselves, and Chinese women as slavishly prone to prostitution. Democratic politicians, seeking to expand their constituencies, responded by promulgating California nativism, labor protectionism, and antimiscegenation laws to the federal legislature. This legislative push led to the first partial restrictionist measure in 1875 and the more robust prohibition in 1882.[7]

Patterns of Chinese migration in the late nineteenth century responded to both these new restrictions and the unraveling of the coolie trade. Chinese migration to Mexico was contingent on these larger patterns. Harsh abuse throughout the coolie system brought heavy criticism of Asian indenture and led the Qing government to pass restrictions on the labor practice. The coolie system was formally dismantled by 1877, but recruiters, shipowners, and industrialists remained dependent upon the traffic in Asian labor. Meanwhile, Chinese migrants anticipated exclusion from the United States when more than fifty thousand Chinese immigrated there in 1881. By the time of Mexico's 1883 colonization law, Chinese people were already seeking entry to Mexico on their own,[8] and operatives of the coolie trade were in search of new markets to continue the circulation of Asian laborers.

In order to understand why Mexican officials thought of Chinese people as an inferior, yet necessary, element of colonization policy, we must examine the historical background of Mexican national colonization. The 1883 colonization law dictated the rights of *colonos blancos* (white settlers) and defined the colonization enterprises that they could initiate. The Indian population was not exempt from this colonization scheme, but to participate they had to relinquish indigenous ties to the land and adopt the modernizing intent of the law. The Chinese people in Mexico were never to become colonos blancos, nor were they simply accidental migrants making Mexico home instead of continuing their journey to the United States. Vera's *Republicano* editorial shows how racial ideology shaped principles of state selection in the recruitment of settlers and laborers for colonization. According to Vera, if Europeans could not be acquired for colonization, then the state would have to look to African and Asian workers. Of these choices, Vera was clear that Asian migrants were preferable both to African ones and to the indigenous population. The advent of intensive national colonization policy in the second half of the nineteenth century brought numerous ethnic groups into the country as potential settlers. Chinese immigrants became instruments of this policy, not as colonos but as motores de sangre.

Foundations of the Mexican Racial State

Mexican immigration policy in the nineteenth century was shaped by the belief that Mexico was potentially wealthy but that the native population was insufficient in number and quality to realize that wealth. The perceived solution was to increase the number and whiteness of the national population through immigration. Criollos thought that the mass immigration of whites would lead to the racial improvement of the Indian population through generations of racial mixing, leading to gradual mixing or racial replacement. Mexico's political class held racist perceptions of foreigners: Europeans were considered to be racially superior, but different ethnic groups possessed unique and useful attributes. The ideal of blanqueamiento shaped the perceptions of foreign immigrants' ethnicity.

The conflation of nation building and colonization was the central paradox of the early Mexican republic. The problem, as Benedict Anderson describes, was how to turn a colony into a homeland.[9] The ensuing transformation was both ideological and structural. Through constitutional independence, the Mexican state reconstructed the extensiveness of sovereign crown authority over colonial territory and its residents. The declaration of independence from Spain was marked by the emergence of a resolute Liberal order concerned with the rights and liberties denied to criollos under the crown. In 1821 Agustín de Iturbide and Vicente Guerrero issued a revolutionary proclamation in the Plan de Iguala to announce three guarantees: the supremacy of Roman Catholicism, complete independence, and social equality. The 1824 constitution extended citizenship to all of Mexico's residents. This was ostensibly designed to abolish race and social class while forming a national communitarian political identity. The articulation of a raceless society in the constitution began a popular mythology that racism had been abolished. Despite the letter of the law, liberal racial ideology continued to shape a graduated citizenship that delimited which bodies and rationalities were appropriate for the privileges of liberty and citizenship. According to this ideology, only the *gente de razón*, or people with Western rationality, could be entrusted with the power of citizenship. Thus, when they proclaimed liberty and justice against far-off rulers, they also denied it to those in their midst.[10]

Race making in the Mexican republic was grounded in problems inherited from the Spanish colonial administration. The contested place of nonwhites in the new republic was historically conditioned, and it distinguished between colonial legacies and emergent national vernaculars of difference. First, the Spanish colonial administration's dealings with Indian republics and enslaved African populations in the transition to an independent nation state in 1821 created a mass underclass. Mexico's national inheritance of Spanish coloniality was based on Indian hatred, African docility, and Asian erasure.[11] After independence, Mexico's ruling elite found mass Indian genocide too costly and moved instead to strip away indigenous culture and convert the masses into a useful class of laborers. The hatred for Indians in early criollo nationalism was based upon colonial perceptions of inferiority and contempt for their lack of enthusiasm for the Mexican republic. Racial blackness differed from Indian contempt and was shaped by an earlier colonial history of slavery. Mexico had the second-largest enslaved African population in the western hemisphere, so black Africans have been a part of Mexican history for centuries—outnumbering even Europeans until the mid-eighteenth century. New Spain did not observe strict segregation and allowed for the gradual emancipation of most African slaves, so by 1790 more than three hundred thousand free individuals with partial African heritage were in colonial New Spain.[12] This level of integration meant that mid-nineteenth-century conceptions of racial blackness retained the Spanish-colonial-caste logic of hypo- and hyperdescent. The perceived racial plasticity of Africans, namely, the potential for children of an African parent to be "improved," were legacies of the social death engendered by enslavement. While "colonial blackness" shaped these perceptions of African Mexican people, their social and political integration reflected far greater complexity and sophistication.[13] African Mexican people drew from a wide range of historical experiences to negotiate their belonging in the Mexican nation, including indigeneity.[14] Yet, Mexican blackness still produced marginalization, relative to the national state and other nonblack residents.

Even after declaring independence from Spain, the new republic assumed the previous colonial mantle. In the months after the declaration of independence,

Juan Francisco de Azcárate y Lezama reported on foreign affairs to the republic's newly anointed Sovereign Governing Council. This report, which outlines the various external relations of New Spain that should be taken up by the new republic, is a valuable artifact of the transition from colony to nation-state. While considering internal strife and external imperial competition, Azcárate lists three straightforward prescriptions: pacify the Indians, increase the population through immigration, and expand trade. As Azcárate notes, the first and most vital subject of "necessity" for the new republic was the ongoing conflicts with the "barbarous Indian nations," notably the Apache, Lipan, and Comanche peoples of the north. He recommended to the council continuous emigration of "civilized" families.[15] Spain's "cruel and bloody war" to settle the northern region was notoriously documented by the ears and heads of indigenous people, which were taken as hard evidence of land won back and the return of stolen horses. Azcárate would have shared the concerns of Spanish colonial officials regarding the "Apache-ization," or incorporation of other indigenous groups (such as Jocomes, Sumas, and Mansos tribes) into the Apache culture and pattern of resistance, as a threat to the inauguration of Mexican sovereign authority.[16] His domesticating language of settlers, not soldiers, was neatly framed by the need to "have enough people to populate" remote lands of the republic. The tempered rhetoric did not lead to conciliation; by injecting settlers into Indian lands, the Mexican state merely invented the need for military protection and a tradition of raising militias from men in settler colonies. For Azcárate and the new national elite, the security of the republic and the unfinished project of pacification and colonization were synonymous.

Speaking to the history of European colonization of the western hemisphere and the policy priorities of the Mexican republic, Azcárate exclaimed, "The progress that results from immigration is astounding."[17] According to the report, the fact that European families crossed oceans to achieve private property was reason enough for generous land grants "to achieve gains in population." Azcárate and the vast majority of ruling criollos understood that their republic was the place from which mountains of silver and gold had sustained the prestige and power of the Spanish empire for centuries.[18] Dwelling upon Mexico's colonial legacy, Azcárate prioritized the establishment of foreign relations with old colonial powers to resume the transpacific Manila trade. He believed that if the silver trade had made the Bourbons rich, it would certainly do the same for Mexican nationals. Because Indian peoples were thought to be incapable, if not inimical, to realizing economic expansion, Mexican elites like Azcárate put their faith in the promise of European settlers.

Comparing Mexico and United States in the 1880s

The extent to which U.S. racial formations influenced the conditions of Chinese people in Mexico can be understood by comparing state architectures and ideologies of rule. U.S. restriction reflected populist disparagement and entrenchment of white supremacy. In Mexico, the government's colonization laws opened the gates of immigration in an effort to attract white racial stock. In the United States, bars to immigration and naturalization underscore the state's articulation of racial citizenship as preserved for the white settler class; in Mexico, citizenship remained ill-defined and fundamentally tied to the recruitment impulse of national colonization policies. In Mexico, citizenship was not a popular domain of mass enfranchisement; it was reserved for the urban ruling class and for recruited agents for capitalist development during the Porfiriato. Only after the revolution did citizenship become a mechanism of political incorporation, cooptation, and discipline.[19] Nationalist ideologies of rule in Mexico have relied upon reworking bonds of dependency, rather than on fostering equal fellowship among citizens.[20] The introduction of antichinismo into Mexico's genealogy of citizenship reveals the ways that racial thought organized collective identity, sexuality, and citizenship for a polyglot heterogeneous indigenous and peasant population—a context quite unlike the United States.

These governments that put racial ideology into practice differ greatly, and comparative racial analysis that contrasts practices of racialization can illustrate why racial politics vary even when the referent is the same. Historical divergences mark the cultural articulations of sovereign authority and the practice of racial governmentality in Mexico and the United States. The Spanish colony has been fragmented by regionalism since the Hapsburg colonization of New Spain in the sixteenth century. For the majority of people in Mexico, these varying patterns illustrate the political utility of ideological flexibility and the people's cunning capacity to respond to elite dictates with mediated self-interest. Both the historical context of nested Mexican sovereignties after the colonial era and the reflexive (state-polity) process of building a "cultural sensibility" of state authority differed dramatically from the practices of state building in the United States.[21]

The most important illustration of difference between these two state regimes is the 1910 Mexican revolution and the crisis of legitimate authority and institutional reconstruction that it fermented. In revolutionary Mexico, popular culture, Indian conciliation, military rivalries, religious revolt, regionalism, and the exigencies of capitalism determined the face and character of state authority, whereas the robustness of imperialist U.S. bureaucratic and white-supremacist legislative institutions combined with well-organized industrial corporations created the conditions for a regulated racial state that was largely consonant with Anglo normativity. In Mexico, law is often not implemented nor applied consistently, and the state's actions are not always legislated. These are certainly concerns in the United States as well, but in terms of racial formations, the United States exhibits much-stricter institutional command than does Mexico. These different state-building projects reflect the differences between political authority based upon the consent of a majority white settler populace in the United States and the accommodationist rule over a multitude of disinterested or rebellious indigenous and peasant peoples in Mexico.

Despite the popularity of antichinismo and the political power of its racial polemic to define the public good, Mexico, surprisingly, did not bar Chinese people from naturalization, nor did the state enact a uniform ban on their immigration. Immigration controls on the Chinese people were constantly discussed and debated but never completely promulgated. Even as some restrictions closed certain avenues, others remained explicitly open. Mexican records show that Chinese immigrants continuously applied for and were granted naturalization throughout this period (1880 to 1940), which is not to say that the Chinese were not at certain times and places prevented from entering or denied naturalization. Rather, it is only to point out that such exclusions were temporary and inconsistently practiced.

Critics may charge that anti-Chinese politics were no different from the myriad other exclusions from Mexican mestizo nationalism. There were parallel programs of exclusion and populist hate speech, as well as a number of other immigrant groups who occupied an ambivalent position in Mexico. All of these Mexican cases demonstrate the absence of a "horizontal comradery" in the preservation of an exclusive "imagined community."[22] The only other form of racialized ethnic difference to achieve the structural level of influence, besides anti-Indian thoughts, in turn-of-the-century Mexico was anti-Semitic prejudice against Jews. Claudio Lomnitz-Adler argues that the widespread denunciation of Porfirian *científicos*, or the ruling class of technocrats, drew from a tradition of anti-Semitism that vilified this elite class as amoral businesspeople and political traitors to the nation. Porfirian officials filled a preformed mold of the economic Jewish person helping to "shape an authoritarian, hypermasculine, and dependent modality of revolutionary nationalism . . . an anti-semitism without Jews." Anti-científico hatred became a common epithet of revolutionaries across the country because its unstable and fungible characteristics fit a broad range of local conflicts. The discourse of anti-Semitism was instrumental to revolutionaries because it emphasized "betrayal, veiled foreign intrusion, and anti-intellectualism."[23] Anti-Chinese and other prejudicial sentiments were conditioned by prior political conflicts, clashes that further distinguish the Mexican experience from that of the United States.

The Conservative-Liberal Fissure and the Colonization Consensus

At the outset of the republic, a Conservative movement sought to fix the previous colonial institutions under the national state to preserve the privilege of the *haciendas* (large plantations or land tracts), the church, and the military. The Liberals, on the other hand, sought to demolish these institutions in order to make individual liberty possible for a new class of criollo nationals. Conflicts between Conservatives and Liberals would continue to fragment and weaken the national state for the majority of the remaining century. Both Liberal and Conservative governances were the basis of ambivalence among Indian *pueblos* (small peasant and indigenous communities) and their future in the republic. The Conservative order offered a continuity of institutional guarantees, whereas the liberal order granted new possibilities for integration. Whatever Indians thought of their role in the republic, the Mexican state, however, pursued economic expansion through foreign investment and advanced the incorporation of what were considered uninhabited Indian lands. To the vast majority of Indian pueblos, the Liberal-Conservative debate amounted to the question of which sets of landlords they preferred: the church and landed elite or the state and foreign capitalists. A common response to these choices was what some scholars have termed *acculturation*, that is, individuals and communities distance themselves from indigenous identifications and cultural markers in favor of a modern comportment and associate with the local arm of the national state, the municipality. Some groups allied with the national government to work in state institutions, such as the police, military, courts, or bureaucracy.[24]

Liberal reforms began a process that eroded the viability and effectiveness of indigenous traditions to meet everyday needs. For instance, agricultural industrialization and railroad construction frequently degraded, depleted, or redirected resources away from traditional usage. This process placed many Indians who were adrift into capitalist labor relations and the state's administrative institutions like the Ministry of Colonization. Adaptation to these structural changes had produced intense regionalism as local actors sought to retain relative positions of power. For the first thirty years of the republic, citizenship laws privileged local residency and intensified regional power blocks in that enfranchisement reinforced fragmentation rather than centralization and homogenization.[25] Not only were Mexican people ethnically different and geographically isolated from each other but intervillage rivalries and disputes also forged strong parochial political allegiances.[26] The colonial imperative of nineteenth-century elites made land reform an important way to negotiate state sovereignty and regional circumstances. Under this regime, Indian volunteers were rewarded with state land. Those who resisted the state would then face armed government campaigns and deputized ethnic rivals, who were rewarded for the extermination of rebel groups.

Liberal reforms increasingly made pueblos more vulnerable and unstable rather than, as was argued in the newspapers of Mexico City, more "vital and productive."[27] This condition led to a pattern where "[t]he dissolution of communal land holdings meant weakening the power of towns over members and so speeded up adoption of new ways."[28] Indian adaptations of Mexican Liberal reforms included seasonal migrant labor in mining and agriculture, as well as military service, to augment rural subsistence. These conditions frequently led Indians back into the arms of Conservative leaders, who promised a return to the stability of haciendas. Each side promulgated the advancement of national colonization, and a modernity without indigeneity. Despite ideological differences, both sides saw promise and peril in Chinese immigration. Yet, the growth of Chinese immigration represented an adaptation by Liberal state authorities to sideline Indian concessions and quicken the pace of industrialization.

Indians in National Colonization

In order to understand the Mexican racial state, examining the historical development of Indian-state relations is helpful. According to historian Charles A. Hale, nineteenth-century Liberal and Conservative criollos "did not hold their Indian contemporaries in . . . high esteem. . . . They saw them as a people who had been socially and politically degraded as a consequence of three centuries of [Spanish] colonization."[29] By the turn of the twentieth century, American anthropologist Robert Redfield, alongside Mexican intellectuals, such as Manuel Gamio and others, maintained, "The 'Indian problem' of Mexico is the problem of converting many little folk societies into a nation."[30] Despite the vociferous conflicts between liberal and conservative doctrines, colonization, pacification, and territorial integration were undisputed commonalities of both sides. As Redfield notes, the challenge of dominating and incorporating diverse indigenous peoples became known as Mexico's "Indian problem." It is also the lynchpin of Mexican racial culture, by which is meant the everyday ways that racial ideology was practiced, experienced, and signified. While the Mexican racial state professed liberal universalism, the actual practice of state authority in local conditions relied upon the customary rules dictated by centuries of colonial racial rule that assumed Indian savagery and European supremacy.[31] Asians had been a part of Spanish colonial society for several centuries, but their integration and periodic expulsion had rendered them culturally and politically indistinguishable from the Indian republics they became a part of during the colonial period.[32]

As the conditions of rule varied, the dialectic between state formations and the popular articulation of race continually sought new equilibrium. Under colonial rule, mestizos, mulattos, and Indians (the lower castes) had been admitted into auxiliary units used as armed patrols against other barbarous Indians. Military service, like civil service, offered prestige otherwise denied to them. Like Sonoran Mayo and northern Mayan peoples, the Serrano population of Namiquipa in the state of Chihuahua was enlisted to fight the Apaches and adopted frontier warfare as a gendered and racial mode of honor, advancing the goals of pacification, and in so doing acquired state-backed titles to Apache lands.[33] The history of Indian-state relations across the republic identified the ways that the Mexican state violently responded to indigenous self-determination. Equally important, it also shows that the culture of colonization created the means by which different Indian peoples could be enrolled in the service of the state, shifting politically from Indian to mestizo. These scenes of violence became crucial sites of state intervention to produce conditions that supported the security and maintenance of the administrative state. The eventual development of widespread antichinismo extended from these violent traditions of negotiating state power among indigenous and peasant populations.

National Colonization as Racial Crisis

Liberal ideals of colonization took the form of regional development projects. These projects were the driving force behind the process of displacement and statist recruitment. New state and territory boundaries were drawn up in 1824 to decentralize authority over settlement policy. In 1833 colonization laws were passed for Jalisco, Texas, Tamaulipas, and the Californias to subsidize settlement of Indian lands. The most successful of these colonies was Texas when U.S. immigrants were enlisted as colonists; however, in 1836 Mexico's greatest hope for effective colonization turned into a national disaster when Texas claimed independence. The crisis of Texas secession led many to question other national colonization efforts. The failure in Texas led to greater support for strengthening the government's powers to dictate national colonization. However, an editorial in the feisty Conservative newspaper *La Lima de Vulcano* in Mexico City criticized the liberal obsession with foreign colonists, arguing instead that Mexico possesses strong institutions and enough settlers to accomplish successful national colonization. The author compared the "joyful conquest of civilization" in the states of Chihuahua, Durango, Jalisco, Nuevo Leon, San Luis, Tamaulipas, and Zacatecas as "the freest in the Mexican confederation." In contrast, the states of Chiapas, Mexico, Michoacán, Oaxaca, Puebla, and Veracruz "will need to experiment with military and ecclesiastical influence."[34] The editorial reflected the Liberal-Conservative conflict but also illustrated the popular sentiment that both sides were committed to national consolidation through colonization policy.

The annexation of Texas by the United States in 1845 and Mexico's loss of its northern portion in 1848 under the Treaty of Guadalupe ended the U.S.-Mexican War. That same year Antonio Garay, secretary of the interior, remained resolute in his characterization of Mexican colonization policy: "The misfortunes that make up the history of the Republic and many other bad omens signaled by the [Indian] rebellions have set all attention on salvation through the immigration of foreigners. Colonization is unanimously supported [in the congress] as the remedy against the endless disturbances and the only hope of maintaining the future integrity of national territory and leading to the achievement of prosperity and greatness."[35] Dedication to colonization by foreigners as a policy panacea to economic development and internal pacification reflected a high esteem for the lackluster benefits of American, British, French, German, Italian, and Spanish settlers. Meanwhile, such inflated expectations ultimately reflected the derision of the Indian population. The continued faith in colonization after the embarrassing Texas failure illustrates how important immigration and land-reform policy was to the reproduction of the racial state. In response to the loss of Texas, Antonio López de Santa Ana, Mexico's president, issued a decree in 1854 to make Mexican citizenship more difficult to obtain by adding residency requirements and stringent naturalization in an effort to ward off future secessions.[36]

Despite a tightening of naturalization policy, foreign settlers enjoyed numerous rights and privileges. The Mexican government, eager to retain whatever settlers it could attract, offered reimbursement for losses due to Indian predation. In 1853 U.S. diplomatic commissioner William Wadsworth presented more than $31 million in U.S. settler claims against American losses in Mexican operations incurred by the predation of "barbarous Indians." The claim not only illustrates the rights of colonos in Mexican society but also the ways that national colonization intersected with the status of Indians as enemies of the state. The basis of Wadsworth's claim for restitution was the argument that the Mexican government held sovereignty over the land but lacked the disciplinary regimes to bring that territory into order. Wadsworth complained that "the ferocious Indians, Apaches, Pimas, Navajos, Uthas, Jaca-rillos, Comanches etc. seem inaccessible or insensitive to the influences of the [Catholic] Fathers, and during the last thirty years have devastated the borders of Mexico with incessant hostilities, especially with regard to the Apaches and Comanches. Actually, the states of northern Mexico (at least Chihuahua and Durango) *offer a prize of 20 to 25 pesos for their men.*"[37] Wadsworth's emphasis on the Indian bounties highlighted his endorsement of this policy as a measure to ensure against future losses. Through colonization law, the Mexican state spelled out the sweeping rights of colonos above and beyond basic constitutional rights of its indigenous residents, effectively undermining the political power of Indian citizenship.

In the 1850s Mexico's colonization policy differed significantly from that of the dominant imperial powers in North America and the Caribbean. In the United States, immigrant settlers fanned out from congested east-coast cities into the American West. New streams of immigrants joined the settlement boom from the Pacific coast. U.S. immigration remained unchecked by policy, save for bans on anarchists and paupers, in order to encourage more potential settlers to occupy the vast lands acquired after the Mexican-American War. The success of U.S. settlement reflected the capacity of the state to organize a settler population that reflected the ideals of Anglo racial supremacy. At the same time, U.S. military campaigns against American Indians sought to clear the land of indigenous inhabitants through extermination.[38] In this context, Chinese immigrants entered into a hostile society but were initially tolerated as commercial functionaries, railroad workers, and farmworkers.[39] By the 1860s, though, white settlers in California marked the Chinese population as queer, slavish drug addicts prone to disease and sick with greed. Westward U.S. expansion, except for Texas, was characterized by the absence of large populations of enslaved Africans and was generally multiracial and anti-Indian. For other colonies, like Cuba, that were engaged in intensification, Chinese coolies were imported to bolster the island's economic output. The widespread extermination of the Cuban island's inhabitants in the seventeenth century, combined with centuries of importing enslaved Africans, led to a type of colonial governance where the racial makeup of the island reflected the various populations who had labored to produce the colony's agricultural exports. In contrast, Mexico's settlement strategy lacked a steady supply of immigrants, a strong state to discipline and protect them from the indigenous population, and an established economic market from which new settlements would expand. Mexico was different from Cuba and the United States primarily because of Indian-state relations. Mexican colonization policy was intended to alter these relationships by introducing settlers. As early as 1857, the Mexican congress authorized the introduction of Chinese workers to aid the settler enterprises of colonos blancos in Colima, Guerrero, Michoacán, and Yucatán.[40]

In Mexico, the hundreds of different Indian republics that formed a mosaic of diverse linguistic and ethnic cultures were stitched together to form the republic's basic social fabric. Each region had established different norms and practices of negotiated autonomy with Indian republics; some were cooperative, others gained favor as recruited foot soldiers against those who resisted. Each built different patterns of rule and consent.[41] As a result, the issue of political legitimacy was particularly salient as regional brokers separately negotiated governance with the centralized state—a social condition that would structure how the revolution unfurled. The multiplicity of regional contexts in Mexico has given rise to the notion that there is not one Mexico—there are many. Nineteenth-century colonization policy envisioned a unified administrative space.

The politics of Mexican colonization were often fought over land reforms, as evidenced by the positions taken by both Liberals and Conservatives. Liberals sought to destroy three colonial institutions that impeded the growth of a new national bourgeoisie: the church, the haciendas, and the Indian republics, the three institutions central to Conservative power. In the 1850s, in the aftermath of the devastation wrought by war with the United States, the Mexican state under Santa Ana expanded its power to be the sole arbiter of legal title, claiming all lands not previously titled and creating new techniques for the administration of land, including price controls and the centralization of immigration and colonization planning under one office. These changes unleashed a bloody civil war called the War of Reform, which lasted from 1857 to 1861.

Conservatives fought off Liberal forces for five years before being decisively defeated in the state of Veracruz. After the Conservative defeat, desperation led to a partnership with French imperialists and the short-lived reign from 1864 to 1867 of Ferdinand Maximilian, an Austrian viceroy. This imperial venture sought to return Mexico to its colonial status and remake the country in the image of France's other colonies. During this period, Maximilian authorized the formation of the Asian Colonization Company (Compañía de Colonización Asiática). This chartered company sought to repurpose Atlantic slave ships, previously carrying chained Africans to the Americas, to deliver Chinese coolies to French Mexico. An 1865 contract Maximilian issued granted Manuel Basilio de Cunha Reis an exclusive ten-year contract to import "workers from eastern Asia."[42] Cunha Reis was a notorious Atlantic slaver and was arrested several times for illegally trading enslaved Africans. Some Chinese coolies might have entered into Mexico under this colonization company, but it and the French regime would be ended in a little more than a year. Despite the likely failure of Cunha Reis's enterprise, other Chinese coolies are suspected to have entered the Yucatán peninsula as escaped workers from British Honduras (now Belize), southeast of Mexico on the Caribbean coast. In 1863 an English company from that colony reported that two hundred Chinese coolies had abandoned a logging project and were thought to have escaped to Chan Santa Cruz on the east coast of the Yucatán peninsula, integrating with local Mayans.[43] Still, the first documented importation of Chinese laborers to Yucatán would not occur until 1892.

Liberal leader Benito Juárez, a politician and Zapotec Indian from Oaxaca, became instrumental in rallying Mexican forces to gain independence from French rule in 1867. Maximilian's reign complicated any progress Liberals might have made during the War of Reform, when French-leaning Conservatives enlisted the support of Indian republics to back the colonial regime. For instance, Yaqui Indians in the northern state of Sonora supported French intervention as they fought the Liberal Mexicans, a mutual enemy.[44] Liberal reforms embodied in the constitution of 1857 had stripped land titles from churches and haciendas, but they did little to respect indigenous sovereignty and independence.

Juárez's 1861 victory over Conservatives in the War of Reform, and his revolt against French occupation in 1867, secured a Liberal future for the government. The progressive constitution of 1857 had created new executive powers that disposed of church lands, created congressional authority to dictate land tenure (article 72), and paved the way for the expansion of ejidos (article 24). The legal articulation of ejidos was designed to combat Church monopolies and weaken the dependency upon large, private, rural estates. The first mention of ejidos occurs in 1523 under Spanish colonial rule to set aside lands to foster agricultural productivity.[45] The use of ejidos varied over time, but most were used to settle Indians close to the Church or grant concessions to cease hostilities. This practice was revived in the Liberal-reform constitution in 1857, this time to take away Church and hacienda land and reallocate them to Indian and peasant communities.[46] The intent was to build village-level support for the Liberal regime, but it accounted for only a minute portion of government-appointed lands. Framers of the law understood that the ejido tied Indians to land for which the government held title. In terms of the letter of the law, the Liberal movement toward nationalization of territory and government-appointed public lands had a mixed impact on indigenous communities but, nevertheless, ended the negotiated autonomy that had been preserved by Conservatives. Ejido lands are frequently thought to be synonymous with indigenous sovereignty or the natural state of Mexican peasants, but ejidos were invented as a state-mediated title to public land. It was a policy that was moderately successful because it sometimes corresponded with indigenous claims.[47] By the end of the nineteenth century, ejidos represented a Liberal program that used economic means of political incorporation specifically for Indians, a practice that evolved from Spanish rule as far back as the sixteenth century.

Principles of State Selection

The constitutional promise of liberal rights, abolition of slavery, and universal equality continually failed to undo inequality because the state relied upon both the stratified structure of society and on the political fictions of its governing institutions. The Mexican state promulgated a racially structured society not through Jim Crow–styled segregation but, instead, by careful recruitment of foreigners and armed persecution of Indian resistance. The Mexican government's principles of state selection for colonos reinforced the inherited inequalities established under Spanish colonial rule; the rights of colonos blancos would always be placed ahead of any non-criollo interest. Colonial racial formations were absorbed into the new republic. Graduated citizenship separated the gente de razón, colonos blancos, naturalized foreigners, and indigenous peoples at various stages of "acculturation." An individual's status could change if his or her career advanced the reproduction of the state apparatus. For instance, Juárez, who was a five-term president, was responsible for inaugurating sweeping reforms that stripped away indigenous claims to land and strengthened the state's authority to do so.

When the political class debated the merits and dangers of incorporating different ethnicities, it began to articulate various other racial positions, a constellation of mutually referential racialized subjectivities—again marked by their utility to state-sponsored projects of colonization. In the second half of the nineteenth century, black African people were still identified as inferior; however, by the 1880s many thought of African Mexican people as a group that had "tried to become property owners, and quickly accepted the language and customs of the nation that they became established in."[48] Blackness in Porfirian Mexico was mediated by elite perceptions of their willingness to assimilate to Eurocentric norms and adapt to capitalism. The opposite might be said of the small colonies of U.S. Mormons who settled in Mexico. Initially welcomed as colonos blancos, they were later expelled for their lack of cultural assimilation.[49] Even as the blackness of African Mexican people was subdued, erased, or overlooked, it was altogether different for African American people who came to Mexico. As threats to racial improvement of national colonization, African American people who migrated to Mexico in the early twentieth century were frequently deported.[50] Unlike the African American population, Lebanese and Syrian immigrants (with Arab, Muslim, and Druze heritage) were received with ambivalence. Theresa Alfaro-Velcamp argues that Middle Eastern immigrants parlayed racial concerns against them by exhibiting exemplary assimilation and emphasizing their Christian roots and an "imagined past" in Lebanese and Phoenician society that corresponded to elite Mexican discourses of Eurocentric modernity.[51]

Mexico's ruling class accepted Middle Easterners as "foreign citizens" and idolized the Japanese as model racial subjects.[52] Japanese recovery from U.S. imperialism in the 1850s, Meiji incorporation of the feudal periphery into the national economy, political and economic consolidation of liberal citizen-subjects, modern industrialization, and homogeneous ethnic nationalism all resonated with the perceived shortcomings of Mexican national development and modernization. Mexican elites romanticized Japan's rapid modernization and began to invent racial genealogies that linked Aztecs to Japan through prehistoric land-bridge migrations.[53] This attitude translated to preferential immigration policies and various state-sponsored programs of settlement for Japanese from 1897 to 1936.

Mexican Liberalism, National Colonization, and Race

Despite the Liberal victory over Conservatives and the passage of a constitution that emphasized individual liberties, in many ways Mexico was unable to make such accomplishments pay off. The realities of rural agricultural instability, Indian insurrections, and foreign interventions weighed heavily on an idealist Liberal government whose administration was geographically fragmented and challenged by professional revolutionaries and widespread corruption.[54] The mounting frustration with utopian ideals led some Liberals to conceive of a conservative liberalism that stressed pragmatic intervention and the science of administration.

Scientific thought guided much of this Liberal reform agenda. Throughout this period, Liberals used European positivist thinking to inform political and policy decisions. This group of technocratic elites became known as científicos. This large cohort of bureaucrats, officials, and other elites initiated campaigns to undermine or transform Indian communities through programs that married science and legal reform. These devoted Liberals began to articulate a vision for centralized, strong, authoritarian government, arguing that doctrinaire rights and liberties had not put food in people's mouths. It was in this context that Díaz, an accomplished military general and Oaxacan mestizo, emerged as a political voice against the high-minded utopian Liberals like Juárez and Sebastián Lerdo de Tejada y Corral that had gone before him.[55] Díaz promised a scientific administration instead of ideological orthodox.

Díaz, the son of an acculturated indigenous mother, rose on Juárez's heels to lead the longest reign in national history and maintained his rule through brutal repression, dispossession, and colonization championed by foreign imperialists. Juárez and Díaz emerged from the lower classes to become the most powerful individuals in the country not because Mexico had created a postracial culture but because of their individual capacities to maintain and preserve the state apparatus.

Díaz's military coup against Tejada introduced an administration that sought results at any cost and by any means. The orthodox Liberal belief that liberty would produce modernization had simply led to greater fragmentation and decentralized state authority. Díaz and his administration took a heterodox approach that rewarded loyalty and demonstrated results with economic advantage and punished resistance or challenges to his authority with the barrel of a gun and a jail cell. Any understanding of immigration to Mexico during the Porfiriato must consider regional variations in Indian-state relations. In other words, the reception and integration of immigrant groups depended in large part on the prevailing conditions of local Indian-state relations.

One indication of the level of conflict between Indian communities and the state was the type of land reform the Díaz regime imposed. In general, the state rewarded compliant and supportive groups by honoring previously held titles. Hostile groups were stripped of their titles, and colonos were invited to settle their land. In this way, Porfirian land reform produced a geography of discontent that dictated the path of Mexican colonization and the reception of immigrants. More than a third of the national territory was in some way altered by the state to induce capitalist expansion by Indian volunteers or by colonos. With the lack of preferred colonos, científicos turned to the declining coolie trade to make up the difference.

The Chinese: Solution or Problem

In the 1870s, Mexican industrial periodicals like *Minero Mexicano* began to use the term *motores de sangre* to discuss the vexed needs of Mexican colonization. The term, borrowed from European engineering and agronomists, was commonly used to distinguish the labor inputs from capital expenditures expected for particular modes of production. In 1858 Eduardo Rodríguez of Spain in his *Manual of General Physics and Application to Agriculture and Industry* detailed the types of actions motores de sangre performed and their expected material effects. Rodríguez describes machines: "All that produces a force is called a machine. Machines are variable in their effect and can be differentiated in each case, by speed, mode of action and duration of working time."[56] His abstraction of the labor capacity of bodies reflected the alienation of commodified labor and the idea of a worker stripped of humanity. In Mexico, the term was used to distinguish imported coolie labor from colonos. At a time when doctrinaire liberalism was criticized for its idealism, the científico technocrats began to think of the pragmatism of an imported class of animal-like disposable workers. It was at this time that intellectuals like Justo Sierro advocated for imported south Asian coolies to aid in colonization with the hope that they would generate "in our tropical coasts the same excellent results found in the islands of Mauritius and La Reunion" in the Caribbean.[57] For Mexican elites, the world's colonies served as experiments in the technique of colonization, which the elites sought to appropriate and institutionalize as national policy. Mexico's complex regional differences, though, made a simple panacea impossible. Elite arguments for and against the incorporation of the Chinese population in Mexico were more of an indication of local en situ state formations than representative of a coherent national agenda. Beyond Mexico, the use of Chinese workers by industrial capitalists and colonial administrations was also igniting international controversy and intense popular resistance in Cuba, Peru, and the United States.

In the mid-nineteenth century, coolies were heralded as suitable free labor alternatives to enslaved Africans. The exploitative nature of the industrialization of plantations, or intensification of cultivation through mechanization, continued the traditions of slave labor through tenuously legal coolie contracts. The system bred abuse, as one might expect. Colonial and national governments attempted to correct the systematic maltreatment; however, the exigencies of capitalist enterprises and wayward colonies rendered the reforms toothless. By the 1870s several governments launched investigative commissions to determine the extent of the shadowy practices found in the coolie trade.[58] Two texts, in particular, helped sway public opinion against the coolie system of contracted south Asian and Chinese laborers, helping to bring an end to the so-called pig trade: John Edward Jenkins's *The Coolie: His Rights and Wrongs* in 1871 and the Chinese Imperial Mission report on Spanish Cuba in 1875, *The Cuba Commission Report: A Hidden History of the Chinese in Cuba*. Jenkins's text, written in the abolitionist tradition, was an exposé and investigative report on the conditions of south Asian coolies in the British colony of Guiana in South America.[59] These types of reports prompted the Qing Imperial Court to conduct a thorough investigation of the most common destination for Chinese coolies, the Spanish colony of Cuba. The commission's report documents the terrifying brutality and careless disregard for life in Cuban plantation society.[60] However, Mexican elites who exploited coolie labor at the end of the nineteenth century were not dissuaded by these reports.[61]

At the same time, the United States was descending into an economic depression, which helped intensify anti-Chinese sentiments in California. Manufacturing slowed and unemployment rose on the west coast. White labor unions blamed the Chinese people and spurred the growth of state-level anti-Chinese measures, some of which were blocked by the U.S. Supreme Court. Initially, popular outrage against the Chinese challenged the terms of equanimity in the Burlingame Treaty between the United States and China, which was signed in 1868. In 1875 California congressman Horace Page authored a bill to restrict Chinese male laborers and Chinese women from immigrating. The bill reasoned that all Chinese workers represent unfair competition for white workers and that the natural immorality of Chinese women led them slavishly to prostitution and racial degradation with the white population. Page's restrictionist bill was constrained by the 1868 treaty and passed the U.S. Congress through a ban on occupational categories, with no explicit mention of race.[62] The Page Act of 1875 began a national conversation about immigration enforcement as a policy instrument to regulate the racial composition of the population.

Mexico's own discussions of Asian racial difference were influenced by much more than U.S. anxieties. In 1875 Mexico was engaged in a diplomatic and scientific mission to Asia, documenting the transit of Venus. This celestial event sparked global interest in the scientific premise that measuring the movement of Venus across the sky from different locations on Earth would provide an accurate measurement of the size of Earth. Statesman Francisco Bulnes and a Mexican cohort traveled across the Pacific Ocean to engage in this scientific exercise. Through Bulnes's travel logs and correspondence, learned Mexican audiences acquired interest in Asia and knowledge of Asian ethnic difference, thus providing crucial sources of racialized knowledge that technocrats translated into policy. Mexicans considered the Chinese and Japanese populations to be very different. Bulnes describes these differences in an illuminating way: "The most surprising fact is that China, having been in contact with European civilization long before Japan, a nation whose power of assimilation is overwhelming, shows astounding resistance to modern civilization and leads one to believe them to be entirely obstinate."[63] His characterization of east Asian geopolitics reflected a deep-seated ideology of state modernity and racial progress. Bulnes's understanding of Mexican Indian-state relations was mapped onto the colonial politics of Asia. The Chinese were likened to the resistant Indians and the Japanese to compliant converts, demonstrating how Indian-state relations became an interpretive lens by which Mexican officials saw the world around them.

Publicity around Mexico's participation in the astronomy study coincided with the incorporation of Asian people into Mexico's culture of colonization at century's end and illustrated the hesitation by elites to give the domestic indigenous population the same privileges and advantages as settlers. José Angel Hernández deftly illustrates that the domestic population became particularly useful for establishing colonies along the U.S.-Mexico border as insurance against further U.S. incursion. However, when such cases are combined with the overall character of Porfirian colonization policy, including the prospects of Asian immigration, the picture reveals mechanisms of racial differentiation, according to the needs of maintaining and intensifying the state's power. The difference between Chinese and Japanese immigration to Mexico was that administrators sought out cooperative agreements with the Japanese government in focused, limited colonization plans. Since the Chinese were not viewed as positive agents of racial modernity, the state simply tapped into existing streams of disposable coolie labor. The figure of the Chinese people imagined by the Mexican intelligentsia shaped the terms under which the Chinese people would be included in Mexican colonization.

U.S. Restriction and Mexican Reform

The integration of Chinese people into late nineteenth-century Mexico was shaped by two policies: the U.S. Chinese Exclusion Act of 1882 and the Mexican colonization law of 1883. These divergent laws established the conditions where U.S. restriction played into the hands of Mexican elites preparing for sweeping economic reforms. The Chinese Exclusion Act was the first immigration law to prohibit entrance to the nation based on racial grounds.[64] The law placed a moratorium on the immigration of Chinese laborers and a revision to the 1868 Burlingame Treaty with China, retaining the trade stipulations but removing free migration from the accord. The flow of tens of thousands of Chinese sojourners to the United States was dramatically reduced to only a few hundred a year after the law. In addition, the act created the first statutory conditions of "illegal" residency, inscribing both bodies and territorial space with new meaning.[65] These laws provided for the authority to regulate the movement of people in and through national space as well as the power to determine the racial composition of the population. Erika Lee argues that this law transformed the United States into a "gatekeeper nation."[66] The laws sought to exclude Chinese bodies from the United States by regulating international migration and broadening racial barriers around both cultural and political citizenship.

U.S. restriction occurred at a time when Chinese people across the Americas were rewriting their destinies as the coolie system was beginning to be dismantled. The restriction instigated vast, coordinated networks to support and enable the clandestine travel arrangements of tens of thousands of Chinese migrants in the late nineteenth and early twentieth centuries.[67] In 1908 the Chinese legation, a diplomatic body, had estimated that more than sixty thousand Chinese had immigrated to Mexico from the United States, though less than fifteen thousand were recorded at the time.[68] Historian Elliot Young estimates a far greater number of Chinese migrants in transit throughout the Americas.[69] These figures illustrate that Mexico was a vibrant hub of transmigration at the turn of the century, not just because of U.S. restriction but also because Mexican policies created favorable conditions for immigrants' arrival and integration.

In 1883 Díaz passed his first of two major land-reform laws. The colonization law reaffirmed and broadened the power of surveying companies, granting them a third of the lands they mapped. The most important statutes for the current analysis empowered the state's prerogative to dictate and evaluate entry of immigrants for colonization and to grant the special privileges of colonos.[70] Second, the law recognized colonos as Mexican citizens and granted them freedom from military service and taxation, as well as other exemptions.[71] However, answers to the Indian lands question were ambiguous, particularly for Indian people with government-appointed communal and ejidal rights or unrecognized or undocumented claims to land. Indigenous communities were reluctant to participate in the surveying plans because companies could legally write Indian people out of their land with no previous claims. This put the burden of proof on the Indian population, the overwhelming majority of whom lacked any previously recognized title.[72] By 1890 Díaz had ended communal land tenure, purportedly to allow Indians to benefit from individual, independent interest.[73] To support the discipline of the market even more, in 1891 Díaz reorganized his administration to consolidate the secretary of war and navy with the functions of colonization and pacification in a new division, Indios bárbaros y colonias militares (Barbarous Indians and military colonies).[74] Centralized authority over both contracts for settlement and military protection of development projects brought unprecedented foreign investment in mining, railroads, and agriculture, which, in turn, created new demands for mobile, surplus, industrial labor.

The needs of colonization projects dictated national policy. The principal concern among these Porfirian bureaucrats was the construction of infrastructure. Railroads were seen both as the best method of cultivating capitalist development and the most effective means of expanding the presence of the central government. In 1880 and 1881 the Mexican government granted nine concessions for major railroad construction projects across the country, amounting to more than 5,500,000 kilometers (3,417,541 miles) of new lines.[75] With tens of millions of pesos committed to these concessions and millions more in interest to be paid on bonds, the Mexican government was understandably anxious to see the completion of these railroad lines. As early as 1870, Mexican railroad authorities expected to use Chinese workers to construct the national rail system.[76]

The demands for labor and the risks of unwanted social integration sparked a debate in the national congress about reforming the naturalization laws. In 1886 the national congress moved to pass a new law regulating foreigners and creating punitive consequences, such as revoking naturalization and the denationalization of women who married foreigners, for breaking with naturalization statutes, while removing obstacles to legal immigration. Debates in congress were driven by discussions of how immigration policy could be made to favor railroad development in states like Durango, a landlocked state whose mines and fertile valleys remained distant from ports and railroad lines.[77]

The widespread expansion of industrial activity under the Díaz regime brought into view the complexity of state and federal laws that had governed colonization and settlement. In 1894 the Díaz administration put into motion its second major land reform. The 1894 colonization law created new legal categories to organize the inconsistencies, ambiguities, and conflicts over land into a unified administration of the nation's territory. The government's capacity to oversee land reforms was expanded through private surveying companies, and for the first time, some Indian people were formally granted lands. Ejido donations from previous administrations were rarely denied in this process for fear of setting off greater Indian and peasant rebellion.[78] From 1853 to 1909, 93 percent of the land adjudications by the state were executed during Díaz's reign. During the same period, only .03 percent of the transferred lands were by ejido provisions. The ejido lands were primarily used in the rebellious states of Sonora and Yucatán to persuade Indians to lay down their arms and settle.[79]

By the 1890s the Porfirian government documented a decline in the Indian population and a rise in mestizos although none would recognize this social category as a national identity. These census numbers are often misunderstood to reflect the biological transformation of the population, but the criteria used to identify individuals relied on social conditions regardless of ethnic background. Such criteria as not speaking Spanish, use of sandals, dirt floors at home, inconsistent income, and lack of savings were all used to categorize individuals as Indian. The population shifts, according to these social criteria, suggest that a political economic and cultural transformation had occurred since independence from Spain. The aggressive policies for land reform in 1883 and 1894 sought to make the territory and resources of the nation knowable as commodities but also to better attach people to particular development projects through various land-rights regimes. Some of the projects introduced by these reforms emphasized the proletarianization of peasants in places like Chihuahua and the wholesale dispossession of entire communities in favor of foreign colonization in places like Sonora. Still others, as in the Yucatán, reinforced local dictators who were loyal to Díaz. The reorganization of Mexican colonization policy under Porfirian rule established the nation's most stable and lucrative period of foreign investment and economic expansion.

Conclusion

One measure of the legacy of liberal land reforms is the population distribution in 1900, with the nation's population heavily concentrated in the country's center, with lower densities in the north and south, and punctuated by zones of rapid development. Despite decades of intense land reform and rapid economic change, Porfirian leaders were unable to more heavily colonize less-populated areas. Mexican colonization policies were not uniform in their application and certainly not uniform in their result. However, these policies were shaped by racialized conceptions of the republic's cultural geography. The north emphasized criollo and colono blanco settlement in the relatively less-populated but more-hostile lands. The middle, the most populated part of the country, reflected a more acculturated Indian population and accommodation to land reforms. The south was a much more densely populated indigenous region, less acculturated with different patterns of resistance and negotiation. These trends are also visible in the figures of land-title transfers divided by state and period of reform.[80]

These figures illustrate that some states experienced more manipulation than others, reflecting the prevailing conditions of Indian-state relations. Sixty percent of all state-adjudicated land transfer in the second half of the nineteenth century occurred in the territories of Baja California, Chihuahua, and Sonora. This concentration of title transfers, amounting to more than twenty-five-million hectares of land from 1877 to 1893 alone, meant that the Díaz regime literally pulled the land out from under the Yaqui rebellion and practically gave it away to anyone else who wanted it. By 1900 Sonoran land was the cheapest in all of Mexico, going for two dollars an acre. This scale of transfer is not just a reflection of the size of states in comparison with others. The surface area of Baja, Chihuahua, and Sonora covered 29 percent of all Mexican territory, but these states received 40 percent of all government-transferred titles.

On the one hand, the legal category "declared not vacant," invented under the 1894 colonization law, was a unique concession by the Díaz administration to recognize lands previously thought to be vacant—in other words, previously unrecognized Indian lands. The majority of the acreage to be granted under these concessions occurred in the states of Durango (109,102 ha), Oaxaca (131,113 ha), Sinaloa (143,214 ha), and Veracruz (91,752 ha)—indicating that securing titles for local Indian pueblos benefited Porfirian progress in some way. While displacement was a common feature of land reform, this legal category demonstrated a formal recognition and incorporation of preexisting rights regimes into the apparatus of state-led capitalist development. The use of this category signaled the desire to preserve and strengthen regions already engaged in agricultural commodity production.

On the other hand, the legal term *vacant lands* (*terrenos baldíos*) had been in use since Spanish colonization. The imperial politics of this term most often represented the removal of indigenous sovereignty in favor of settlers with exclusive rights backed by the state. Nomadic peoples were the most vulnerable to these assaults because their claims to land were only recognized where permanent settlements were located. By 1900 more than 7 million hectares were designated "vacant" in the northwest borderlands. Baja California (2,979,364 ha), Chihuahua (1,711,156 ha), Coahuila (1,079,106 ha), Sinaloa (1,285,306 ha), and Sonora (2,147,284 ha) were the states with the highest number of designated vacant lands.

In many ways, the sparse population in these regions is a testament to the effectiveness of indigenous struggles against the Mexican state. From this perspective, colonization policy was a systematic effort to inject market forces into these remote zones of conflict. A disaggregation of these trends illustrates that when the Chinese were excluded from the United States, they were welcomed to Mexico, not as colonos but as motores de sangre or surrogate capitalists, to be used in the state's most hotly contested regions.

Later chapters illustrate that antichinismo became a part of the revolutionary state's solution to Porfirian colonization. If land reform in the Porfirian era was defined by its alienation from previous claims and by consolidation among capitalists, the revolution introduced a method of national colonization that recruited peasants and Indians as settlers in fulfillment of the revolution's promise for the redistribution of land. Less than .01 percent of all lands adjudicated before the revolution were ejido land. After the revolution, ejido land was the most important and predominant form of land adjudication and most frequently the end result of nationalist expropriation; from 1930 to 1970 more than half of Mexico's total area was ejido land. The articulation of social rights in the revolution's 1917 constitution responded to a need to side with the discontented peasant masses; however, the implementation of redistributive measures satisfied the administrative fantasy of discipline and universal institutionalization—an experiment in mestizo racialization as agrarian citizenship. The ejido system established by the Mexican state has relied upon racial stereotypes of Indian communes as an "aboriginal method under which agriculture was made the basis of society in Aztec and pre-Aztec times."[81] Emilio Kouri has recently written about the racist underpinnings of the assumed collectivity among Mexico's indigenous populations to question the national mythology that ejidos answered revolutionary demands for land reform.[82] The strategic integration of Chinese people into zones of conflict further illustrates how race and land were intimately tied. Chinese people were first infused as nonsettler labor to satisfy a colonization imperative, and then they became the racial threat to the revolution's agrarian reforms. Mexican racial formations were fundamentally organized by the so-called Indian problem; however, anti-Chinese politics successfully intervened in the racial politics of postrevolutionary reconstruction because of their historical role in national colonization.

2

Motores de Sangre

They Do Not Think, or Assimilate, or Master

In 1907 the steamer *Maori King* arrived in San Diego, California, harbor in a state of siege. The vessel intended to deliver eleven hundred Chinese (and two hundred Russian) workers to armed guards and the field manager of the Southern Pacific de Mexico railroad company in Guaymas, Sonora.[1] The Chinese passengers aboard the *Maori King* overcame their captors during the voyage across the Pacific Ocean only to be handed over to the captors' Mexican counterparts by U.S. Marines. Little is known about these workers after they disembarked, but they serve as an example of ways Mexico became a new market for the trade in Chinese workers after the coolie system was dismantled in the 1870s. Evelyn Hu-DeHart's seminal work on the Chinese immigrants in Mexico interprets the Chinese people as opportunistic immigrants and accidental settlers, but the Porfirian period of migration illustrates a system of labor recruitment that was akin to the coolie trade.[2] This chapter extends the contention by Moon-Ho Jung and Elliot Young that the networks of sojourners and those of the coolie trade were intertwined, though neither migrant stream was free from exploitation, despite the voluntary nature of sojourning and the legal codes of coolie contracts.[3] In the late nineteenth century, Mexico's technocratic ruling class devised plans to use Chinese people as human instruments of national colonization. Mexican colonization policy was a deliberate program to recruit foreign settlers, or colonos, and expand capitalist industrialization. Chinese workers were imported and permitted to immigrate in order to serve specific commercial and labor needs but were not considered ideal. These conditions shaped how the Chinese people were perceived in different regions and, ultimately, determined their vulnerability in the 1910 revolution.

This chapter follows a genealogy of the Mexican racial formation of the Chinese population as motores de sangre. Porfirian officials responded to Mexico's perceived failure to attract great numbers of white settlers with open migration. A history of colonization policy reveals how Chinese-ness was wedged between Indians and the state. In this respect, Mexican racialization adds to Asian Americanist understandings of racial triangulation by illustrating the conditions of contested indigeneity that structured the integration of Chinese migrants. Efforts by Porfirian leaders to introduce Chinese workers were hindered by interference from Britain and the United States. Chinese workers arrived through private initiatives and clandestine channels to expanded infrastructure and colonization projects. The use of unregulated Chinese workers illustrated that Mexican policies favored contracted Chinese labor in regions with the most intense conflicts with indigenous peoples: Sonora and Yucatán. Because Chinese people were injected into regions of violent Indian wars, they occupied an ambivalent position in programs of economic development for both local and Mexico City bureaucrats and politicians. Eventually, comparisons between Chinese motores de sangre and the domestic workforce led to the articulation of a self-colonization policy—a set of programs to discipline and reconstitute Indian people as scientifically administered settlers. These debates centered on a commission to study Chinese immigration and its role in Mexican modernization. The commission's report predictably recommended restriction and nativist protections; however, a new cadre of technocrats rose to power and introduced reforms that preserved the subordinate role of Chinese people in the aggressive expansion of irrigated agriculture. As the current chapter traces this history, we begin to understand why the Chinese people were targets for revolutionary retribution in 1910. Their exclusion from early formulations of self-colonization presaged their subsequent massacre, segregation, relocation, expulsion, and marginalization during revolution and reconstruction.

Contentious Modernization

In 1864 the first group of workers imported from China arrived to build a portion of the Central Branch of the railroad. Mexico was under French rule and, like many other colonies around the world, had pondered the mass importation of Chinese and south Asian coolies.[4] The importation and use of Chinese workers in Mexico were embedded in a web of relationships that tied trade, steamships, immigration, and colonization together. The period of more-regular migration would not begin until decades later in the 1880s, and by the second half of the nineteenth century, Mexico's international trade and migration became increasingly regulated and subjected to the scrutiny of British colonial administration as well as the U.S. government. These regulations complicated Chinese migration to Mexico because the route to Mexico fell under the jurisdiction of different governments.

From 1874 to 1899, stalled negotiations of a binational treaty with China granted Mexican officials flexibility and discretion in the use of Chinese workers in the country's most contentious zones of hostility between Indians and the central government. Officials and businesses explored the possibility of Chinese labor throughout the 1880s and 1890s but were constrained by the formalities of an international treaty. Historians have long considered the 1899 China-Mexico treaty a feeble accord—the result of decades of disagreement and missed opportunities. Recent studies by Roberto Romero and Grace Delgado highlight the vulnerability of Chinese workers in Mexico after the treaty was in force.[5] The traditional scholarly focus on China-Mexico diplomacy has led to an overemphasis on the unstable conclusion of the treaty in 1899 but lack of discussion about the negotiation process.[6] The failed negotiations continued while Mexico turned a blind eye to clandestine use of Chinese labor. This policy failure was, nevertheless, successful in maintaining murky conditions that facilitated the delivery of Chinese workers to sites of national colonization.

The issue of Chinese immigration first gained national prominence in the context of Asian trade prospects and Mexican speculation on Chinese demand for pesos. During the 1880s one of China's trade concerns was a reliable source of silver specie that bypassed European intermediaries.[7] To Mexican bureaucrats Asian interest in the peso could not have come at a better time. China was willing to pay more for specie than the Europeans, and precious metals accounted for 80 percent of Mexican exports. As a normal part of negotiating international trade in the nineteenth century, immigration was a regular concern. However, the prospects of Asian trade alone were never enough to endorse the mass importation of Chinese labor. The most important influence came from European and American investment interests in Mexican industrialization. Debates in English-language newspapers, such as Mexico City's *Two Republics* and *Mexican Herald*, demonstrate that business elites had a familiarity with the international coolie trade as early as the 1830s. Manuel Vera, a Mexican diplomat, became the first editor of a major business daily, *El Economista Mexicana*, which regularly highlighted the accomplishments of coolie labor and advocated for the expansion of the coolie trade in Mexico.

By the 1870s Europeans began making proposals to the Mexican government that included plans to import Chinese workers in large numbers. By the 1880s the Mexican government could not have made it any easier. The opening of Pacific trade routes coincided with a dramatic increase in government funding to subsidize foreign colonization. In 1880 Carlos Pacheco, secretary of development, began soliciting foreign legations to open trade and invest in Mexican colonization. In 1881 Pacheco saw the ministry's budget increase from twenty thousand pesos a year to nearly a million.[8] The expansion of the secretary's charge required new partnerships with Ignacio Mariscal, secretary of foreign affairs, as well as with industry leaders and state governors. This policy approach emphasized the invitation of well-funded foreigners for targeted projects of colonization and industrial development.

Mexican colonization policy favored settlers; however, the Chinese people in Mexico occupied an ambivalent position as an instrument of industrialization. Despite the preference for colonos blancos, the Mexican government did not block the immigration of wealthy Chinese people as surrogate capitalists. Mexican land reform and colonization policy created two important structural conditions that shaped the integration of Chinese immigrants. First, the reform and policy put the rights of settlers ahead of the native population articulated in colonization contracts. Second, the reform and policy emphasized the rapid expansion of infrastructure to connect sites of commodity production with access to markets. Railroads, port facilities, and steamship service were critical to attracting potential settlers, delivering imported laborers to remote sites, and extracting commodities for sale on the international market. Railroads granted access to the interior of the country, and steamships connected Mexico to the rest of the world.[9] Part of the Ministry of Development's budget was dedicated to subsidies for steamship service to make sure transatlantic and transpacific steamships made regular and scheduled stops at Mexican ports. Despite diligent efforts by bureaucrats, administrators, politicians, and private contractors, these public works projects were continuously mired in labor shortages, rebellion and Indian sabotage, lack of support in remote areas, and intermittent funding. As problems mounted, the promise of imported Chinese labor grew, and Chinese investors and entrepreneurs seemed undeterred by Mexico's political instability.

As they weighed the needs of national colonization, Mexican elites were skeptical about the potential racial fallout from mass integration of Chinese workers, even for the most important public works projects. News of Chinese coolies and racialized projections of them circulated among Mexico City elites through newspapers and the *Diario Oficial*, the congressional digest. Some cautious *diputados* (congressmen) proclaimed, "We don't think the question of Chinese immigration to Mexico can be resolved in the single stroke of the pen. We need to consider all possible detours of colonization."[10] Científicos were envious of the material progress that Chinese labor brought to other places. For example, an 1871 article in the newspaper *El Federalista* compared the prospects of European, Asian, and African immigration for Mexican colonization, highlighting the role of Chinese workers in the completion of the transcontinental railroad in the United States and "plantations of the Antilles."[11] Still, the criollo ruling class saw detours everywhere. Racist perceptions of this path of industrialization focused speculation about the effects of miscegenation in a multiracial workforce. Elites were encouraged to imagine the impact of the Chinese people on the domestic population. One editorial said, "The mixture of his race . . . will produce a generation whose quality we leave to the judgment of ethnographers."[12] By the 1870s Chinese labor was widely known as motores de sangre—factors of labor that lacked humanity and intelligence.[13] News of Chinese workers elsewhere contributed to popular Mexican thought about racial difference. For instance, in 1873 a Mexico City newspaper exposé on Peru's use of coolie labor in the progress of railroads, guano exports, and agriculture called the Chinese workers "no more than slaves by another name."[14] In the 1880s, while officials debated the use of Chinese labor, British railroad contractors in Mexico, such as Pearson and Son, had already begun to use African labor from a host of nearby Caribbean and North American sources.[15]

After the passage of the U.S. Chinese Exclusion Act in 1882, Mexico became an increasingly important destination for Chinese people, which reinforced U.S. immigration officials' suspicions that Chinese people were flocking to Mexico to gain illegal entry to the United States. Anti-Chinese politics in the United States had grown to influence both immigration law and a sense of national security. This anxiety led to forceful pleas by U.S. officials for Mexico to adopt restrictive laws—pleas that were mostly ignored.

Despite pressure from the United States for restriction,[16] the Ministry of Development created the Compañía Navegación Mexicana del Pacífico (Mexican Navigation Company of the Pacific) (CNMP) in 1884. The company was formed to begin regular transpacific service from a few Mexican Pacific ports. Salvador Malo, an agent of a British commercial house, authored the original charter for the company and sought to expand trade with Asia.[17] Even though this shipping company had ample financial backing, the slow progress of treaty negotiations and interference from British and U.S. officials snuffed out the efforts. After international criticism of the British handling of the

coolie trade, officials blocked all labor streams that were not covered by a rati-
fied treaty. While treaty negotiations continued between China and Mexico,
Malo attempted to use his British contacts to circumvent British and Chinese
emigration restrictions. In Malo's correspondence with the British Foreign
Service, he frequently argued with British officials that since Chinese coolies
were freely transported to Australia, Peru, and Cuba, "it seems somewhat
anomalous that they should be prevented from [being shipped] to Mexico."[18]
Claims by the Chinese government that its subjects would be treated as slaves
in Mexico heightened British resistance to Malo's plans. Malo quipped back to
British bureaucrats that Chinese workers could be easily acquired outside of
Hong Kong and Macao, beyond the reach of Qing officials, a proposal that the
undersecretary of state in London flatly rejected.[19] Other British subjects in
Mexico also petitioned the crown for permission to bring Chinese laborers to
Mexico. For example, one British investor asked—and was denied—permis-
sion to import hundreds of coolies to Campeche for timber extraction.[20]

    Still, vessels sailing under a number of different flags provided regular trans-
pacific service that delivered Chinese workers to Mexican shores. Hundreds
of Chinese people found opportunities as industrialization and land reforms
created new demands and made different resources available.[21] Chinese merchants regularly sought authorization to build Mexican franchises, or new
branch outposts of established merchandise stores in North America into
their transnational circuits. For instance, in 1886 the Wing Wor Company, a
powerful Hong Kong brokerage, requested an audience with President Díaz
to modify the CNMP contract to accommodate Chinese settlers. Wee Pack, a
representative of Wing Wor, made direct appeals to the Díaz administration for
permission to begin settlement of Chinese people on the Mexican west coast.[22]
However, like Malo's steamship plans, Pack's appeal to alter the terms of the
original CNMP charter were snubbed by British officials.[23] Chinese businessmen in the United States were much more successful in establishing Mexican
operations because they were not subject to the scrutiny of transpacific regulations. A man named Woo Soo, for example, ventured away from agricultural
work in Los Angeles, California, to start a small general-merchandise store
south of the border in Baja California, later becoming a transborder cotton
broker.[24]

    In 1886 the CNMP was granted permission for a single voyage to bring
workers to Mexico. By this time, Porfirian officials, foreign businesses, and
Chinese labor brokers had begun to take advantage of the shadows of legal
ambiguity left in the absence of a formal treaty. Mexican laws did not present
obstacles for Chinese immigrants who wished to pursue formal recognition

and documented migration; however, those caught in coolie circuits remained on the periphery until released from their work.

Despite unsuccessful attempts by the Mexican ambassador to the United States to find a quick remedy for establishing formal ties, the promise of the CNMP for Chinese merchants went cold. By the 1890s, however, Chinese labor brokers were supplying foreign contractors of the Mexican railroad with hundreds of Chinese workers each year. The continued entry of Chinese immigrants into Mexico ahead of a formal treaty reflects the agency of Chinese brokers and migrants to take clandestine action. By the 1890s thousands of Chinese could be found across Mexico working in railroad construction, cotton fields, and mines and on plantations and irrigation canals.

In a telling correspondence, Secretary Mariscal in an 1882 letter to the Mexican ambassador laid out the Díaz administration's plan on Chinese immigration and described the prevailing belief among Mexico City politicians and científico elites that Mexico would not experience Chinese labor competition as had happened in the United States. Because the Chinese were to be specifically used in colonization projects in unpopulated areas, they would not intermingle or compete with domestic workers. Furthermore, the letter argued, should the Chinese be used in areas with Indians, "the problems that result from the mixing of the races" would not occur because Chinese people always seek a return to their homeland.[25] Mariscal argued that widespread racial antagonism was unthinkable in Mexico because of the reticent nature of the Chinese people, as well as their being restricted to remote regions. Confident that the Mexican populace would be untouched or disinterested in the Chinese populace, Mariscal's attitude reflected both the low estimation of Mexico's Indian people as well as the imagined role that the Chinese people were thought to perform. Motores de sangre were envisioned to fulfill a discrete and strategic function in Mexican colonization.

Chinese migration to Mexico in the second half of the nineteenth century was shaped by several intersecting factors: national colonization policy, foreign contractors, Chinese labor brokers, and the obstruction of legal protections. Mariscal's policy formula blurred international law, but it also increased the availability of global resources (finance and Chinese labor) for national colonization. The absence of a treaty meant that Chinese immigrants were without rights unless they pursued naturalization. The flexible approach allowed politicians and bureaucrats to experiment with imported Chinese labor before forcing the issue upon congress, which was split between Eurocentric nativists and capitalist technocrats. The Chinese question at that time would have forced Mexican statesmen to confront the nation's presumed racial innocence. The racial discourses produced by Mexican colonization policy granted bureaucrats the capacity to construct a system of graduated citizenship that ordered colonos, chinos, and Indians in relationship to the goals of national colonization. Vera's *El Economista Mexicana* was frequently the site of open discussion of strategies within Mexico's unlegislated response to the Chinese question. The newspaper's writers advocated for strict domestic oversight of contracted Chinese workers, stating that they would "serve the development of agriculture in those regions where there is not competition, not for reasons of supply and demand, but by the very lack of laborers."[26] The justifications for additional infusions of Chinese laborers relied upon a contradictory plan where state authorities were empowered to direct and allocate the labor. The absence of formal regulations provided the conditions to administer nonsettler labor in national colonization projects, with railroads, in particular.

As a treaty became more plausible in the 1890s, clandestine practices had practically become institutionalized. An 1889 editorial summed up a growing consensus among Mexican technocrats: "Immigration other than Chinese or African will be very difficult, if not impossible. In addition, the streams established by *private initiative*, will remain effective so long as their demand remains steady. This approach is capable of leaving other interests unharmed as it would if it were officially legislated for the whole country."[27] The author of the editorial advocated for no formal treaty with China but, rather, asked for permission to continue using Chinese workers contracted by private initiative. The eventual passage of the China-Mexico treaty in December 1899 did little to challenge or alter this practice among industrialists and Chinese-labor brokers. Rather, the treaty opened an additional pathway for independent migrants and merchants, illustrating that the Mexican state could achieve the desired racial management of the country through the absence of legal instruments rather than explicit discriminatory measures.

Inaccuracies and the clandestine nature of smuggling make records of the importation of Chinese people during this period difficult to trace. However, the example at this chapter's beginning illustrates one botched smuggling attempt in 1907 that shows the conditions for imported Chinese labor. A Russian named Zimmerman, who was a naturalized U.S. citizen but conducted business out of Shanghai, made the initial commission with two other Russian associates for the *Maori King*'s voyage.[28] With the help of Chinese and U.S. accomplices, they successfully deceived with fake labor contracts eleven hundred Chinese men in Vladivostok, near the Russia-Korea border. The recruiters sold the idea that workers would be taken to Shanghai to work on farms in China. After weeks at sea, the passengers knew they had been duped and were going to be captives in Mexican work camps and organized a mutiny. Twenty Chinese passengers were killed.[29] At San Diego, California, armed American marines boarded the ship to ensure delivery of the human cargo to its destination. Once in the Gulf of California, the entrapped Chinese over-ran their American guards and pleaded with Mexican authorities for protection. Mexican officials commandeered the vessel, quarantined the passengers, and ignored their appeals to prevent their delivery to the Guaymas contractor for the Southern Pacific de Mexico (SP de Mexico) Guadalajara line.[30] Chinese officials brought suit against the Mexican government, and British agents filed fraud charges in China's courts. No convictions were ruled, and the crew was absolved from charges. The case left the question of kidnapping and forced labor untouched; the central drama focused on recouping the cost of returning the *Maori King* to Asia.[31]

Only failed or troubled voyages attracted public attention; successful clandestine voyages were quiet affairs, often arriving under the cover of night.[32] Mariscal's formula for utilizing Chinese workers by private initiative in remote regions created brutal conditions without accountability. Such circumstances are not easily compared to the experiences of other more well-known accounts of Chinese Americans or those of the coolies in Cuba. Because Mexico raised few restrictions to Chinese immigration in this era, there are fewer instances of the use of fraudulent documents to claim birthright citizenship, or "paper sons," as practiced in the United States. Yet, Chinese migration to Mexico was unevenly documented and regulated. Imported laborers to Mexico were often contracted workers like those in Cuba; however, most Chinese workers were largely imported as mobile construction crews, with the exception of those sent to Yucatán. Chinese workers in Yucatán closely resembled those in Cuba, where Chinese workers were largely located within an existing plantation system organized by slavery. In Mexico, the combination of government neglect, industry prerogative, and ongoing Indian wars made the Chinese population extremely vulnerable. While Chinese passengers of the *Maori King* affair were coerced into railroad construction, local Yaqui rebels, elsewhere in Guaymas, were hunted down and their families deported. As motores de sangre, the Chinese immigrants unwittingly played a role in Indian-state hostilities. Acknowledging the introduction of Chinese people into landscapes of racial violence is critical to comprehending the role of immigration in Mexico and exposing the racial designs of Porfirian colonization policy.

By 1900 most Chinese immigrants resided in Sonora and Yucatán. When Chinese merchants and laborers settled in these states, they entered into regions of violence, genocide, and struggle by indigenous people for survival against state persecution. The management of national territory through the category of vacant lands created hostile conditions. This policy used the rights and interests of settlers as a weapon against the indigenous inhabitants who resisted programs of Mexicanization. The open door for Chinese immigration was cloaked in shadows and conditioned by the character of indigenous resistance. It seems that the Chinese people were tolerated as long as they continued to advance the expansion of industrial capitalism and maintain the criollo racial order.

Of Mexico's imported Chinese workers before 1900, the majority supplied labor to railroad contractors. Railroad construction extended the sovereign reach of the central government and brought agents of the state and market forces deeper and more reliably into peripheral territory of the country. Chinese labor on the Tehuantepec Railroad served as a crucial transition between conscript and wage-labor regimes among Indian people in Oaxaca and Veracruz.

If not for the infusion of Chinese railroad workers on the coastal spur of the SP de Mexico's Sonora line, Mexican military campaigns would not have been successful in subduing Yaqui rebels in the 1900s. The 1907 extension of the telegraph and railroad network to the Bacatete Mountains in Sonora became the death knell for the Yaqui resistance, leading to the surrender at Ortiz of hundreds of rebels.[33] These conditions are significant not because the Chinese workers were directly involved in these military campaigns but because they demonstrate the social conflicts that Chinese immigrants entered into when they arrived. More important, these conditions created the potential for the revolution's vehement anti-Chinese attitudes and the then-unimaginable success of mestizo national identity decades later.

At this time, nearly every state in the republic registered a Chinese presence. The total number of Chinese people, though, came to less than ten thousand across the country, and it would be fair to ask how such a small group could have such a significant impact. Before the 1880s, public works projects, such as railroads, were built using colonial traditions of *presidio* (military conscription), convict (imprisoned), and *corvée* (drafted) labor—all unpaid work. Although free, the labor was unreliable. Construction suffered not only from an intermittent supply of workers but also inclement weather and a lack of funding. Infusions of Chinese workers into the development of the national rail network proved crucial to the completion of difficult, dangerous, and remote lines.

Chinese participation in the construction of the transisthmusian Tehuantepec Railroad is a good example of how the Mariscal formula supplied vulnerable and considered disposable workers to nascent industrial modes of production (map 3). Commercial rail was an attempt to preserve Mexico's colonial position as a leader in interoceanic commerce. A land grant in 1823 was the first step toward making the Tehuantepec "the center of commerce and navigation for the world."[34] The failure of domestic contractors to complete the line led to a windfall contract for the British firm Pearson and Son in 1848. The unpredictability of forced-labor regimes with largely Mixtec and Zapotec Indian people forced Tehuantepec railroad companies to lean on imported contracted labor. Excitement over the promise of a new contractor led one railroad supporter to propose the importation of eighty thousand Chinese workers.[35] Such plans never came to pass. However, CNMP engineer Malo regularly brought Chinese workers to Oaxaca to lay track.[36] In 1890 he commissioned six hundred workers from China and scattered them along the isolated construction route from Salina Cruz, on the southern coast, north through the lowlands to build a bridge at Malatengo, and along the way to Sarabia and La Puerta, all in Oaxaca. Malo also delivered these same workers to railroads in Suchil, Veracruz, on the Caribbean coast.[37] The workers were poorly supplied and fell ill in a few weeks. The following year, the Hei Loy Company of Hong Kong supplied Malo with several hundred more people.[38] The use of Chinese workers on railroads helped transition from

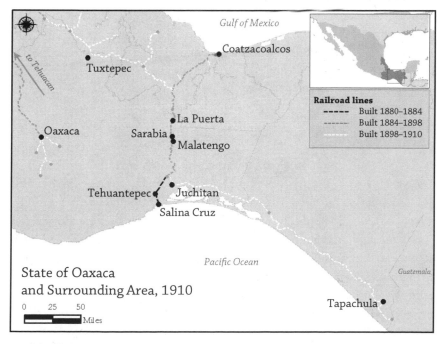

MAP 3. Railroad lines built in Oaxaca and surrounding area, 1880–1910

practices of coerced labor to capitalist forms of wage and contracted labor. The introduction of Chinese laborers taught Mexican industrialists the financial and social pitfalls of managing a dependent work crew.

By 1899 Pearson and Son took control of construction and steadily employed hundreds of Chinese workers at the coastal terminals in Salina Cruz, Oaxaca, and Coatzacoalcos, Veracruz. Chinese workers improved the port facilities, increasing the capacity of the ports to disembark supplies for the railroad. Once the line was completed, the Chinese construction crews became stevedores and lighters who regularly worked nights to improve the pace of development inland with reliable and timely supplies.[39] The establishment of Salina Cruz as a reliable Mexican port drew hundreds of Chinese people to clandestine journeys. Night landings at this port provided a reliable location for clandestine entry until bans on nocturnal disembarkation in 1919.[40] Pearson and Son's successful management of Chinese laborers trickled down to smaller railroad contractors. For instance, in 1899 the On Wo Company supplied the San Luis–Potosi-Tampico Railroad on the Caribbean coast with five hundred workers.[41] On the Pacific Coast, Wong Kong Chong, a railroad-labor contractor, brought several hundred workers to lay track in the state of Colima in 1903.[42]

The integration of Chinese workers in remote construction sites and in the urban port economy did not accompany the decimation of Indian people. In this case, the railroad provided for upward mobility and integration of Indian people into the project of modernization. This is not to say that conflicts did not arise. Zapotec and Juchitan people frequently resisted railroad incursions. However, the degree of accommodation practiced by the railroad at the isthmus permitted the region's Indian population to use the iron-horse economy to their advantage.[43] In Veracruz, Indian claims to land were upheld in Díaz's land reforms, which institutionalized and verified indigenous claims.[44] A report that reflected the accommodationist attitude reasoned that the great machete skills possessed by the Indian people of the region warranted regular wages as expert loggers. Higher pay and legal title strengthened these communities' responses to the impact of railroad development. The Tehuantepec Railroad fit into established patterns of accommodation with Indian republics, in that the Chinese people did not fill ancillary positions within hostile national-colonization programs, as they did, for example, in Sonora. Responses to the railroad expansion and the 1883 colonization laws varied enormously. In Sonora and Yucatán, Yaqui and the Mayan people considered national colonization policy to be an act of war.

Mexico's Indian wars were the defining political context for the majority of Chinese workers in the late nineteenth century. By 1904, 63 percent of the

Chinese people in Mexico resided in the states of Sonora (3,670) and Yucatán (approximately 1,510)—the two territories with the longest-running indigenous rebellions.[45] As steamers disembarked Chinese workers, the government waged wars of extermination. From these violent struggles over sovereignty emerged the revolution's anti-Chinese politics. The complexity of Mexico's Indian wars is derived from the way that government and military leaders mobilized interethnic rivalries. The political practice of recruitment in state-sponsored campaigns is a crucial cultural logic of consent that would later inform membership in anti-Chinese organizations, detailed in chapter 4.

Since the colonial period, Indian people had been systematically recruited into the rank and file of the military and police institutions of the state, even as they were considered to be incapable of modernization. The Mexican military and its frontier forces extended colonial traditions that aggravated interethnic rivalries. Officers would recruit one subordinate group to police or wage war against another. Such military service was attractive to many Indians because it often carried with it a salary and title to land, frequently the lands of their victims. Recruitment into the Mexican culture of colonization granted marginal privileges, stability, and resources for some Indian pueblos in exchange for advancing the capacity of the state to facilitate industrial capitalism and extinguish challenges to its legitimacy. Because colonization policy depended upon these negotiations, local officials and political bosses helped author regional patterns of interethnic conflict and violence. The following sections explore some of these regional patterns and what they meant for the Chinese immigrants there.

Sonora and the Northern Deserts

The highest concentration of Chinese people in Mexico in the late nineteenth century was in the state of Sonora. Its position on the U.S.-Mexico border and the rapid pace of industrialization made this region attractive to many segments of the Chinese diaspora. This region appealed to wealthy merchants, modest entrepreneurs, and laborers. Unlike the isthmus, however, the northern states (particularly, Chihuahua, Coahuila, and Sonora) were sites of intense and brutal warfare between Indian people and the central government, which dated to before independence from Spain. Scholarly literature on the Chinese settlement in Sonora occasionally highlights the campaigns against the Yaqui population.[46] Interpretations of the political context where Chinese immigrants arrived has not been adequately framed with the Mexican government's genocidal campaigns against rebellious Indians. That these immigrants found niches in an economy of warfare, and not merely in a remote frontier, helps to explain why violence against Chinese people during the revolution had political meaning beyond nationalist xenophobia. While the north was less populated, it was also much more violent, characterized at the time by state-led massacres, public lynchings, and mass deportations of Indians.

The most successful of Mexico's Chinese railroad workers in Porfirian Mexico were those on the SP de Mexico line, which ran from Arizona in the United States south into Sonora through the heart of Yaqui territory.[47] SP de Mexico's extension of the U.S. rail network into Sonora in 1880 granted Chinese people on the Mexican Pacific coast easy transit to and from the border with the United States. The industrial giant's previous experience with Chinese labor in the construction of the U.S. transcontinental railroad meant that workers did not suffer the same lack of management as those on the Tehuantepec line. As late as 1907, the Southern Pacific was still contracting Chinese workers from China, a preferred source of labor for SP's chief engineer, E. A. McFarland.[48] After completing the railroad, many of Sonora's Chinese population became residents of the Mexican northwest. They were well positioned as nonsettler immigrants to fill the emerging petit bourgeois niches in the rapidly industrializing landscape, yet as nonsettlers they did not readily occupy newly acquired lands. Contrary to the predictions by Secretary Mariscal and others, Chinese workers frequently married or lived with Yaqui, Mayo, Kumeyaay, and Cocopah Indian women.[49] Chinese marriage with Indian people defied dominant characterizations of these migrants as disinterested sojourners or motores de sangre.

Chinese-Indian intimacy poses many questions about indigenous perceptions of the Chinese people. Imported laborers could have expected to be targeted as enemy accomplices to the government's campaigns of extermination. Yet, the Maori King affair clearly illustrated that the Chinese were neither willing workers nor a warring class of settlers. Is it possible that Mexican disdain for the Chinese made them acceptable partners to persecuted indigenous women? Speculation into the gendered dimensions of Sonora's Indian wars suggests that Chinese men possessed important qualities that signaled stability and security in uncertain times. Indian male soldiers often lived separately from women, mobile male raiding parties decreased the number of potential co-ethnic partners for Indian women, and the establishment of Chinese businesses did not seek to exclude Indians nor cater exclusively to Mexican settlers, making the Chinese presence open to interpretation. Chinese immigrants' access to transnationally circulated capital made them economically successful and independent from Mexican colonization subsidies, and the decimation of Indian families may have put a premium on finding mates to sustain the Indian culture.

Rare photos of Mexican government campaigns to exterminate Sonora's Yaqui people help illustrate the dire conditions under which Indian women entered into intimate relations with Chinese men. Photos by Charles Chester Pierce, an American photographer, in the 1900s document the capture of Yaqui women and children and their transit from an inland fort to the port of Guaymas for deportation (figures 5 and 6).

FIGURE 5. Yaqui captives. Undated photo by Charles Chester Pierce.

FIGURE 6. Deportation of Yaqui captives. Undated photo by Charles Chester Pierce.

These roundups frequently occurred after raids conducted by Yaqui spouses, brothers, and sons. Figure 5 shows soldiers, civilians, and Indians. The Mexican soldiers on the left and right extremes flank three generations of Yaqui women and children. Behind the prisoners stand onlookers, whose hats and light-colored shirts mark them as civilian peasants, distinct from the armed soldiers wearing darker clothes. Rounding up three generations was meant to cripple Yaqui society permanently.[50] By attacking the family unit, military campaigns decreased the Yaqui's ability to mount future attacks in the short term and to continue traditions of resistance in the long term.

The meager belongings that adults carry in figure 6 suggest preparation for a journey; however, most were drowned at sea or delivered into slavery.[51] This traumatic scene was a social backdrop to Secretary Mariscal's formula of the injection of motores de sangre into contested lands because Yaqui deportations during the Porfiriato foreshadowed the expulsion of Chinese immigrants and their Mexican families in the 1930s. The genealogies of violence that informed the anti-Chinese politics were rooted in Mexican-Indian state relations.

Deported Yaqui women and children were regularly sent to Yucatán to work on henequén (agave) plantations that produced valuable fibers for woven products. Enslavement there was designed as penance for their participation in the Yaqui insurgency, and their contributions to Yucatán's plantation economy supported the ability of the *hacendados*, or landed elites, to continue to wage war against the Mayan people there in the south. The complementarity of this policy between the Sonoran and Yucatecan theaters of war and the high concentrations of Chinese people illustrate a national level of coherence among the issues of colonization policy, economic development, race, and intolerance for resistance to that agenda.

Yucatán and the Caribbean

The second-largest concentration of Chinese people in Mexico was in the state of Yucatán. Chinese migrants entered Yucatán in two ways: as ex-coolie Caribbean migrants or indentured workers. As the sugar economy of Spanish Cuba began to hemorrhage at the end of the nineteenth century, the Yucatecan cities of Progreso and Mérida became key destinations for ex-coolies leaving the island (map 4).[52] Throughout the last decades of the nineteenth century, Chinese workers from the Caribbean, Central America, and China were funneled into the plantation economy of the isolated peninsula as contracted workers. While xenophobic politicians and ambitious railroad magnates of Mexico City made the most visible and vocal expressions of Mexican attitudes

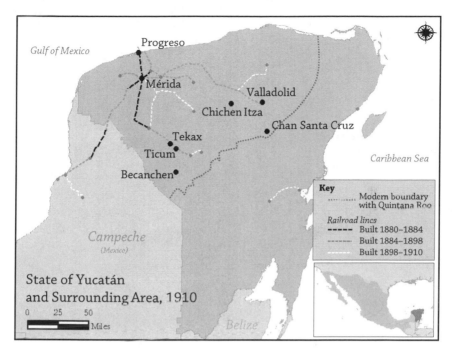

MAP 4. Railroad lines built in Yucatán and surrounding area, 1880–1910

about the Chinese people, those in the Yucatán worked far more quietly to expand the Chinese presence. However, the pattern of economic development in the peninsula was dictated by indigenous rebellion, the reach of international markets, and the scale of railroad construction. These patterns also shaped the contours of life for Chinese migrants in the remote peninsula from plantation work, small agricultural colonies, and urban enclaves.

The Mayan revolt in 1848 ignited a prolonged war of pacification by the Mexican government called the Caste War, which shaped the political conditions for the Chinese population in the region. The insurrection against criollo hacendados, elites known as the *casta divina* (divine caste), brought severe consequences for the plantation economy, from struggles over land to destroyed fields and a strained level of henequén production. Chinese workers are known to have fought alongside Mayan rebels, as many ex-coolies shared the hatred of the plantation system, and some had intermarried with Mayan people, especially the Chinese people of Chan Santa Cruz.[53] The architect of the Yucatecan counterinsurrection was the henequén kingpin Olegario Molina, who employed a totalizing strategy that combined social, economic, and military responses to quell the rebellion. He alone controlled a mind-boggling fifteen million acres of henequén plantations radiating from Mérida, the state capital. This civil war disrupted henequén production and threatened to collapse the plantation system.

In Molina's vast plantations, hundreds of thousands of enslaved Mayan, Yaqui, and contracted Chinese and Korean workers suffered brutal repression. The first Chinese plantation workers were brought to the Yucatán in 1892.[54] They joined a sad lot of Mexico's most vulnerable populations, including local peasant farmers and the unemployed from central Mexico, political dissidents from the north who opposed Díaz, criminals from around the country, and Yaqui deportees—all of whom were usually delivered in chain gangs and kept in barbed-wire enclosures. Other sources indicate that African people from the Caribbean and Canary Islands were also unfortunate enough to work on the plantations. The vast majority of the workers were Mayan peasants stripped of their ancestral lands in the expansion of the henequén plantation. Mayan workers lived as prisoners on the large estates but were returned to their villages as cultivation and harvest dictated.[55]

Most Chinese people in the Yucatán either worked on the plantation or in the cities, however. Small Chinese agricultural colonies were established in Becanchén and Ticum in the southernmost province and Tekax. In May 1892 a Chinese labor broker named King Wing was awarded a colonization contract and authorized to bring Chinese workers to work collectively on ejido plots. Tekax was home to armed Mayan people who had resisted the expansion of the henequén system for decades.[56] Wing had plans to build gardens and tramways to facilitate the circulation of goods and people; however, the state legislature disqualified Wing's project later the same year, fearing that Chinese workers would side with the Mayan people as those elsewhere in the region had already done.[57] The majority of the Chinese people who came to Yucatán via Cuba arrived by their own means, not as imported labor, and the ruling class appears to have considered them radicalized by the coolie experience and, thus, a threat to Mexican colonization of Mayan lands.

By the 1890s Chinese workers could be found on the plantations, in the swamps, on surrounding causeways building roads and tramways, and in the cities selling fruit and vegetables. Reflecting the broader conditions established by Secretary Mariscal, Chinese workers came to Yucatán in a variety of ways. In 1895 a group of 250 ex-coolies from Cuba were caught crossing through Mexico into the United States via Yucatán.[58] It was quite common for Chinese-contracted workers destined for Mexico to be transported across the U.S. rail network. In 1897 U.S. observers began to note the transit of hundreds of Chinese immigrants in bond to the Yucatán from San Francisco down Mexico's main rail line to Veracruz.[59] Independent Chinese contractors were not far behind the *henequéneros* (henequén plantation owners) in their desire to increase the Chinese presence. Despite the demand for Chinese labor, Yucatecan plantation society did not hold them in high regard. In an 1891 article in the newspaper *La Revista Mérida*, plantation advocates, complaining that Chinese plantation workers would not stay on the plantation but preferred the commerce of the cities, carped, "The Chinese are all Indians."[60] The isolated Yucatán peninsula attracted coolie traders and recruiters, although they were limited in their ambition due to the constraints put on them by the hacendados. The zeal for coolies in Yucatán was reflected in 1894, when a naturalized Chinese merchant living in Mérida sought support to bring two hundred thousand Chinese to expand the region's monoculture amid the booming export economy.[61] Even though other Yucatecan hacendados expressed dissatisfaction with the Chinese workers, Molina celebrated their contributions and advocated increased immigration, arguing that the Chinese people were treated well and paid high wages.[62] Yet, public discourse about the Chinese population rarely revealed suspicions that Chinese might sympathize with Mayan rebels.

Even as victims of the brutal plantation mode of production, the Chinese people still occupied an intermediary position. Historian Gilbert Michael Joseph argues that on the Yucatán plantation, little difference existed between the ways different workers were treated, including the application of the whip. However, important differences were engineered by the henequéneros in the use of the Chinese workers.[63] The most vivid descriptions of life on the Yucatecan henequén plantation come from U.S. journalist John Kenneth Turner in his book *Barbarous Mexico*. Turner conducted his research in Mexico in the 1900s and reported on the inhumane conditions of the plantation, with particular details about the participation of the Chinese laborers, who have escaped mention in the scholarly literature.[64]

One of the first scenes Turner describes in Yucatán is the whipping of a resistant Yaqui rebel named Rosanta Bajeca, who had been deported to Yucatán. In the early-morning scene, the administrator made a signal and "there stepped from the host of waiting slaves a giant Chinese. Crouching, he grasped the wrists of the silent Yaqui. The next moment he was standing straight with the Yaqui on his back in the manner of a tired child being carried by one of its elders." In another passage, Bajeca was "given fifteen lashes across the bare back with a heavy, wet [henequén] rope, lashes so lustily delivered that the blood ran down the victim's body. This method of beating is an ancient one in Yucatán and is the customary one on all plantations for boys and all except the heaviest of men. Women are required to kneel and be beaten in the fields as well as at the morning call."[65] In this manner, the Chinese people were incorporated into the system of coerced labor, becoming a corporeal extension of the henequéneros' domination. While the Chinese people labored in the henequén fields alongside Mayan and Yaqui slaves, they were also used as a means to further demoralize the Yaqui population. In another account, Turner details an encounter with a group of Yaqui women who tell him about being forced to "marry" Chinese men or be prostitutes for them.

The forced unions between Yaqui women and Chinese men were supposed to further degrade the Yaqui, "to keep the contracted Chinese satisfied," and "to give birth to children who could be sold into slavery."[66] In the plantations, contracted Chinese workers were given access to Yaqui women to rape them. Perceptions of Chinese sexual perversion were used to inflicted greater symbolic violence in the forced sex of Yaqui women by Chinese men. Constructions of racial difference were not only used as a means of racialization of individual groups, but I also interpret it as an intergroup logic of racial domination in the plantation system. This system sold mixed Chinese Yaqui infants into slavery and thus reflected the devaluation of both the Chinese and Yaqui people in the Mexican colonization agenda.

The history of Chinese migration to the Yucatán demonstrates how Mexican officials opportunistically appropriated circuits of the Chinese diaspora to augment the racial rule over Mayan people. In the peninsula, the terms *Indian* and *mestizo* were categories of domination. Henequén workers were only known as mestizos to symbolize their incorporation by criollo domination. *Indian* reflected an indigenous identity that was the basis of sovereignty claims and the primary challenge to henequénero colonization. In this regional racial hierarchy, the Chinese people were situated as forced laborers and urban merchants or were absorbed into Mayan society. The most numerous class of Chinese people was agricultural workers, many of whom circulated between the cities and the fields. Their vulnerability to plantation abuses was enabled by dubious labor contracts, yet for those who escaped the orbit of the plantation, co-ethnic connections in the diaspora provided cultural capital to take advantage of commercial niches in the cities.

Yucatán never implemented segregation orders like those in Sonora; however, Chinatown enclaves did develop in Progreso and Mérida and reflected the class stratification of the Chinese diaspora. Wealthy merchants like Wing used Mexican colonization policy to advance their own capitalist enterprises, and a small bourgeois class composed of middle-class migrants and henequén workers were able to save or borrow money and enter commercial trades, mostly as grocers or laundry operators.

As Mexican businessmen gained political influence, they brought their regional experience with the Chinese workers into the national arena. For example, Molina's Yucatán henequén empire catapulted him into the position of national chief of development and shaped how Chinese immigrants would serve colonization projects. In 1902 Molina became governor of the peninsula and brokered a deal with U.S.-based International Harvester, the most important buyer of Yucatecan henequén rope. He combined market manipulation and military action to tighten the grip of the henequén elites over the Mayans. For the next four years, Molina's rule over Yucatán captured the attention of Porfirian officials in Mexico City. Rather than relying upon foreign capitalists to bring modernization and industrialization, Molina had accomplished the same goals with repressive policing and exclusion of competitors. Molina's success was contrasted with the prescribed Mariscal-Pacheco approach to development: recruiting foreign capitalists. Part of Molina's plan included specific racialized attitudes toward the Chinese people as motores de sangre, attitudes that he thought were essential for modernization. From 1902 to 1906 Molina demonstrated that government-led programs for industrialization could be effective at colonizing territory and fostering industrial modes of production.

In 1907 Molina replaced Pacheco at the Ministry of Development and held the post until the revolution in 1910. The previous sixteen years of development policy were characterized by luring investments to Mexican shores, resulting in an ad hoc mosaic of laws, concessions, and programs. Molina's policies created colonization contracts that focused on infrastructure and expanded agricultural capacity.[67] During his tenure, the federal government acquired more power than ever before to direct agricultural production and helped preserve the role of Chinese labor and capital in national colonization.

The Chinese Report and Modernization

The experiment with imported Chinese workers under Secretary Mariscal's formula created problems. Policies that injected Chinese workers into sites of economic transformation in politically contested territory led to unintended consequences: long-term settlement, sexual relations with Indian people, and class ascendancy. Against the expectations of Mexico City bureaucrats, the settlement, intermarriage, and economic integration of Chinese people across Mexico raised fears of racial and cultural degeneration in the populace, as well as a fear of unchecked migration. Observers from different regions began to sound xenophobic alarms about the use of unregulated Chinese workers on important national projects. Industry advocates continued to voice support for the recruitment of wealthy Chinese investors and of contracted workers with guarantees for return to China.[68] In response to the rising tide of complaints in the 1880s to the secretary of development, Pacheco oversaw a multiyear study that compiled data regarding the economic, social, health, hygiene, and immigration effects of the prevailing colonization policy. The completion of the report in 1891 evaluated the effectiveness of existing policies to encourage modernization, highlighting recommendations for changes in immigration policy and specifically mentioning risk of exposure to unchecked Asian immigration. Meanwhile, Pacheco continued to approve colonization contracts that used imported Chinese labor by private initiative.

Public debate about Chinese immigration among the ruling class around 1900 set certain conditions for Mexican colonization policy. New streams of independent, documented Chinese immigrants after the 1899 China-Mexico treaty had proved to be useful counterparts to foreign- and state-sponsored projects of colonization in the northern border region. Questions of labor, investment capital, and technology animated the discussion of Chinese racial qualities as irrigation and agricultural settlements became the focus of the Ministry of Development under Molina. These concerns did not shape debates about Chinese participation in railroad construction because the discrete and transitory condition of laying track was fundamentally different from agricultural settlements, as colonization policy concerned issues of land and people's rights to it.

Over the course of Molina's tenure as secretary of development, he instituted reforms to centralize policy. He equalized colonization laws and infused regional agricultural banks with cash. He eliminated the gratuitous concessions developed in the 1880s to encourage hesitant foreigners or to purchase loyalty from regional *jefe politicos* (political bosses). He centralized decision making and created increasingly strict boundaries on the use of public lands and water.[69] Molina offered an industrial vision of agricultural expansion that catered to domestic cries for relief from famine. In essence, Molina replaced foreign contractors with the state bureaucracy and regional agricultural banks funded by foreign investors.[70] After decades of sweeping land reform, the promise of progress was eclipsed by the persistence of famine across the country. Public debates about domestic agriculture were shaped by ideas of race, modernization, nutrition, health, and biology. In this climate of national crisis, broad public concern turned to the issue of Chinese immigration.

In 1903 President Díaz commissioned a study on Chinese immigration, led by a seasoned politician and accomplished civil engineer named Genaro Raigosa.[71] Raigosa gained notoriety for his role in the construction of the Gran

Canal de Desagua, a plan to drain the lakebed that Mexico City was built upon. The drainage of the Mexico City basin was a massive public campaign that Díaz had hoped would make the capital "one of the most sanitary and beautiful cities of America."[72] Arguments for the canal were organized around the scientific understanding of biology and disease in the city's poor population. Discussions of fecal waste, the formation of swamps in building basements, and the way that such conditions made the "pernicious" diseases of typhus and scarlet fever among the poor created an assemblage of powerful images to capture public support.[73] The project was designed to modernize the city and decrease illnesses aggravated by high humidity and standing water.[74]

The formation of the immigration commission reflects early links between anti-Chinese attitudes and a notion of the public good that reinforced the necessity of the state. Raigosa's appointment to the 1903 commission was a political choice that positioned him as a competent antagonist—someone who could articulate the need to drain the nation of the Chinese affliction. The language regarding the hygienic effects of the drainage plan foreshadows Raigosa's appointment as chair of the 1903 Chinese immigration commission. To accompany him on the commission were other científicos, like engineer José Covarrubias and an ambitious senator from Morelos named José Maria Romero.

The 1903 commission sought testimony from across the country regarding attitudes about the Chinese people. Responses to its surveys reflected a spectrum of opinions, from racist condemnations to calls to bring a hundred thousand more Chinese to the *tierra caliente*, or hot coastal lowlands. However, the work of the commission became politicized by an outbreak of plague across the northern states that claimed 365 lives.[75] Beginning in Mazatlán, a port of the Pacific coast state of Sinaloa, Chinese arrivals were blamed, although records indicate that no Chinese immigrant had disembarked during the period of incubation and infection.[76] Nevertheless, accusers suggested that rats carrying the plague had been transported from San Francisco's Chinatown to Mazatlán via unloaded cargo. The Chinese people and disease were thought to be so closely related that the congress passed new health regulations for Chinese immigrants, requiring inspections similar to those at Angel Island in California, complete with sanitary standards and barracks of observation. The commission and bubonic plague helped transfix Mexican perceptions of the Chinese people as a serious public health threat.[77] The resulting immigration restrictions introduced significant barriers to Chinese immigration into the country, with the exception of Baja California, described below, where new settlements expanded rapidly.

Ideas relating health to the racial body in Mexico were in wide circulation by
1900. The Gran Canal de Desagua, for example, tried to combat all that was pernicious, pestilent, and infectious among the city's poor.[78] Xenophobes similarly
applied these traits to the bodies and living quarters of Chinese immigrants.
State ideologies mapped the language of the body and health onto national
territory. In 1886 the Mexican congress passed immigration legislation, Ley
de Extranjería y Naturalización (Law of Foreigners and Naturalization), to
reform the ongoing colonization effort. Despite the benefits conferred upon
potential colonists, the law specified the right of the government to expel
"pernicious foreigners" that might infect the nation.[79]

While the policy did little to stem the importation of Chinese workers, it,
nevertheless, established a national discourse of health and racial regulation
via immigration policy. By 1899, after the treaty with China had been formalized, the image of infectious Chinese people had become so widespread that
their allegedly diseased bodies signified the degeneracy of repugnant customs,
a lack of Christian morals, and poor hygiene.[80] The fact that Chinese living
quarters were thought of as "sites of infection" reflected an ideology that the
government treated the population as a doctor would an ill patient. Like U.S.
patterns of racialization, racial difference linked the notion of "contagion"
to Chinese immigrant settlements.[81] Unlike the United States, discourses of
disease and health did not exclude Chinese immigrants from naturalization.[82]
Attention to health concerns thought to be related to Chinese racial difference served to construct a benevolent image of state intervention in the lives
of common people. The efficacy of health issues in defining popular ideas of
Chinese racial difference illustrates that Mexican racial ideologies extended
beyond class antagonism and highlights the competencies of governing institutions as a key mechanism of popularization and racial formation.[83]

The commission released its report to congress in 1904, after five years of
the treaty with China. The report recommended suspending open immigration
of Asian people altogether.[84] Its stated goals were to elevate Mexican immigration policies to those of other industrialized nations, ramping up health
regulations, documentation, and liability of steamship companies for cost of
deportation or termination of labor contracts.[85] While the report's recommendations were unwavering, it did not fully reflect the attitudes of its members.
Covarrubias, one of the more moderate members of the commission, wrote
elsewhere,

> There is no danger that contact with the Chinese will change our people favor-
> ably or unfavorably, mainly because that contact cannot be verified. There has
> neither been assimilation nor submittal to our customs by the Chinese, and as

for the other part, their labor is an economic necessity for our country. They do not think, or assimilate, or master. We should only try to consider them as a partner, counseled by the government, not their systematic exclusion, as has been done in other countries in economic conditions different than those of our own. Only by *constant intervention of immigration by the government can it be directed to certain points* where they are needed, to reduce our loss to convenient terms, and always retain the hand of government in the direction of its movement.[86]

Covarrubias echoed the formula Secretary Mariscal articulated years earlier. The government would exercise constant vigilance over the use of Chinese workers. As motores de sangre, they would be governed by immigration laws and colonization laws, even if they became naturalized, due to their perceived racial qualities. The restrictionist report created an impasse between científico developmentalists who saw Chinese immigration as a strategic policy instrument and political nationalists who vied for education, recruitment, and discipline of domestic workers. In other words, debating the Chinese question became a choice between colonization as foreign recruitment or domestic conscription.

The more that Mexico City elites considered Mexican peasants to be agents of capitalist industrialization, the more anti-Chinese politics acquired political value. When the vast rural population was written off as incompetent savages, Chinese motores de sangre become an attractive alternative. This ideological binary shines a profound light on Raigosa's work on the Gran Canal of Desagua. While the public health charges of the project bolstered his credentials, the real value of Raigosa's leadership in the canal's construction was that it was built with domestic peasant labor. After the completion of the canal, Díaz nominated the republic's top civil engineer to evaluate the potential of Chinese immigration against the existing pools of labor. The last section of the immigration report to congress paid considerable attention to the social and economic virtues of Mexico's Indian population. The accomplishments of Chinese contracted workers were weighed against those of millions of indigenous peons across the territory's diverse regions who were charged with establishing military fortifications, opening carriage roads, and constructing railroads. Furthermore, the inspection of various public works, which have been admired for their moral stricture, showed the incredible seriousness and extraordinary corporal strength that characterizes the indigenous workers of Mexico, Raigosa said.[87]

The commission concluded that unlimited Chinese immigration for the purposes of colonization or for temporary labor was no longer "convenient" for the nation. Its recommended restrictions reflected the emerging idea of self-colonization.[88] As either motores de sangre or yellow peril, the racialized figure of the Chinese people was important in the formation of nationalistic ideas about modernization and the public good.

Public works like the Gran Canal fed fantasies of self-colonization among the ruling class. The successful completion of massive public works projects gradually began to shift expectations of development and colonization. Instead of merely being recipients of development and beneficiaries of colonization policy, the Mexican peasant was beginning to be considered as an agent of modernization. This characterization of the average Mexican worker was novel. An example of the ideal Mexican worker can be found in the image blazoned opposite the title page of Raigosa's final report to congress on the Gran Canal work (figure 7).

Figure 7 creates an optical illusion and helped symbolize Mexican projects for modernization. A railroad line is being extended across an enormous lake via the construction of a dike. The track and dike are overshadowed by a mass of workers, who extend to the vanishing point of the visible horizon. The extension of the line straight to the horizon makes it appear that the line of track and workers continues indefinitely, perhaps forever. The geometrical lines produced by the image's forms correspond with an orderly vision of development that weds modern engineering with Indian bodies. Images from projects like this helped generate the idea that domestic Mexican workers were capable and competent conscripts of modernity, a concept that pushed

FIGURE 7. An ideal image of the Mexican worker from Raigosa's final report on the Gran Canal. Photo in Raigosa, *Desagüe de la Ciudad.*

against a century-old assumption that development would only come at the hands of immigrants. These types of images, produced by the Mexican state, document how projects of modernization were sites to observe how popular culture and state power intersected.[89] They offered hard evidence of an orderly nation imagined and legislated by elites, yet unrealized by those captured in its frame. Given the mixed performance of Mexican workers on other railroad projects and the state preference for Europeans in colonization policy, images like this introduced new meanings for the placement of Mexican workers in the social order.

In the end, however, political concerns might have trumped both the high-level status of the report and the momentum against the Chinese people after the bubonic plague. After the commission delivered its findings, it was adjourned, and the report was shelved. Raigosa, the public and intellectual leader of the commission, passed away shortly after the commission was dissolved, as did Matias Romero, Mexico's diplomatic representative in Washington, D.C., and an ardent supporter of the China-Mexico treaty.

Even if they had lived, powerful business interests would not have allowed these restrictions on Chinese immigration to take hold.[90] Molina, for one, stood to lose much if new limits on Chinese immigration had been passed.[91] In his 1903 annual governor's address to the Yucatán legislature, he had cited particular interest in advancing Asian settlements in the tropical peninsula.[92] Covarrubias continued his independent accolade of Chinese motores de sangre through three essays published in the top policy journal *Revista Positiva*.[93] These attitudes likely earned him the position of chief engineer in the Ministry of Development under Molina in 1908.[94]

Still, some antichinista self-colonization advocates like Senator José Maria Romero did not give up the fight. In 1908 Romero raised the issue of Chinese restriction to the legislature for a second time and successfully led an amendment to the Mexican constitution's article on immigration and sanitary laws to prevent unrestricted immigration.[95] While the law itself does not single out the Chinese people, the preamble to the amendment is directed at científico excess: "It is undisputed that the prosperity of Mexico is principally based on immigration . . . but what Mexico needs is a blood transfusion that is pure and vigorous, by the importation of healthy men of sound mind and body. The government not only has the right but also the duty to make a wise and prudent selection of immigrants."[96] Again, economic development was envisioned through notions of the country's racial composition. Prosperity and the public good were dependent upon the capacity of the state to bring about racial improvement, and immigration policy helped articulate this ideology.

The 1908 reform did slow Chinese immigration to Mexico. Pacific ports were closed (although many places along the U.S. border remained open to Chinese immigration). Medical inspections blocked the arrival of hundreds of potential Chinese immigrants that year. Although the attitude behind the amendment was aggressive, it was inconsistently applied throughout Mexico, perhaps illustrating Covarrubias's position of flexible enforcement. Contradictory positions regarding the Chinese people reflected a broader ambivalence of colonization policy. The continued reliance upon Chinese labor after 1900 indicated that institutions would rather import Chinese workers than give Indian peasants greater political and economic power.

The 1908 amendment reflected a growing obsession with the racial development of the population through guided evolution and prudent selection. In 1909 Andrés Molina Enríquez, a public intellectual and científico, wrote that a figurative mestizo (mixed Indian-European population) would absorb indigenous qualities and assimilate foreigners to evolve the nation into a distinctive race of people endowed with a capacity for industrialization.[97] The redemption of the Indian peasant through discourses of mestizo industrialization were to be the supporting ideological architecture for self-colonization policy and revolutionary agrarian reform. The structural role of Chinese immigrants during the Porfiriato situates them as a crucial obstacle to the realization of state-sponsored self-colonization—a conflict that will play out through revolution and reconstruction.

Since the 1830s the Mexican government tried desperately to implant foreign settlers in the barbarous north. Pacheco's development bureau oversaw a widespread surge in colonization contracts that granted concessions to a number of foreigners, particularly in the Comarca Lagunera where the town of Torreón is located, which covered municipalities in Coahuila and Durango, where irrigated agriculture grew 400 percent from 1880 to 1890.[98] In this expansion, capital investment outpaced labor supply, creating a number of opportunities for which diasporic Chinese immigrants were well suited to take advantage.

Molina's self-colonization plans gained popularity because they were designed to increase agricultural productivity of staples, rather than that of the cash-crop exports that dominated the agricultural settlements of the previous decades. According to statesman Francisco Bulnes, the economic depression that set in around 1907 created a significant problem of growing enough food for the country. For Bulnes, irrigation "was the only means of saving and enriching the people . . . and above all, [to] reclaim that great portion of the arable land which is most depleted, by permitting the introduction of intensive methods of agriculture." Rather than address existing inequalities in Mexico's food production systems, the specter of famine was used to advance a wave of industrialization. From 1908 to 1910 the Mexican government spent $45 million on the agricultural improvement of the country—primarily, irrigation enterprises. Finance Minister José Limantour, along with a number of wealthy hacendados, created the Loan Fund for Agricultural Work and the Development of Irrigation for exclusive use by Molina's office.[99] Despite the populist discourse surrounding these public works projects, the funds were accessible to only the largest landholders. Ranchers and Indian communities stood little chance in acquiring new land titles in Molina's irrigated colonization. Molina's funds exceeded $30 million, dwarfing the colonization blitz under Pacheco in 1881 and illustrating the turn by Mexican elites to spend heavily to enrich an emerging class of domestic industrialists, rather than entice foreigners. Yet, Chinese immigrants were crucial informal functionaries to the expansion of this phase of agricultural development, particularly, in Baja California.

Despite the quiet preservation of elite interest in sustaining the Chinese presence, popular riots against the Chinese were not uncommon. Mobs targeted the small Chinese communities of Mazatlán and Mexico City in unrelated events in 1886. A strike erupted against Chinese people in a Sonora lumber mill in 1891 and another in Monterrey in 1895. These attacks became increasingly common by 1900.[100] The increased predation on Chinese communities seemed to reflect frustrations of their growing integration in Porfirian colonization.

Abarroteros Chinos and the Pacific Commodity Circuit

Chinese intermediaries could be found across northern Mexico's newly irrigated settlements. From the peasant perspective, they began to fit a preexisting stereotype of a foreign merchant, broker, or trader only concerned with exploitation and political treason that furthered their economic success. According to xenophobes, Mexico had been plagued by a "regime of abarroteros" (grocers, but more generally merchants); however, Chinese immigrants were not equivalent to the agents of Mexican, British, and U.S. capitalism that they were being compared to. In Baja California, Chinese migrants were the sole source of labor and commercial know-how in the isolated peninsula and were the majority of the population until 1930. Chinese immigrants filled intermediary roles in domestic retail sales or transpacific trade, rather than extractive industries. The larger patterns of Porfirian colonization created key dependencies upon Chinese immigrants that gave the impression of a slow-moving invasion to everyone except científico elites.

The Baja California case is instructive because it demonstrates how and why the discourse of motores de sangre intersected with Porfirian colonization. Like many other irrigated colonization schemes in northern Mexico, foreign contractors made cotton colonies an attractive place for the Chinese people to migrate to. Immigrants were directed to Baja California and other northern border states and were discouraged from settling in other regions. For instance, Albert Owens, an American investor with an agricultural colonization contract for Topolobampo, Sinaloa, was denied permission to develop direct steamship service with China for fear that Chinese immigration would become too prevalent in Sinaloa.[101] The irregular application of Chinese restrictions and approvals reflects the científico paradigm of privileging private initiative and government discretion. Leaders in the west-coast cotton industry were convinced that strong demand for their exports in Asian markets guaranteed a brisk trade and quick profits.[102] Harrison Gray Otis, Southern California owner of the *Los Angeles Times*, was of the same mind, as he invested millions to develop the Colorado River delta and its Baja California basin. Otis and real estate tycoon Harry Chandler partnered with Baja California elites to execute a contract to colonize the desolate borderland through the Colorado River Land Company (CRLC). The contract granted enormous power to the CRLC as it began to develop irrigation infrastructure.[103] Through its financial largess and the integration of transnational Chinese networks, the CRLC overcame obstacles that stopped others from developing the region.

Otis's industrial syndicates created the single-largest, irrigated colonization project on either side of the border, boasting more than twenty-five hundred miles of canals. Efforts to relocate Mexican farmers to CRLC lands failed because better conditions existed on the northern side of the border, so Otis and CRLC ranch managers turned to the Chinese people. By 1908 Otis had begun recruiting laborers directly from China,[104] and advertisements for Mexicali, Baja California, appeared on the streets of Canton and Hong Kong, offering opportunities to work, rent, or own land in the pursuit of cotton cultivation.[105] Eventually, the CRLC joined with Hong Kong labor recruiters of the Mi Wah Company. This Cantonese brokerage house furnished five-year CRLC contracts for Chinese laborers.[106] The Mi Wah contracts promised wages of $24 per month (almost $700 today) with extra wages for "diligence" and the option to lease company lands.[107] The promised wages exceeded those paid to other Chinese people already working in California fields.[108] The possibility of working and leasing land for a cash crop booming in China was of immense interest to laborers, farmers, traders, and financiers throughout Hong Kong and Canton. Over the next three years, U.S. immigration officials reported a dramatic influx of Chinese migration to Mexicali, with more than two hundred Chinese immigrants per eastbound steamer.[109] The mass arrival of Chinese immigrants to Mexicali transformed the border region into a bustling agricultural depot: a site of cotton cultivation and export for the industrialization of textile manufacturing in east Asia.

Communications between CRLC ranch managers and the Los Angeles CRLC office indicate a complete reliance upon the Chinese immigrants, not only for labor but also in organizing the social relations of production.[110] The CRLC, being primarily a real estate–development venture, was ill-equipped to facilitate international trade in commodities, and its managers tried using the Chinese businessmen who were already in Baja California to establish links with other co-ethnic businessmen throughout Mexico. The CRLC's main attorney wrote to an American friend with diplomatic connections in China to discuss methods of attracting more Chinese workers for the colonization enterprise:

> [W]e are just as anxious as ever to secure coolies at a cheap rate and work them upon our Mexican property, but we have had so many disappointments that we have dropped the matter because we thought it was impossible to secure them. We have a very few on the ranch now who wander into the country by way of Ensenada, but they are costing too much money to justify us in having many. . . . Or, if it would be possible to make an arrangement with some rich Chinese house to lease part of our land and bring their people over to work, I think possibly that would work out to a better advantage all around. It is quite a hard matter to get the Chinaman to stay south of the line at the small wages we are willing to pay, when the imaginary line on the north is the only thing between them and the high American wages if they can successfully cross and keep out of the clutches of the American officers. But if they were working for some of their own people it might be different.[111]

The attorney's coy plea for help straddled the difficult situations of bringing Chinese people to Mexicali and getting them to stay. Eventually, the CRLC found success in leasing out parcels to mutualistic Chinese fraternal associations. The informal and flexible terms of the leases allowed groups of Chinese men to overcome the single major obstacles to growth in Mexicali—labor supply and market access. Chinese associations had advantages over others because the Chinese associations shared start-up costs between partners, labor was organized through co-ethnic networks, and harvests were marketed internationally through established commercial networks.[112] The CRLC colonization scheme did not result in productive enterprises until managers could solicit Chinese recruiters and east China cotton brokers to organize the harvest and export.

The CRLC offered irresistible lease terms to encourage workers to endure the hardship of desert colonization. The ranch managers found the Chinese people to be so enthusiastic and capable of delivering results that the managers charged no money down to open new leases. Furthermore, lease agreements in 1908 offered plots with no rent for the first year although they did require significant improvements of no less than $2,000 worth of fencing, irrigation canals, and clearing of the land.[113] These contract terms ensured that the CRLC would spend no money on land improvements while quickly populating its agricultural land. A mix of Chinese, Mexican, and American farmers signed these early leases. However, the Chinese farmers became a clear majority when Mexican ranches failed and American farmers subletted to other Chinese farmers. As tenants became established, the lease terms changed to fulfill the rent-seeking aspirations of the CRLC. Still, lease agreements encouraged the expansion of Mexicali's agriculture with graduated terms of payment in cash or in kind. By 1911 American leaseholders of CRLC lands began to subcontract to the Chinese farmers, using contracts of indenture.[114] American farmers held more than fifty thousand acres of Mexicali farmland and went so far as to petition the federal government to allow the flow of Chinese laborers to their Mexican fields.[115]

Molina's agricultural loan fund sparked a wave of new development, which made the Chinese people a consistent presence in irrigated colonization. In 1908 Pearson and Son, the Tehuantepec Railroad contractors, won another lucrative contract for the construction of a dam on the Rio Nazas in Durango to deliver water east to the Comarca Lagunera (the lake region), near Torreón, Coahuila. Mexican finance minister Limantour touted the project as the first large-scale irrigation project funded by the Mexican government.[116] Pearson not only brought Chinese people to help build the dam but also worked to establish them as farmers and beneficiaries of the irrigated lands, further encouraging the development of the Chinese community. In addition to Chinese workers, African American immigrants were also brought to these irrigation projects; in 1895 the Tlahualilo Colonization Company, north of Torreón, imported an estimated eight hundred African American immigrants to work the irrigated desert. Shortly after their arrival, the workers were plagued by illness and racially charged attacks by members of the surrounding *rancheros* (ranchers). When some workers tried to leave the colony, armed Mexicans killed them.[117] In these cases, blackness and Chinese-ness were crucial frames that common people in the north contested. Regardless of the popularity of anti-Chinese discourse circulating in Mexico, officials and industry leaders continued to utilize Chinese workers and appropriate their expertise and social connections for the purposes of Mexican colonization. These structural conditions gave rise to a class of Chinese petit bourgeoisie across northern Mexico. The Chinese population became a group managed by the Porfirian state and remained distinctive from European and American colonos blancos and the mass Indian peasantry.

Mexico's Chinese population had become associated with what Bulnes refers to as the Mexican "regime of abarroteros." Bulnes argues that the Mexican republic chronically suffered from the capitalist and extractive nature of a colonial economy plagued by traders and merchants who inspired political assassinations, demanded tyranny, profited from war, corrupted politicians, funded vice, and supplied weapons to enemies of the republic. Bulnes also argues that divisions between the conquerors and the conquered kept the mestizo from expressing "the strength of [their] blood."[118] This strain of populist thought became exceedingly common in the lead up to, and aftermath of, the 1910 revolution. Widespread classist, anti-intellectual denunciations of liberal Porfirian científicos drew from earlier traditions of anti-Semitism.[119] If Díaz and his cronies were characterized as the villainous abarroteros of the republic, then the Chinese people had become the pernicious abarroteros of the villages and towns.

Conclusion

Imported Chinese laborers were an economic policy prescription that joined a host of other programs aimed at either exterminating "unruly" Indian republics or recruiting Chinese laborers into modernization schemes. The Mexican state did not consider the imported Chinese workers as political subjects or social actors; however, their presence in Sonora and Yucatán placed a political charge on their presence. The problem of labor scarcity that Chinese workers were intended to resolve was a manufactured crisis; the lack of labor required to produce surplus value in export industries was positioned in regions where federal control was weak and labor could not be supplied or coerced. Zones of conflict were hot spots precisely because of capital's penetration and state campaigns of submission. While the Chinese people remained vital to various types of colonization projects, they became highly visible members of a society built by technocrats. In essence, the Chinese people became associated with the regime as the social residue of a dictatorial period. These Porfirian colonization projects not only determined the manner of incorporation but also determined the character of local rebellions where revolutionary actions delivered violence against the Chinese population.

As the next chapter will make clear, the rise of the mestizo as a figure of national identity coincided with the proliferation of anti-Chinese organizations and episodes of state-endorsed racial segregation and expulsion. Anti-Chinese attitudes in the revolution connected ideas of economic redistribution, female dependency, cultural unification, and populist nationalism. The following chapter also shows the role of race in the armed rebellion and a return to the Asian Americanist critique of warfare as a crucial arena where racialized Asian-ness is articulated.

3
Violent Imaginaries and the Beginnings of a New State

On April 10, 1911, *El Tiempo*, a Mexico City newspaper, published "Chinese Immigration for the Development of Agriculture, a Mexican Prejudice," a letter from José Díaz Zulueta, the Mexican consular representative in Chile. Zulueta took issue with the declaration from a prominent agronomist that imported Chinese labor was the best method to expand irrigated cotton cultivation in Mexico's arid highlands. Having witnessed firsthand what imported Chinese labor had wrought in Chile's neighbor Peru, Zulueta warned against such proposals. The letter criticized Mexican policies of the last decade that augmented irrigated colonization with Chinese *motores de sangre* instead of "our Indians."[1] He painted a picture of Mexican pueblos transformed into the Chinese slums of Lima and used rancorous language against importing coolies, applying common anti-Chinese epithets. According to his letter, Chinese laborers turned themselves into merchants from their greed and intermarried with the local population from their perversity, thus promoting a dangerous moral and racial denigration. Zulueta's diatribe added to the growing association between anti-Chinese vitriol and support for programs of self-colonization—that would become central to revolutionary agrarian reform. Throughout Mexico, people began to envision broad social change through violence directed at the Chinese people. Unlike the anti-Chinese campaigns in the United States thirty years earlier, the racism developing in Mexico was tied to revolution, reconstruction, and reworking rule and consent within industrial agriculture.

Experience did not prepare the Chinese diplomatic corps for the changes brewing in Mexico. However, the Chinese diplomatic staff in Mexico City did not take Zulueta's letter lightly. Days after its publication, Li Chung Ping, chancellor of the Chinese legation, replied to *El Tiempo*. Ping's response, "In Defense of Chinatown," made economic development his central thesis: the Chinese people generated great wealth because they were essential collaborators for speculation in land improvement. Ping's letter plainly spelled out the vital role that Chinese financiers, merchants, and laborers had served in the advancement of Mexico's and Peru's agriculture over the previous decades.[2] Ping's confident rebuttal failed in one crucial way—admitting that Chinese were collaborators with the Porfirian regime represented a grave self-indictment. Because the Chinese people were introduced into Mexico under a colonization plan, they were not simply immigrants who settled into emerging economic niches. By 1910 any justification for the Chinese presence was associated with Porfirian national colonization and assumed to involve support for its underlying ideologies of Indian racism and widespread dispossession. The chancellor's miscalculation illustrates how unsuspecting Mexico's Chinese population was of the coming revolution. Just six months earlier, Francisco Madero, a wealthy Coahuilan, had announced his Plan de San Luis Potosi, inciting rebellion against the aging Porfirian regime. Unrelated to Ping's letter and only weeks apart, Maderista soldiers and civilians brutally butchered 303 Chinese people in the streets of Torreón—the most violent episode of anti-Chinese violence in the western hemisphere. It would seem that no defense could surpass the cultural and political value of violence against the Chinese people. This chapter shows several ways anti-Chinese violence was mobilized in warfare as a vehicle for collective imaginaries, panethnic mobilization, and battlefield tactics.

Largely forgotten or disavowed, anti-Chinese collective violence was a regular feature of the revolution's frontlines. The waves of insurrection that spread across Mexico from Madero's defiance of the Díaz regime resulted in several large-scale demonstrations against the Chinese population. Before Madero claimed the presidency in November 1911, three major uncoordinated demonstrations against the Chinese population erupted, the first in Torreón, Coahuila, in May; the second in Tapachula, Chiapas, in June; and the third in Pilares de Nacozari, Sonora, in August. The Torreón massacre was the most horrific. All three were woven together with insurrection in boomtowns that emerged through científico colonization. The policies of both Mariscal and

Molina created distinct patterns of Chinese settlement at sites of colonization and rapid economic development. In all three locations, the Chinese people were the most numerous among a cadre of foreigners. These Chinese settlers occupied an array of class positions from menial laborers to wealthy magnates but were predominately small- and medium-sized businesses of retail merchants and brokers—signaling Bulnes's so-called vile regime of abarroteros. This violence contrasted with anti-American agitation, which was frequent throughout Mexico. Anti-U.S. demonstrations did not systematically result in homicide, even when hundreds shouted "death to the gringos" in street parades.[3]

Anti-Chinese violence during the revolution can be compared with the Japanese experience. While Chinese immigrants abstained from entering the revolution's military factions, Japanese immigrants were prized combatants racialized as martial experts. Historian Jerry Garcia uncovers important dimensions of this practice, although not discussed in the current pages. Differences between the Chinese and Japanese people during the revolution illustrate the importance of an immigrant's home country's standing in the global order. However, the influence of foreign governments upon their respective immigrants within Mexico was uneven during the revolutionary years. Comparisons of experiences of Chinese and Japanese immigrants in revolutionary and postrevolutionary Mexico must keep in mind that the Japanese population was even smaller than the Chinese one, never exceeding more than ten thousand in the first half of the twentieth century.[4] The small population size compared with the cultural and political weight given to racialized discourses about differences between Chinese and Japanese populations reinforces my central argument that Mexican Orientalism was concerned with the internal coherence of a state-organized racial order. In this sense, anti-Chinese and pro-Japanese attitudes acted as guidelines for modernist aspirations during the collapse of the Porfirian state and the rise of the revolutionary order.

Since the decline of the Porfirian order after 1900, dictatorial rule had produced a cacophony of incongruent discontents—who, nonetheless, all seemed to agree that the Chinese population must go. Madero's call for revolt against Díaz and the despised científicos represented a landed middle-class segment of Mexico's north. His insurgent strategies focused on urban assaults and a takeover of the political class of appointees and local political bosses. His platform did not include agrarian reform but, rather, expropriation and a democratization of bureaucratic posts. Despite being conservative, "Maderismo" became a viable alternative to the Porfirian machine; borrowing the legitimacy of his name, many raised his banner for their own unaffiliated causes. Although in his writings Madero himself did not single out the Chinese people, others included anti-Chinese positions as they took up his cause.[5] Madero, as a leader of the rebellion, never disabused them of this association. Still others, like Ricardo Flores Magón of the Liberal Party (PLM), who challenged Madero's bourgeois revolution with an anarchist platform of syndicalism, were more explicit. In his party's newspaper, *Revolución*, an unnamed author called the Chinese "Porfirian lackeys."[6] This more radical proletarian strain of the revolution expressed mixed feelings for the Chinese people, calling for their removal and alternatively asking for their solidarity.[7] However, such positions appear paltry in the face of Francisco "Pancho" Villa's call to kill all the Chinese people his troops encountered—orders that his famed Dorados followed to grim ends.[8] Leaders of Mexico's revolution could not imagine change without tearing Chinatown asunder.

This chapter examines three distinct practices of anti-Chinese violence: mass killing in uncoordinated assemblies, tactical assassinations, and other violent rituals. The mass killing of Chinese people in the early revolution was a symbolic rejection of Porfirian colonization that gave life to a new kind of public imaginary. The 1911 Torreón massacre and its historiography, along with several other popular antichinista demonstrations, are detailed to discuss the generation of a racialized public space. The coordinated assassination of Chinese functionaries in colonization schemes illustrates the way that battlefield tactics contributed to making anti-Chinese violence legitimate, and violent rituals including looting of Chinese businesses demonstrates how the structural position and legitimized violence against them transformed their resources into wartime assets. Competing groups vied for these resources and opportunistically appropriated them. These types of violence were cathartic outbursts that condemned decades of national colonization and opportunistic responses to vulnerable Chinese communities during wartime conditions.[9] A decade of these types of collective violence against the Chinese people established a popular cultural logic of hate and a history of persecution. Both outcomes became vital political resources for the Sonoran inheritors of the revolution, Álvaro Obregón and Plutarco Elías Calles, who used the effects of racial violence to build approval for institutionalized discrimination of the Chinese people as well as consent for agrarian reforms of self-colonization. Anti-Chinese politics bloodied the ground from which diverse people stood to claim citizenship in the revolutionary order—a mode of political incorporation for state capitalism in the revolutionary government.

This chapter departs from the premise "Violence needs to be imagined to be carried out. Groups do not strike out at random."[10] In other words, group action is not idiosyncratic, without meaning, or without a perceived conflict.[11] The chapter's focus on collective or cooperative violence seeks to underscore the web of social relations that reflect both the large structural conflicts that anti-Chinese violence sought to resolve and the symbolic value that practices of collective violence had upon future confrontations. Rather than calling upon the sinophobic boundaries of Mexican nationalism and a supposed tran- scendental mestizo collectivity to explain patterns of violence against the Chinese population, this chapter shows how anti-Chinese violence rose from perceptions of the structural conditions of Porfirian colonization and a com- petition for scarce resources. The cultural articulation of these anti-Chinese behaviors leads to a rejection of revolutionary xenophobic nationalism as its sole cause. The xenophobic explanation is incomplete because it too hastily constructs the formation of mestizo collective identity as its origin. In other words, the mestizo racial form did not become an "imagined community" until the institutionalization of the anti-Chinese ideology described in the next two chapters. At this early stage, as this chapter discusses, the revolution was nei- ther politically coherent nor unanimously popular. Xenophobia is also a poor descriptor because, during this period, it included other foreigners besides the Chinese people, as well as hostile suspicion of Mexicans from other regions. Lastly, any gesture toward nationalism as horizontal social bonds, such as that witnessed in the 1920s and 1930s, can only be said to exist as aspirations of intellectuals, bourgeois revolutionary generals, and the cohort of Porfirian bureaucrats that carried the mantel of self-colonization into the revolutionary regime. For these reasons, revolutionary xenophobic nationalism clouds our understanding of role of violence in identity formation. Cooperative incursions against the Chinese people provided opportunities to explore new social and political associations in the redefinition of state authority and legal violence. Anti-Chinese violence gave life to both peasant and elite ambitions for struc- tural change. These group projects reflect what I call *grotesque assemblies* that later form the basis for a more coherent and compelling nationalist project that centers a mestizo racial discourse and subjection to the institutions of the revolutionary state.

Dawn of the Revolutionary State

Violent assemblies against the Chinese people formed in both organized and unplanned ways. However, each event reflected local hierarchies, existing ten- sions between factions, and the Chinese role in Porfirian colonization. After Díaz was deposed and exiled in 1911, Madero's forces began to fray. The ins and outs of Mexican revolutionary leaders and factions are dizzying and have been explored at length by other scholars.[12] The focus here is on the factional divisions between Constitutionalists and Conventionists and the consequences for anti-Chinese violence. After Díaz loyalists withered, conflicts between these rebel groups, the Constitutionalists and the Conventionists, shaped both the battlefield and the aftermath. Upon Madero's assassination in 1913, Venustiano Carranza took up Madero's role as commander of the revolution and moved to ratify a new constitution, which gave the revolutionaries the title of Constitutionalists. Meanwhile, Villa and Emiliano Zapata broke away from this conservative cause, forming a loose alliance established at a conference, giving them the name Conventionists. The constitutional congress under Carranza's administration wrote into being a completely new government and retained much of the liberal 1857 constitution but added new sections that articulated the social rights of Mexican people. This document responded to a world in upheaval and authored the most protectionist language of any constitution of the time. Under these provisions, the revolutionary government derived its sovereignty from the mandate to care for the most vulnerable populations. These social rights spelled out guarantees for education, health, worker protections, and rights to ejidos. This last provision, authored by politician Luis Cabrera, latched onto the ejido as a valuable government-owned asset that uniquely tied recipients to the land *and* the new regime.[13]

The revolution's ejido was legally different from that under the Porfirian colonization laws because the new laws were to be broadly applied to all peasants who wished for them, rather than as individual concessions. Yet, the notion that ejidos recruited peasants into national colonization objectives was preserved. As early as 1909, Porfirian bureaucrats were drafting such agrarian policies that used public credit to support widespread ejido donations. For example, in a 1911 editorial, Carlos Negrete, a close associate of Carranza and president of the Mexican National Railroad before the 1910 revolution, pleaded with *El Tiempo* readers to support the Porfirian model of a balanced agrarian policy in Madero's new Ministry of Development. Negrete's program for self-colonization called for mass recruitment into twenty-year leases on small ejido plots funded by small-scale public credit and sharecropping for domestic staples. Negrete called the ministry of development the most important branch of the Mexican government because it engineered the economic organs of the national body.[14] He knew that self-colonization was not just an economic policy but also a political project necessary for the intensification of industrial capitalism and security of the Mexican state. In the 1917 congress, Cabrera crafted ejido laws to appeal to broad audiences, specifically, the Zapatista supporters who fought for outright ownership. The ejido was a bargain for peace that mixed Zapatista demands for redistribution with racist characterizations of national indigenous collectivity and Indian savagery as proof of the inappropriateness of private property.[15]

Carranza's new constitution prioritized mass political integration through the gratification of the social-rights mandate and self-colonization through collective land rights. However, the full force of this strategy of conscription would be stalled until the administration of an antichinista, General Abelardo Rodríguez, and his more famous successor, General Lazaro Cárdenas. In the meantime, reluctantly implemented land reforms became a method of negotiating the ongoing conflict and the numerous competing forms of regional military rule. In the three years until his assassination, Carranza distributed 132,639 hectares to 59,846 *campesinos* (peasants). Conventionists criticized these handouts and fought for a more open institutional process instead of constitutional dictates. Villa and Zapata fought for a more immediate and transparent redistribution of land. The eventual defeats of Villa in the north and Zapata in the south ultimately allowed the Sonoran Constitutionalist generals, Obregón and Calles, to claim victory and begin a consolidation of power and the reconstruction of the state under the new constitution.

The Torreón Massacre: "Malicious Spirit" or Grotesque Assembly?

The massacre at Torreón occurred in the context of revolution but was produced by decades of intense economic transformation and regional growth. Madero's family had been at the center of these changes because Madero was the heir to large holdings in the states of Coahuila, Durango, and Chihuahua. The family's most valuable possessions were in the Comarca Lagunera, whose hub is the city of Torreón. By the 1880s Torreón sat at a junction of railroad lines (map 5) and thrived from explosive growth in agricultural exports, primarily cotton. Population growth was rapid and drew in people from the surrounding mineral-rich mountains and fertile valleys. Maintaining control over this region in the insurrection against Díaz was both matters of pride and strategic importance.

After the defeat of federal forces at the city of Juarez in 1911, Madero sought greater control over the north. He sent his brother Emilio Madero to ensure the installation of a sympathetic senator, Carranza, at Torreón as governor.[16] The revolution's onset coincided with regional protests over drought and a deep depression in mining operations.[17] The previous decade of Molina's development program had rolled back marginal gains made by peasants and replaced

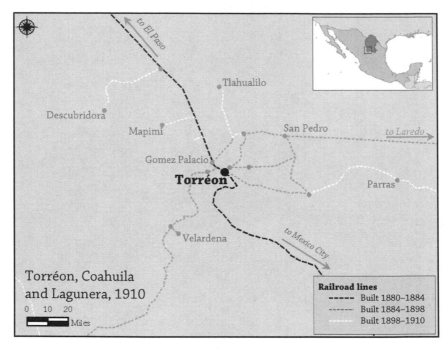

MAP 5. Torreón at a junction of railroad lines, 1910

them with foreign-owned, large estates that often hired or contracted Chinese workers.[18] Despite the hardships workers faced, Torreón produced cotton for export valued at more than $30 million.[19] The Chinese people were a visible part of Torreón's growth, appearing in the fields, residential areas, and the urban center.

On May 13 Emilio Madero's battalion of troops arrived in the rural outskirts of Torreón. With their forces divided among five lieutenants, Sixto Ugalde, Jesús C. Flores, Agustín Castro, Orestes Pereyra, and Gregorio García, the rebels surrounded the city. Ugalde approached from the east and Flores from the west via a mountain pass while the others secured the rail and roads.[20] When Ugalde's troops arrived in Torreón's agricultural fields, they entered Lim Ching's farm, where eleven Chinese workers resided. A few soldiers went into the house, robbed the residents, and killed one. Ugalde's men shot the other seven Chinese workers in the fields as the soldiers departed. Another Maderista unit entered a larger farm, also owned by Ching, which employed twenty-four Chinese workers. The troops demanded money and killed three workers. The remaining were "gathered together and [driven] to Torreón through the mud and water, forcing them to run, and every time a Chinaman slipped and fell to the ground, he was shot and trampled upon by the horses."[21] On an adjacent farm that Dan Kee and Wong Sam owned, the Maderista forces ransacked the living quarters of the Chinese workers. Eighteen were shot and killed there. The gruesome advance of Maderistas through the countryside to the city's edge brought them within range of federal gunmen.[22]

A large farm owned by Wong Foon-Chuck became a significant site of engagement between Maderistas and federal troops. Seeing the farm's tactical advantage, Ugalde's men forced Ung Shung Yee, Foon-Chuck's superintendent, and the thirty-eight workers under him to serve them food and suffer their maltreatment as the fighters made a stand against federal forces.[23] General Emiliano Lojero's troops defended the city despite being outnumbered and repelled Flores's entry from the mountain pass, killing the rebel lieutenant. The following day saw further skirmishes and more rebel losses. Gunfire ceased on the second night of the battle, and General Lojero fled the city with his men for lack of ammunition.[24]

The next morning, rebel soldiers entered the city from their entrenched rural positions. The soldiers' entrance, which had been vigorously defended only hours earlier, was marked by the looting and destruction of Chinese stores and businesses. Park Jan Jong's restaurant, Hoo Nam's grocery, Mar Young's leather shop, and Yee Hop's general-merchandise store were among the first to be attacked. In each instance, soldiers forced their entry, shot the inhabitants, and destroyed what they did not take with them. Many Chinese residents suffered a grisly death, being dragged into the street and butchered with knives and hatchets. Continuing to the heart of the city without their commanders, rebel soldiers amassed in the central plaza opposite the prominent Yah Wick building that housed El Banco Chino and La Compañía Shanghai.[25]

In the plaza the city's residents mingled with the troops and rural peasants from the surrounding area. The Maderista victory over Lojero's federal troops was a highly anticipated event and drew the whole region's attention. In the plaza that morning, roughly four thousand men, women, and children gathered to witness a crescendo of attacks on Torreón's colonia china. Amidst the commotion, a Torreón man named Jesus Maria Grajeda, mounted on horseback, invited those gathered to sack the town's Chinese businesses.[26] Around noon, the crowd entered the Yah Wick building and brutally murdered seventeen bank employees, tossing their severed body parts to the street below. The safes, containing $30,000 in cash, were blown open, and the building's interior was destroyed. Similar scenes were repeated at other establishments like Yee Hop's, where eighteen were killed. Eleven more were murdered at Hung Lee's place. Their bodies were dragged out into the street and further butchered in a search for money thought to be hidden in shoes and clothing. One victim's body was quartered between drawn horses.[27] Chinese children were not spared: one child was swung by his feet, his skull slammed into a light pole until he died. By two o'clock in the afternoon, the streets were strewn with corpses. Bodies were trampled as Torreón's residents scavenged their remains for valuables.[28] Uniformed Constitutionalist troops and civilians both participated in the looting and killing. Troops marching in formation through the streets left civilians engaged in the riot unharmed.[29]

A small number of people in Torreón risked their lives to save their Chinese neighbors. As the crowd spread through the streets, a young boy climbed to the roof of the Café Oriental, waving his arms and shouting that all the Chinese people had left the restaurant and were headed south toward the railroad. His claims directed the rioters away from the residents and saved the Chinese residents' lives.[30] The Cadena family hid 22 of their Chinese neighbors. J. Cadena placed his young daughter at the front door to announce to anyone who approached that no Chinese were hiding there.[31] Several other poor families hid fearful Chinese residents in their houses. At least nine individuals hid 137 Chinese people from the surrounding violence that day.[32] While the mob remained in the town, some soldiers returned to the rural outskirts. One group went back to Foon-Chuck's farm and killed the workers that had hosted them during the siege. The soldiers proceeded to attack the workers on neighboring farms owned by Wong Quam, killing 6, and Mah Due, killing 38 of 40 workers. In all, fifty-nine establishments were visited, and 303 Chinese individuals were killed: 62 merchants, 110 farmers, 65 employees, 56 travelers or newcomers, and 10 unknown minors.[33]

Later that day, General Emilio Madero went into the city with his four remaining commanders and found the colonia china atrocity. The troops were ordered to remove any other Chinese residents. Under Madero's orders, the 180 to 200 of Torreón's surviving Chinese residents were detained in the city's military barracks. For two days, his troops beat the prisoners, harassed them, and withheld food. On the day after Madero's arrival, corpses were cleared from the streets and farms. Prohibited from the municipal cemetery, the dead were buried in unmarked trenches outside of the city or disposed of in open wells.[34] That night the troops held a dance on the second floor of a Chinese laundry adjacent to the Cadena residence. After escaping detention in the barracks, the 22 hidden Chinese residents at the Cadena home endured a terrifying night amid the macabre celebration next door.[35]

Although the atrocity quickly garnered international attention, locally it was almost immediately overshadowed by the rebel victory. In a matter of days, Senator Carranza was appointed and confirmed as a Maderista state governor. The Maderista hold on Torreón was realized through coordinated military campaigns, a fact that is well established among historians. However, it also unleashed less well-known popular cooperative violence. The shift in northern Mexico's balance of military power was matched by the eruption of political actions that put anti-Chinese violence at the center of shifting social relations. The massacre is frequently absent in books, relegated to footnotes, dismissed as exceptional, or framed as self-evident nationalist xenophobia. The massacre's patterns of violence, composition of participants, and position in the larger socioeconomic context of Porfirian colonization suggest otherwise. This collective act of slaughter was a grotesque assembly when rules and inhibitions are suspended during an unplanned cooperative gathering to act out a new social order through violence.

Social Significance of Collective Violence

The political framing of the Torreón massacre occurred almost immediately. Three Mexican factions, as well as the U.S. and Chinese governments, all contributed official interpretations of the event. Four inquiries were made over the following months. In a matter of days, General Madero appointed a Mexico City deputy to investigate his soldiers' role in the atrocity. U.S. consular agent George Carothers, stationed in Torreón, made an in-depth report to the U.S. State Department and acted as liaison for the Chinese government, which later agreed to an independent investigation to determine reparations. The prospect of an enormous indemnity to China provoked the Díaz cabinet to select a Mexico City judge to examine General Lojero's culpability. Another inquiry, largely duplicating the two previous Mexican investigations, was made in 1913 when General Victoriano Huerta, a Porfirian officer, inherited the Mexican obligation to China after his 1913 coup over Francisco Madero. A comparison of the reports reveals a diversity of sources but also different provenances of responsibility.[36] They do not help build an understanding of the event's violence as a social practice because each of them focused on liability rather than signification.

Interpretations of the Torreón massacre reports are important because these interpretations have been central to the misconception that the Chinese community was targeted because of exclusion from mestizo nationalism. From the ways that violence was rationalized to the personal politics of the examiners and the legal resolution of the case against the assailants, nationalist xenophobia provides a tidy veil for what was, in other words, the expression of an experimental unity through violence. The nationalist interpretation operates by casting mestizo nationalism backward in time to account for the cooperative and systemic elements of the event. The success of mestizo national ideology is that it has covered up the process of its own formation within anti-Chinese politics.

Predictably, the three Mexican reports blamed Chinese residents for their own murders and cited armed Chinese participation and firing upon Maderista rebels as the main cause for the massacre. Emilio Madero held that the Chinese people were to blame for firing upon the Maderistas.[37] Soldiers' testimonies included sightings of armed Chinese people or shots heard from their direction, but no conclusive proof could be found. The defeated Porfirian General Lojero produced a signed statement from Lim Ching, a prominent individual among the Torreón Chinese population, stating that he and other Chinese had taken weapons from the federal troops and fired them against the Maderistas. Later, to Carothers, Ching testified that he signed the statement under duress. Neither Carothers nor the independent Chinese inquiry could find a single civilian witness to corroborate claims that the Chinese held and fired weapons that day. Nevertheless, the Huerta investigation replicated the statements of both Lojero and Madero.

While at odds on the battlefield, federalists and Maderistas conspired to make the Torreón Chinese population an accessory to their conflict over state control. While both generals were eager to escape liability for the incident, Porfirian officials and Maderistas had different concerns. Porfirian officials feared that the massacre would discourage foreign investment. Maderistas distanced themselves from the image portrayed in Mexican newspapers of unruly lower-class passions; such savagery was not to be associated with the elegant oratory of democratic change wealthy urban Maderista sympathizers espoused.[38] The Mexican studies also referred to rumors that Ung Shung Yee and his employees attempted to poison soldiers while they were encamped on his farm. Illnesses among the troops were blamed on the Chinese people, and some allegations were that troops might have sought retribution once in the city for the supposed offense.

The news of the Torreón massacre took a week to reach Washington, D.C., and the Peking government. In June, the following month, U.S. consul Carothers was thrown back into action when Maderista supporters advertised an anti-Chinese demonstration.[39] Still reeling from the May 15 massacre, Carothers extended protection for the remaining Chinese population in Torreón and pleaded that the rally be blocked.[40] Shocked by the massacre, the Chinese government sought monetary restitution, and a U.S.-backed investigation promised results and the perception that justice had been done. By July twenty of thirty-five accused Maderista soldiers had been detained, but no convictions were ever issued.[41] This unresolved blame led Chinese officials to hastily adopt a legal team the U.S. State Department endorsed. The Chinese legation in the United States approved the third-party evaluation of the U.S. Court in Shanghai, headed by Judge Lebbeus Wilfley.[42] Wilfley, the presiding official over the 1907 *Maori King* affair, once again shaped the outcome of a Chinese-Mexican conflict to limited fiscal ends. In the *Maori King* affair, Wilfley judged the only penalty to be resolved was the cost of returning the ship to Chinese waters, not the damages or loss of life the coerced passengers experienced. As with the *Maori King* affair, Wilfley's decision in Torreón foreclosed other possibilities.

Wilfley took eight months to submit the final report to the Chinese minister, Chang Yin Tang. Indemnity was calculated at $1,137,227.04, the largest amount of individual reparations ever granted for noncombatants during civil wars. Wilfley framed the massacre in terms of "injuries inflicted upon neutral aliens by soldiers" in relation to mutual obligations established in the 1899 China-Mexico treaty for claims by individuals. A Mexico City newspaper chided the Chinese for further wringing Mexico of its wealth.[43] In establishing a legal precedent, the judge, in assigning culpability, defined the tragedy and the Chinese population as individual victims of the lawlessness of war where the "animus" and "malicious spirit" of Mexicans are "the serious feature of the whole situation."[44] This charge obscured the general state of banditry practiced by the rebel volunteers and the larger conditions of poverty from which they were frequently recruited. Recruiters' promises of land allotments, salary, and plunder mixed personal interest with military duty. This condition of the troops, combined with the racialized discourse of Chinese depravity, encouraged victimization of Chinese people. The charges of animus and malicious spirit are disingenuous because they replace the potentialities of predatory self-interest, following orders, and opportunistic survival with a blunt and nebulous prejudice.

The definitive legal measures that Wilfley employed hid the spuriousness of their rationale. Contorted by the legal categories established by international case law, claims in the Torreón massacre case were attached to the prevailing political leadership of the country. The indemnity report was designed to produce a monetary claim and formal resolution. This legal framework, which substituted litigant individuals or subnational institutions (e.g., the military) for national states, operates with the assumption that national states have perfect representation and are completely sovereign. The problem inherent in Wilfley's construction of the Torreón case is that ascribing damages and responsibility in this manner removed the victims from political visibility and hid offenders within the apparatus of the national state. Wilfley was successful in producing a tidy end that pleased Chinese officials with an enormous indemnity and protected Mexican generals from further fallout. The U.S. State Department also celebrated the indemnity report because it set a precedent for financial recuperation from potential American losses as a result of the revolution. Not only were the Chinese and Mexican states in shambles at this time but also the use of the nation as a political unity falsely coheres the assailants as mutually and unquestionably nationals. What remained unresolved was the way that anti-Chinese violence became an important expression of revolutionary action.

The investigators' own interests also conditioned these two accounts of the massacre. Carothers was the official representative of the U.S. government and was under orders to extend protection to the remaining Chinese people. Carothers had a personal stake in their safety, as well. He served as the standing secretary for the Compañía Guayulera, a rubber-refining subsidiary of a New Jersey company.[45] Compañía Guayulera carried out official meetings in the conference room above the Banco Chino in the Yah Wick building—a privilege given only to partners and loan grantees. Carothers's report reflected a need to document material losses and to judge whether U.S. citizens should fear the same treatment. Judge Wilfley's motives are questionable, as well. He was known for using his appointment to the U.S. Court in Shanghai for personal remuneration and was accused of bribery, abuse of power, and the illegal appointment of his district attorney.[46] He was known to the U.S. State Department's Chinese consuls as a "scoundrel" for his handling of other cases.[47] Furthermore, he took a percentage of the indemnity as payment for his services in the investigation and was personally invested in finding a conclusion that all parties could agree upon.

Many historians emphasize the class dimensions of the Torreón massacre, and the debate over the preeminence of class over race in Mexican politics does a disservice to understanding the ways that material conditions take on a racial meaning. For instance, the looting of the Chinese bank building and murders of its employees illustrate how certain features of the material economy took on particular meaning. The American, British, and German banks in Torreón, institutions with far greater capitalization and influence upon the Mexican landscape as a force of imperialism, remained intact. One estimate of foreign investment in Mexico around 1920 valued U.S. and Spanish holdings at more than a hundred million each, with more than fifty million in British investments, compared to a meager five hundred thousand in total Chinese investments.[48]

Historians have largely relied upon Wilfley's report to interpret the Torreón incident. While it contains important details and the official proceedings of a legal resolution, it also reflects a calculated, imposed causality intended to make larger economic and political structures invisible. His report hinged upon the claim that a large measure of responsibility rested upon an incendiary speech General Madero's Lieutenant Flores gave in nearby Gomez Palacio only days before the siege. In his call to arms, Flores pleaded with his audience to support the revolutionary agenda and to rid Torreón of its burdensome Chinese population. The garden-to-market grocery and laundry businesses, an investment bank, large irrigated cotton and vegetable farms, and municipal tram construction projects were used as evidence of Chinese racial depravity and unnatural success. He continued by condemning their presence, which took work away from Mexican women and hemorrhaged Mexican wealth when the Chinese people sent remittances home across the Pacific—all common and widely circulated racial tropes of the Chinese population.[49] Wilfley tied this speech to the Torreón massacre by supposing that Flores's words created the inspiration for popular discontent. Focusing on Flores was also convenient because he had perished at the hands of federal troops during the attack, closing any avenue of further questioning or alternate trials. Why should one speech in an adjacent town hold such sway over the course of the following days in the siege of Torreón? Flores's speech would not have been the only source of anti-Chinese vitriol. A more sensible assumption would be that Flores's speech was but one identifiable example of a more diffused and common discourse and speech practice that permeated the popular imagination of insurrection.

At the time, other sources of anti-Chinese propaganda in proximity to Torreón illustrate the ubiquitous presence of racial hatred as a part of the social field of revolutionary action. Another one of Madero's lieutenants, Benjamin Argumedo, who was previously affiliated with the anarchist Liberal Party, might also have been responsible for encouraging his troops to loot and murder.[50] The PLM listed Chinese exclusion as a tenet of its revolutionary platform and had orchestrated several anti-Chinese demonstrations in the previous years. Several other historians point to the yearlong drought and the mining recession for the exaggerated expression of violence.[51] Alternatively, Madero might have sought to settle a dispute with the Chinese bankers. A Mexico City newspaper printed a rumor that the Maderos had been attempting to buy out the Banco Chino a year earlier.[52] Speculation about the macrostructural and individual catalysts of the massacre has continued, but a different line of questioning has yet to be taken in the historiography, largely due to the veil of nationalism. Because violence is always more than an instrumental behavior in the resolution of a competitive conflict, interpretation of the massacre must appreciate the experiential and cultural dimensions of a grotesque assembly. The causality of the massacre must be linked to the social significance of this act of collective violence to understand its political meaning.

Five months after the massacre, in October, José Maria Romero, the Porfirian deputy from the 1903 Chinese immigration commission, republished the commission's findings. In the prologue, Romero appropriates the massacre as evidence of his report's alignment with revolutionary ideals: "The current practice of Asian immigration has a strong influence upon the social and economic opinions of our working classes—they might have considered this publication to be useful and beneficial—as recent success in Torreón has shown. The social and economic disadvantages attached to Asiatic immigration put the future peace of the republic in serious danger. A true congestion in our economic and social body can arise from the permanence of compact, dense groups of Chinese in certain areas amid our heterogeneous population."[53] Porfirian politicians were able to dress themselves as revolutionary nationalists through antichinismo.

The massacre and its appropriation illustrate how violence constituted a new political subjectivity. It did so in two ways. First, enacting violence upon Chinese people altered one's relationship to a perceived social order. Second, the participation and cooperation of strangers in anti-Chinese collective violence built new social bonds. The Torreón massacre illustrates how notions of race were constitutive of the political economy, state formations, and ideologies of rule. This analysis of the massacre has sought to underscore the ways that anti-Chinese violence ushered into being new political subjectivities.

The Cultural and Tactical Logic of a Racialized Battlefield

The organizing logic of anti-Chinese collective violence is absent in the history of rebellion and national-identity formation. The U.S. State Department consular records speak to this silence. The agency reported over 650 Chinese deaths from 1910 until 1919. If the total ethnic Chinese population was between 15,000 and 20,000, then at least 1 in 25 was killed as part of revolutionary violence in the first years of fighting.[54] The Torreón massacre was but the most horrific example of patterned collective violence against the Chinese people. U.S. State Department records have been vital to the recovery of anti-Chinese incidents; after the Torreón incident, U.S. consular agents were often granted authority to act on behalf of Chinese citizens. While the U.S. State Department did liaise Chinese concerns, requests for protection, and indemnity, the extent of the protection was limited.

Until now, anti-Chinese violence during revolutionary fighting was interpreted as cruel opportunism or vicious, individuated attacks.[55] While others have mined the State Department's Chinese Problem in Mexico file for exemplary cases of anti-Chinese violence (no comparable compilation exists in Mexican records), I read the entirety of the collection as an archive of racialization through warfare, that is, a conception of the battlefield as a social structure—not just the setting where organized violence takes place. The patterns of violence scattered throughout the consular reports illustrate the extent to which soldiers and civilians interpreted the revolutionary battlefield through constructions of Chinese racial difference. Anti-Chinese discourses, originating in the Porfiriato, created a violent imaginary that elevated the significance of violence against the Chinese population as more relevant and valuable in the armed revolt. Even as "the mass of the population takes no side" in the revolution, they do seem to participate in anti-Chinese demonstrations.[56]

Such a reading provides a more robust understanding of the genesis and foundations for the popularity of anti-Chinese politics once revolutionary fighting subsided under the Obregón presidency. This interpretation also runs counter to the argument that violence against the Chinese was arbitrary or incidental in nature. Arbitrary and incidental cases did occur, but the overall pattern of the historical violence illustrates that revolutionary ruthlessness exhibited a cultural logic and rationality that did not extend from sinophobic mestizo nationalism. In these events, homicidal ideation and violence against the Chinese population allowed Mexican people to experiment with a new subjectivity produced inside evolving relations of power. Anti-Porfirian discourses of Chinese racial difference convinced many that Chinese expulsion was a step toward the resolution of deep structural issues of racial inequality reinforced by corrupt and rigidly undemocratic institutions of governance.

Revolutionary antichinismo might be the first truly national identity to emerge from Porfirio Díaz's fall. In addition to Torreón, Tapachula and Pilares de Nacozari in 1911 also marked the rise of insurrection through violent assemblies against the Chinese people. The state of Sonora, being home to the highest concentration of Chinese people, reflects the higher incidence of violence; however, anti-Chinese demonstrations could be found in every state. Because attacks were not directed at a competing military campaign, they have evaded historians' attention. Punitive campaigns against the Chinese people and assassinations of Chinese functionaries show how warfare and collective violence were crucial avenues through which racial difference was realized and revolutionary visions enacted. Mexican anti-Chinese collective violence during the revolution was built upon memories of the Porfiriato and aspirations for structural transformation through violent revolt.

In northwest Mexico, insurrection was an invitation for anti-Chinese collective violence. After the Torreón siege, Maderistas expanded their campaign to the west to join forces with other local groups. The initial military campaign was successful, but maintaining control was difficult. Accompanying this wave of insurrection was a rash of violent attacks that rocked Chinese residents of Sonora and Sinaloa. In early spring, five hundred troops from Cananea, Sonora, a mining town that had been hostile to the Chinese people since 1906, descended to the coast to skirmish with federal troops at the coastal port of Mazatlán. Their attack on the city led to a rampage through the Chinese district.[57] As the rebel campaign strengthened later that spring, Cananeans tried to expel two thousand Chinese residents—a move the mayor rapidly blocked at the behest of the U.S. consulate.[58] Among those who led the westward campaign was Argumedo, a lieutenant at the Torreón massacre. In the summer of 1912, he led a thousand troops to Sinaloa to force out the remaining federalist troops in Mazatlán.[59] Again, Argumedo's soldiers sacked the commercial district, targeting Chinese establishments, although no deaths were reported that day.[60] By the fall, Maderistas held the northern Pacific coast by means that included the destruction and looting of Chinese settlements from Guaymas to Culiacán and Mazatlán.[61] Under the leadership of Macario Gaxiola Urias, the rebel hold on the region was strengthened after he arrived in Mazatlán in December. Aspiring to greater authority, Urias announced orders for the city's Chinese people to leave. More than 570 Chinese residents of Mazatlán sought protection with the U.S. consulate.[62] Urias rescinded the order, but many departed, nonetheless. The following year, 600 Chinese residents of Guaymas fled the city onto the USS *Pittsburgh* and USS *Glacier*, which had been conveniently docked in the harbor and whose presence likely saved the residents' lives.[63]

The violent imaginary of revolutionary structural transformation identified the Chinese people as key symbolic targets. The Chinese population became such a salient symbol of change that anti-Chinese demonstrations often involved premeditation and homicidal ideation. In February 1914, another mass demonstration shook the Chinese settlement in Cananea, where the staunchly anti-Chinese Mexican Liberal Party held sway. This time, the attack coincided with the surge of Villa's forces to retake the north from the Constitutionalists, which invoked a new challenge to the town's corporate sponsor. The demonstration began when eight miners organized a protest against James

Douglas of the American-owned Consolidated Copper Company. Workers believed the Chinese people and the American company had artificially raised prices for basic staples to rob Mexicans of their wages.[64] The Women's Union, wives of the miners, held a rally in the town's Ronquilla district, where many of the Chinese stores were concentrated, calling for the expulsion of the Chinese residents. The mob approached a nearby Chinese laundry, destroyed it, and looted its contents. One laundry employee escaped while the other two were beaten with stones. One of them, José Lee, was severely injured. The mob drove the Chinese residents into the streets and out of town. Local officials and police were completely overrun while the mayor requested reinforcements.[65]

The U.S. consulate noted that images of executed Chinese people contributed to the agitation, mentioning that a picture postcard of two Chinese men, one of whom was lynched and the other lay decapitated on the ground, was in wide circulation among Cananea residents.[66] A causal relationship between the circulated images and the riot is unclear, but what seems more certain is that envisioning anti-Chinese violence was a social experience. When eyes were transfixed on the spectacle of anti-Chinese violence, men and women stood shoulder to shoulder, class divisions evaporated, and interethnic tensions dissolved. The fact that these grotesque assemblies formed so frequently and without coordination between subsequent events suggests that anti-Chinese discourse had become ideological in the sense that Mexican people understood their relationship to the Chinese people as an experiment in altering the social order and acted upon this idea collectively, not because they individually held dear to an imagined mestizo nation. The sanction of anti-Chinese violence by insurrection forces, combined with the regularity of targeted attacks, created a kind of ritual script of racialized democratic revolution.[67]

Economic Sabotage and Assassination

These racialized, violent rituals targeted large groups of Chinese people, but individuals who served as vital functionaries to economic operations were also singled out. For instance, Joe Wong of Durango was murdered by Mónico Rodríguez, a Carrancista soldier.[68] Wong's murder was motivated by Rodríguez's speculation that a Chinese truck farmer would have cash on hand from door-to-door sales.[69] Rodríguez's attack, and so many others, took advantage of the soldier's possession of the means of violence and the probable impunity of his actions. Competing revolutionary factions frequently identified Chinese functionaries for assassination in order to disrupt their opponent's economy, denying them resources or tax revenue from Chinese businesses.

After Madero was assassinated in 1913 and Villa and Zapata broke away from the Constitutionalists, a new round of battles ensued. In the scramble to reset the battlefield to secure vital railroad sites, mines, and ports, Porfirian concessions for colonization and development became strategic targets, including crucial members of the Chinese labor regime. In January 1914, an American colony near Tampico became a target for Constitutionalist forces as they stormed the oil-rich coast. Pleas by U.S. consular agents to Huerta convinced the forces to spare the American residents and the Chinese laborers in their colony. The next day, however, an unnamed Chinese cook was singled out and kidnapped by Constitutionalist soldiers and was executed later that day.[70] If the soldiers could not destroy the colony without diplomatic fallout, they could at least disorganize its operations by removing a key functionary among the Chinese workers. A similar scene took place in Túxpam, Veracruz, where rebel soldiers killed a Chinese employee of an American settlement.[71]

Chinese cooks, a seemingly mundane occupation, were actually crucial players due to the internal structure of the Chinese diaspora as well as the Porfirian practice of injecting workers into remote regions. The use of Chinese labor required a degree of organization and regulation that neither Mexican officials nor foreign investors could supply. The most effective form of regulation was co-ethnic subordination under a labor contractor, and the title of cook often combined the roles of a labor contractor and general manager. Chinese managers were also recruited as a link between capitalist employers and the Chinese laborers, serving in mediation and providing direction across the language divide.

As Villa won the north from Constitutionalist forces in May 1914, Lewis Fong fled for his life to El Paso, Texas, from Pearson, Chihuahua (now Juan Mata Ortiz). In advance of Fong's arrival in Texas, his employer, Lewis Booker of the enormously profitable Booker Lumber Company, telegrammed the U.S. consulate in El Paso, requesting temporary asylum for Fong, who was his cook. Booker's sawmill and lumberyard moved twenty thousand board feet daily and drew from a 165,000-acre nearby pine forest. Booker's investment helped spur the development of Fredrick Stark Pearson's expansive Mexican Northwestern Railroad. Pearson's use of Chinese workers to build the railroad provided a ready supply of laborers for the sawmill once the railroad was completed. The most difficult task in Booker's operation was getting timber to the mill and then on mule carts from the mill to the train station.[72] In this remote location, Booker employed about 130 Chinese men at Pearson's sawmill and lumberyard.[73] Given the scale of Booker's operation, the fact that only the cook should be sent for safety is a clear indicator that Fong was one of Booker's most prized employees.

Another incident in Jimenez, Chihuahua, underscores the practice of assassinating Chinese functionaries. In February 1916 Constitutionalist soldiers under the authority of General Prieto stopped at the Hotel de Nueva York as they moved north into Villista territory. The hotel was a favorite with foreigners, including John Reed, the author of *Insurgent Mexico*, and provided board to a number of Chinese workers. The hotel was a fixture of the community because of the magnanimous owner, Charley Chee, a well-known Chinese merchant and manager of an important silver mine in Guanacevi, Durango. Chee and his cousin Foo had married "respectable Mexican villagers."[74] On the twenty-fourth, Carranza soldiers were conspicuously monitoring the hotel's traffic. Later that night, they stormed the hotel, taking five high-profile prisoners, all agents of large companies, each from a different nationality (British, American, Spanish, Turkish, and Chinese, Chee being the Chinese one). All six were taken to the railroad and locked in a freight car. In the morning, the American agent and Chee were moved into the brush a hundred yards away, where Chee was executed by pistol upon the order of the general, sparing the American.[75]

Chinese Settlements as Wartime Assets

The association of Chinese with money, business, and commodities was particularly accentuated during the years of intense fighting because of the severe shortages of money, food, and basic necessities. This was not only true of the majority of civilians but also of the various revolutionary factions. Survival of the small dispatches of soldiers in the battlefield often relied upon their ability to fund or sustain their own forces. When troops of any faction departed from the railroad's supply lines, they often looted or paid with worthless paper money for the supplies necessary for their mission's survival. Although the Chinese people were not the only group singled out for this treatment, Chinese sites of economic exchange were targets for soldiers and civilians. The widespread disdain for the Chinese people illustrates a unique convergence of anti-Chinese politics from different factions that hinged upon tactical convenience and populist appeal.

The broad distribution of Chinese people across the country and in remote areas made them reliable sources of supplies and capital for raiding parties and looting. The transnational commercial orbit of Chinese merchants and diasporic credit networks allowed Chinese general-merchandise stores to rise above the limitations of the region's turmoil to continue operating when others were forced to close. The persistence of Chinese stores amid the economic depression reinforced their image as unnatural, greedy abarroteros. While looting, forced loans, and theft from non-Chinese people were common throughout the revolution, two things make the Chinese people different. First, the consistent presence of the Chinese population throughout contested territory made them routine targets. Second, looting, forced loans, and theft from Chinese people systematically included ritual humiliation, vandalism, and execution—experiences that other victims were largely spared. The tides of rebellion, insurgency, and counterinsurgency during the revolution resulted in a continuous competition for increasingly scarce resources. A wide array of destructive forces crippled the Mexican economy as competing factions tried to reduce their opponent's ability to continue fighting.[76] While preying upon Chinese establishments sustained the violent imagination of structural transformation, it also became a means of survival.

The lines of fragmentation and opposition help illuminate the ebb and flow of violence. A formal opposition to Díaz had been mounted, and that opposition quickly fragmented into other factions. Madero's assassination and the 1913 coup by Huerta, a Porfirian officer, fractured the loose alliance of rebels. The following year Huerta was exiled when Carranza, a Maderista Constitutionalist, called for a convention to bring revolutionary forces together. Villa and Zapata both opposed the Carrancista return to strict constitutionalism and waged a counter-rebellion against the Carranza government. In this volley between Villa's and Zapata's forces and the Constitutional army, violence against the Chinese people became a crucial wartime asset. At times, the Chinese were protected to ensure a margin of economic activity and, thus, tax revenue, such as occurred in March 1915 when Villa issued orders to his commanders in Chihuahua not to attack the Chinese residents.[77] Villa knew that if the Chinese stores were protected, they would continue to supply people who might pose a problem should they be driven to desperation by hunger. Economic integration made small Chinese businesses important for local and regional political stability.

Collective violence against the Chinese population also became a new expression of the existing tensions of Indian-state conflict. In Sonora, the Yaqui people engaged in the revolution with skepticism. It is easy to imagine why Yaqui leaders would have thrown their support behind the Constitutionalists, given the Porfirian extermination-and-deportation policy. Most of all, Yaqui people hoped Constitutionalists would uphold legal covenants of their sovereignty, as the Conservatives had done in the previous century. However, these hopes were pinned to vague promises by local officials with uncertain political futures. Yaqui attacks on Chinese stores were a response to the government's collapse and reflected a limited set of political alternatives. Boomtowns like Cananea and urban centers like Hermosillo, Sonora, had experienced food shortages, inflation, and other exasperations, yet the situation in the Rio Yaqui hinterlands was even more dire. As they toyed with alliance and opposition to Constitutionalists, the Yaqui population relied on the looting of the Chinese people to survive. By the 1920s the Yaqui population had abandoned both tactical attacks on Chinese stores as well as the practice of trading military allegiance for political protection.[78]

At the outset of Madero's call for rebellion in 1910, Governor José Maria Maytorena ardently supported Díaz's ousting. As an intermediary for Pedro García and José Valenzuela, the Yaqui tribe leaders, Maytorena played a key role in supporting Madero's revolt. Maytorena offered the restitution of lands and the return of those deported to Yucatán in exchange for their military support and the cessation of raids.[79] The Yaqui people had no interest in the political agenda of the revolution, so they sided with whoever would negotiate with them. After Madero's assassination and Carranza's victory over the Huerta coup, Maytorena rejected the conservative Constitutionalist platform and, instead, sided with Villa and the Conventionists. This put Maytorena at odds with Carranza's secretary of war Obregón and Sonoran general Calles. The fragmentation of the rebellion resulted in competing promises to the Yaqui people, which explains why they participated in so many different factions of the revolution. While raiding and looting Mexican pueblos was a part of the Yaqui tradition, the Yaqui people could jeopardize alienating their allies by continuing what would be seen as a breach of a tacit agreement with Maytorena. While the Sonoran colonias were outposts of Mexican colonization, they were in locations meant to interfere with and subvert Yaqui sovereignty and sustainability. Raiding these colonies was a mode of Yaqui survival for decades. However, since the 1880s the state had attracted a growing population of Chinese people. Their roles in providing general merchandise and groceries permitted a more reliable source of goods for the colonias, but, more important, they became a dependable wartime asset the Yaqui people used to sustain their communities.

In January 1915 Yaqui troops under the command of Constitutionalists ran through their ancestral lands and looted the Chinese community. In the lower Yaqui River valley, the deployment of Indian troops triggered locals to clear out the Chinese stores in Torin and Cocorit, both in Sonora. The scramble for resources left the franchise retail stores of Quong Chong Lung, Fook Chong, Man On Wo, and Sin Chong in ruin. Cocorit was primarily served by Fong Hong y Cia, Hay Loy, Hing Chong Lung and Company, Lay Wah and Company,

Quong Hong Chong and Company, and Tai Kee and was likewise sacked by local residents. Given the economic context of war-torn Sonora, the stocks taken from Chinese stores were a valuable resource that could sustain Yaqui soldiers' families until new supplies could be acquired.[80] The Constitutionalist looting of Chinese stores may have also served as an impetus for looting by Yaqui soldiers loyal to Maytorena in Nacozari in the subsequent weeks. Looting Chinese stores both garnered resources for those soldiers and denied those same resources to the competition. Under orders by Yaqui general Francisco Urbalejo, who was loyal to Maytorena, the retail-merchandise stores of Jim Wong and Company, Kim Sing, Louie Lung, and Louis Quintero and the Mee Lee grocery in Nacozari were completely looted.[81] No matter which faction the Yaqui people aligned with, Chinese stores could be looted without drawing the ire of their allies' constituencies. Chinese stores were intended to play a role in the Yaqui-Conventionist alliance, not because of their exclusion from mestizo nationalism but because of their caches of supplies.

In the struggle to control the two parallel north-south routes through Sonoran mining country, Calles, a Constitutionalist, ordered Colonel Michael Samaniego and several hundred troops to lay waste to the Chinese communities from Agua Prieta (a northern border town in Sonora), along the border and south through Arizpe, Moctezuma, Cumpas, Nacozari, and Fronteras (map 6). While they encountered no resistance from Conventionist forces, they, however, used the military campaign to annihilate Chinese settlements. It is unclear if the orders were motivated by the resource needs of the soldiers, to keep those assets from enemy hands, or to simply rid the region of the Chinese presence. In any case, the effect was the same. The Chinese legation and U.S. State Department pleaded with Sonoran leaders to abstain from brutal violence against the Chinese population, but in Agua Prieta, Chinese people were still driven from their homes and left without food.[82]

As Samaniego's troops traveled south, their violence increased. Drunken troops were killing fleeing Chinese storeowners.[83] A 1915 U.S. consular report stated that in these deployments, "one of the favorite pastimes of the soldiers seems to be to tie the Chinese up to a post or tree after having taken all their clothing and money, leaving them at the place until someone happens to pass and release them. This is done in out-of-way places. None of their property is safe."[84] The humiliating ritual illustrates how coherent the racial scripts of revolution had become since their cathartic origins in 1911 and how anti-Chinese violence was variegated by different factions.

The Sonoran coast suffered heavily from war-related scarcities, increasing retribution on Chinese businesses. Guaymas erupted with riots led by

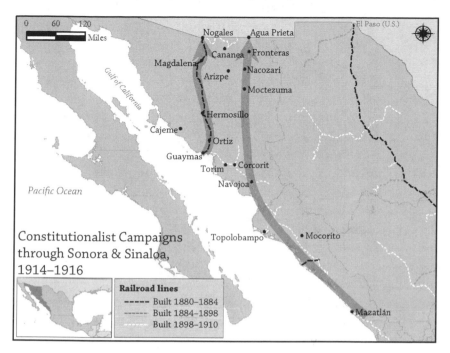

MAP 6. Constitutionalist campaigns through Sonora and Sinaloa, 1914–16

Constitutionalist soldiers against Chinese people, where 60 percent of the stores were looted and destroyed. Wai Chiao Pu, president of the Chinese Association in Guaymas, beseeched the Chinese legation and U.S. consulate for protection from the swift and ruthless devastation.[85] Several days later, farther south in Sinaloa, seven hundred Chinese people fled Mazatlán as the "situation became more and more tense," as one U.S. consulate member reported.[86] Although the Yaqui River valley had been completely looted in January, Maytorena's troops returned in April to secure more resources, leading to the killing of Chinese Lee Yan You and Wong Toy near Ojo de Agua.[87] None of the murders that spring led to arrests or convictions. While the Chinese people, like Wai Chiao Pu, saw themselves as hapless victims of discrimination, the U.S. consulate viewed them as unwitting casualties caught in the crossfire of a civil war. However, both characterizations ignore the fact that the Chinese structural positions as motores de sangre and agents of economic exchange made them valuable nonmilitary assets in the rapidly changing landscape of warfare. Li Chung Ping, introduced at the chapter's beginning, might have framed his defense of Chinatown differently had he known how quickly stability in Mexico would deteriorate. Even still, any defense he could offer might have fallen upon ears made deaf by decades of Porfirian colonization. In other words, anti-Porfirian sentiment was more important than alleged mestizo nationalism.

The variations of collective violence against the Chinese people discussed thus far have shown the ideological, structural, and tactical origins of new social and political subjectivities. Racialized scripts of democratic revolution heightened the saliency of anti-Chinese violence in the inauguration of revolt in the form of grotesque assemblies. Sonora was a particularly intense location for these violent expressions of political invention because of the multiple sovereignties that struggled for survival.

The northern mining town of Cananea demonstrated these tensions clearly in the summer of 1915, balancing the shifting military, commercial, labor, and indigenous influences toward the resolution of the armed conflict. That year, Maytorena's Conventionist forces retreated and began looting the Ronquilla commercial district of Cananea. Their willful destruction and theft of Chinese property inspired a mob, in which "about half of the Mexican population of town" participated.[88] Later in the summer, Urbalejo's Conventionist-loyal Yaqui soldiers sacked the Chinese stores in nearby Nogales.[89] By the end of the summer, Cananea had become completely unsafe for the Chinese population as soldiers and civilians had begun killing them and running them out of the town.[90] The departure of the Chinese people sent economic shockwaves through the mining town. When U.S. consul Friedrich Simpich sought recourse from Calles on the matter of the devastation to the Chinese people, Simpich was instructed to relay the message to the Chinese Association that assailants would not be prosecuted but that the general would ensure their future safety if the Chinese people would return to open their doors for business.[91] Calles knew that if the Chinese population never returned to Cananea, food shortages would result in a complete breakdown of authority and undermine his control over a known PLM stronghold. As Calles gained ground in Sonora, sustaining the economic productivity of the region became just as important as armed milieus. Earlier that year he had written to Carranza, suggesting they must "resolve the issue of striking workers in order to get the mines working again and gain the support of the workers in Agua Prieta."[92] If the Chinese people were despised, they, nevertheless, appear to have been found useful for the stability of the region's economy. The Yaqui people, on the other hand, were not viewed in a favorable way, even if they had contributed to Constitutionalist victories in the state. Calles's chief of staff Arnulfo Gomez confessed to U.S. consul Lawton, "The Yaquis are to be exterminated," adding that the campaign would begin in the coming months.[93] Not only were the Yaqui people seen as a burden to the local economy but also their demands for restitution were not congruent with agrarian reforms designed to continue Mexican colonization with Constitutionalist veterans and other displaced agrarians. However, the Chinese people continued to serve Constitutionalist needs to wage war against Maytorena, Villa, the Liberal Party, and the other unaligned forces.

A similar pattern of balancing various military, economic, and political influences can be seen in Chihuahua as Villa lost ground to Constitutionalists in 1916 and 1917. In these northern highlands, desperate retreats spurred increased violence against the Chinese people, and worsening economic conditions made Constitutionalists more interested in the well-being of Chinese merchants. Villa's forces even revisited Torreón, executing thirteen Chinese storeowners in the streets.[94] These opposing influences led to more than two hundred Chinese fleeing for El Paso, Texas.[95] Nonmilitary tactics contributed to the character of the revolution and eventually came to a head in the Battle of Agua Prieta, when Calles's forces won control of Sonora in the fall of 1915. Reed's *Insurgent Mexico* describes the tactics invented by Villa, such as the night raid and other guerilla techniques. To this repertoire of warfare should be added the assassination of Chinese functionaries and the looting of Chinese businesses. Syrian minorities in Mexico, who occupied a similar structural position as the Chinese people, did not experience the same disavowal and rejection.

Lethal Agency and the Turn to Institutions

The processual nature of the development of anti-Chinese sentiment from a lethal experiment in social relations to racial scripts of democratic revolution needs to be emphasized. The violent imaginary of structural transformation through attacks on Chinese people has been misunderstood as either arbitrary and incidental or as xenophobic nationalism. The specific patterns of attack illustrate the racial dimensions of revolutionary fighting, revealed in the treatment of noncombatants and the social and tactical value of Chinese retail assets in a wartime environment. The efficacy of anti-Chinese violence was founded in both tactical advantage during revolutionary fighting and in racial scripts of structural transformation.

In 1916 Calles began to institute new policies that took advantage of the Chinese population as a source of capital. In March he increased monthly taxes on Chinese merchants from five to thirty pesos to fund Constitutionalist forces and local government payroll. Two months later Calles issued orders to segregate the Chinese people in Hermosillo and prohibit their travel to the surrounding area. In the following month, he called for all Chinese merchants from Nogales, along the border south to Magdalena and west to Hermosillo, to close their stores. Calles essentially sought to formalize the thievery that troops had previously engaged in under the authority of the state government. Because the Chinese people remained unpopular with civilians, corralling the Chinese population would have met with approval and support, and he was stopped only after intervention from the U.S. State Department.[96]

By the end of the decade, Carranza's Constitutionalist forces had subdued Villa and assassinated Zapata, yet the battle against the Chinese people continued. In 1919 the anarcho-syndicalist PLM continued looting and killing Chinese people in Agua Prieta. Several months later, Cananea officials issued an expulsion order for all Chinese people to leave the city. As before, a large majority of the city's residents favored the expulsion, yet President Carranza vetoed the municipal order, fearing economic collapse. A similar municipal order appeared in Juarez, Chihuahua. Chew Look, the leading Chinese merchant in Juarez, conferenced with local officials who promised protection.[97] This failed experiment to transplant anti-Chinese proclamations from Sonora to Chihuahua foreshadowed the contentious local politics that would unfold during the 1920s as antichinistas built a national campaign.

In Juarez, local officials tolerated the Chinese people for their role in border commerce. In the state of Yucatán, other troubles plagued the Chinese residents, but Governor José María Pino Suárez saw the Chinese population as a part of Yucatán's economic stability and supported the unionization of more than three hundred Chinese henequén workers in the Liga de Trabajadores de la Colonia China en la Península (League of Workers from the Peninsula's Chinese Colony). Despite these positive examples, anti-Chinese politics was beginning to emerge as a cultural logic of governance, especially as local revolutionaries attempted to secure their military victories by exercising legal authority. Independent from the Cananea expulsion orders, Mocorito municipal authorities in Sinaloa wrote into law the power to segregate Chinese people in formal *barrios chinos* (Chinatowns) that would be inspected and regulated for density, sanitation, and certain economic prohibitions. Mocorito's segregation orders illustrate one of the ways that revolutionary leaders wrote racial ideology into their exercise of state authority to indicate their revolutionary authenticity.[98] Physical anti-Chinese violence dissipated in some places after the fighting ended, but the Chinese presence continued to draw attention from those who found racial scripts of structural transformation useful when they established new relations of rule and consent. Anti-Chinese violence on the battlefield coded antichinismo as revolutionary. The next chapter discusses the social organization of anti-Chinese collective violence that helped institutionalize the racial scripts born out of the violent imaginaries of structural transformation.

Conclusion

A key question emerges at the intersection of physical violence against the Chinese people and the psychology of homicide. What problem did killing intend to solve? The evolution of anti-Chinese politics illustrates that killing Chinese immigrants in revolutionary Mexico was an adaptation to new circumstances. In the revolutionary context, physical violence against and the killing of Chinese people emerged out of a set of other possible nonlethal alternatives.[99] Imagining murder and actually killing the Chinese population helped resolve the cognitive dissonance many Mexicans experienced. Despite military triumph, peasants languished in the countryside and remained dissatisfied with Constitutionalist victories. Chinese homicidal ideation provided a populist enemy that revolutionary leaders could extract material benefits from without major repercussions from an unruly, unorganized constituency. The political benefit of this strategy was that extracting wealth and stability from a minority community made the power players appear socially and economically benevolent toward an increasingly urban peasantry. Constitutionalist leaders drew upon, amplified, and codified anti-Porfirian hatred and rejection of the Chinese people in the construction of a new agrarian regime of political incorporation.

The patterns of violence discussed in this chapter document the development of racist discourse within revolutionary ideology. From unorganized, uncoordinated grotesque assemblies to ritualized collective violence and centrally organized campaigns, Mexican actors built new social bonds through anti-Chinese behaviors. Ping from the Chinese legation made an argument for the defense of Chinatown based upon economic collaboration with the Porfirian regime. After the revolution, the Chinese spokesmen no longer used such language to argue for the defense of Chinatown. The revolution upended the landscape of power, including the cultural basis for sovereign state authority. It was only in this context that anti-Chinese violence became filled with new meaning and purpose. Yet, the act of meaning making is unstable and holds the possibility for different outcomes, none of which guaranteed a widespread mestizo nationalism. Anti-Chinese violence was not a side effect of the fog of war. Antichinismo allowed Mexican people to experiment with new political identities and associations. During the rebellion, violence became a powerful expression of ethnicity and political affiliations and, thus, helped shape the character of warfare. The types of anti-Chinese violence discussed here were more than just instrumental to local conflicts or the needs of the battlefield. They were deeply symbolic of an anti-Porfirian redemption, a cathartic demolition, that fostered the emergence of a nationalistic public sphere. Anti-Chinese events became cultural referents that would later be appropriated and employed in populist discourses of mestizo nationalism.

Scholar Edward Said articulated Orientalism as an ideology of Euro-American imperialism, a culture of empire.[100] U.S. Orientalism in the mid-nineteenth to early twentieth centuries racialized that Asian figure through legal exclusion, militarized conquest, and trade imperialism. Mexican Orientalism, on the other hand, racialized the Chinese people via battlefield violence, economic populism, and, as the next chapters will show, a polemic nationalistic discourse to expand and legitimize the postrevolutionary state. Mexican antichinismo illustrates another valence of Orientalism that is not geographically expansionary or primarily actualized through legal racial codes but that is a set of political and cultural practices that naturalized a government imperative for racial rule and domesticated political discontent through racial populism. Even as Mexican and U.S. Orientalism share the same referent, the distinction between their objectives and political mechanisms relates the Mexican case more closely to other postcolonial nationalist revolutions.[101]

The next chapter will trace reconstruction as a transfer of violence from the battlefield to institutions. The rise of mestizo nationalism out of the ashes of the revolution solved a long-present problem of governance and political legitimacy. The demobilization of the revolution became a political necessity as the victors sought to cement their rule through agrarian recruitment. This approach introduced new forms of exploitation and domination by the revolutionary national state to institutionalize the nation's Indian population. These changes were facilitated by emergent political discourses about citizenship, ethical governance, and an ideology of racial futurity, or the progressive potential of racial improvement. Mexican people who practiced anti-Chinese violence utilized racism to transform their political identities. The Chinese population became what intellectual Frantz Fanon refers to as a "phobogenic subject," or a catalyst that ties violent revolt, new social bonds, and political incorporation together.[102] In this case, it became an identity that served the new state because it tamed revolutionary furor and was the basis for new modes of production. The following chapters explore what might be referred to as the wages of mestizaje whereby Mexican people used the effects of antichi nismo for political acceptance even when it led to marginal or no material improvement in their lives.[103] Mirroring David R. Roediger's argument, the wages of mestizaje in revolutionary Mexico point to a kind of social standing that arises from the adoption and practice of antichinismo.[104] Discourses of Chinese alterity became expressions of recuperation and self-transformation that had been building over the previous decades. Due to this structural position, the Chinese people became a catalyst for a new political subjectivity.

Violence had become a prominent feature of early twentieth-century Mexican ethnic identity because it was an irrevocable social act that changed one's relationship to authority and forged new subject positions in the social order. Other antiforeign politics did not produce this effect because the constellation of antagonisms embodied within them did not correspond with the needs of reconstituting state power. For example, anti-Americanism was anti-imperial and, thus, bolstered protectionism but did not constitute a racial threat. On the other hand, anti-Semitism was based on racial threats to the republic, but it failed to become popular because this racial ideology constructed the majority of the Mexican populace to be savages. Anti-Chinese politics was successful in ways that other forms of racial culture were not.

The codependent rise of mestizo nationalism and anti-Chinese politics was not spontaneous but structured by a process of development and discovery. This process was subject to dynamic conditions that could not have been planned or designed. More important, it was a process that could not simply be lifted from the pages of public intellectuals like Manuel Gamio or José Vasconcelos, who has been given too much credit for the rise of mestizo nationalism. Many leaders and organized groups discovered the efficacy of anti-Chinese politics through the exigencies of wartime conditions. Each turn of events generated favorable circumstances for a different set of events. In other words, these acts of anti-Chinese cooperative violence became historical precedents that later became effective for the mobilization of collective action in labor unions and agrarian reform. Furthermore, populist politics of land reform built upon existing anti-Chinese attitudes that were tied to self-colonization. The anti-Chinese violence described in this chapter did not engender the broad-based claims of mestizo nationalism represented in the following chapters. These acts of collective violence set into motion a means for identification that became the basis for other more organized and institutionalized approaches—approaches that could not have succeeded without this prior stage of enacting a violent imaginary of revolutionary potential.

4

Abajo Los Chinos

The Political Invention of Mestizo Nationalism

In the summer of 1922, hundreds of residents of Hermosillo, the capital of Sonora, took to the streets to protest shoot-outs between rival Chinese groups. Rising interethnic Chinese violence, rooted in homeland politics, was considered to be further evidence of the danger the so-called yellow race posed. That day, the assembly of concerned and agitated Sonorans did not strike out against the Chinese people. Instead, they marched to a meeting hall and convened to discuss plans to push for their removal by the government. While violence against the Chinese population continued throughout the 1920s, violent fantasies were transformed into popular discourse by the growing imperative to participate in the institutionalization of the revolutionary state. A decade of revolution led to a contentious scramble to redefine legitimate state authority and national identity—a context of multiple sovereignties.[1] This process was structured by competing nationalisms of the *patria chica* (locality; literally, small country) and indigeneity, as well as by ideological divisions over religion, liberalism, and socialism. During this cacophonous period, antichinistas helped develop a regionally contingent, culturally based understanding of state authority, because they demanded government action based on a newly imagined racial profile of the republic—a mestizo nation.

This chapter places the anti-Chinese movement within the field of Mexico's contentious politics during the 1920s and details the conditions of the movement's emergence, consolidation, and ascendency to national power. By tracing antichinista organizations in the swirling waters of competing nationalisms, the aim is to denaturalize Mexican mestizo nationalism. The chapter attempts to account for the uncertainty of the political process and the ambivalence of actors in that time. Take, for instance, Secretary of Education José Manuel Puig Casauranc, who in the early 1920s wrote with bewilderment about the advent of the use of the term *mestizo* in political writings and speeches of the revolution, questioning how and if such a term would become popular.[2] To counteract the historiographical tendency to represent the Mexican nation as monolithic, we need to begin by understanding that mestizo nationalism was never inevitable—it had to be won. This point of departure requires tracing the process of articulation, dispute, and dominance that had to have occurred for this ideology to become hegemonic.

The history of anti-Chinese organizations runs through the revolution and reconstruction because antichinismo intervened in a nationalistic public sphere that was just being constituted. The public records of state legislatures and official correspondence reveal that state-level officials were key architects of the anti-Chinese movement. They were different from other political or social actors at this time because they were charged with constructing new statutes that aimed to create the revolution's institutions. They created both the instruments to impose rule and their measures of evaluation. What distinguishes the antichinista movement in Mexican politics is that its political ideology transcended class. Social actors who occupied an intermediary position between the forces of a centralizing federal state and the search for consent among their rebellious, disinterested, reluctant, and defensive constituencies were the ones who fomented antichinismo. In addition to instigating popular violence, antichinistas employed political strategies to intervene in formal civic institutions. Leading politicians used antichinismo to advance and steer institutionalization, public debate, and juridical reform. These political strategies are distinct from more popular forms of activism because they engaged the process of state craft. Grassroots antichinistas negotiated their terms of consent to the revolutionary order by articulating a racial program for reconstruction. Still, when Obregón claimed to be the revolution's victor in 1920 and the Mexican state apparatus was in shambles, it was antichinistas, more than any other political group, who gave a distinctive "national" coherence to the reorganization of the state. Other bourgeois generals who were appointed to favorable positions frequently used those positions for personal enrichment and gave little regard for what antichinistas argued was a true public good: a state-disciplined mestizo future. The task of transforming Obregón's military victory into a political one ran parallel with a plurality of regional revolutions and a diverse field of nationalisms, some of which were enthralled with mestizophilia. However, none were more tightly organized, well positioned or better able to foster national unification and present a popular notion of ethical governance than the antichinistas. Antichinistas offered a virtuous rationale for government authority based upon racial protection and improvement. Even though it was openly racist toward Chinese people, anti-Chinese politics became a panacea to Mexico's perennial "Indian problem" because it allowed people to think of themselves as citizens living under a necessary and munificent bureaucratic state. The hysterical fantasy of the so-called yellow invasion created a racial imagination, by which the fragmented republic could be thought of as a mestizo nation under siege.

This chapter will reveal that antichinismo was not just a racist condemnation of Chinese people; it was a rational, ethical model of rule—one where Indians and women were the most visible objects of its domination. Antichinistas were most successful when they linked the Chinese threat to the racial evolution and capitalist development of a purportedly mestizo nation. This strategy made gender and sexuality central sites of contestation. Women's participation in Chinese antimiscegenation campaigns illuminates the centrality of the biopolitical features of female biological and social reproduction. *Biopolitics*, famously defined by Michel Foucault, is a term used to describe the management of life through a politicization and instrumentalization of the basic components necessary to sustain the human species.[3] Nutrition and disease are clear examples, but the most important object of biopower is sexual reproduction. For this reason, antichinismo among women provided an explicit sexual and gendered dimension of mestizo nationalism that other visions of the nation neglected. Their racial claims to a gendered citizenship made the mestizo figure a tangible policy object that created heterosexual women as a juridical subject. Because anti-Chinese politics gave voice to debates about collective identity and structural change of the economy, it became vital to the formation of an official national ideology that invented the conditions of national belonging. This symbolic economy constituted the wages of mestizaje, a racist practice that purchased political inclusion for its adherents. This chapter provides regional examples of the national antichinista campaign from Tamaulipas to Colima and Tlaxcala to Baja California to illustrate the different cultural registers and sets of interests, in which antichinismo became understood.

Continuous rebellion, an uncertain competition between nationalisms and regions, and the persistence of the Porfirian economy are all basic conditions that shaped how antichinismo was voiced and heard. Anti-Chinese politics was even influenced by political rivalry among Mexico's Chinese population.

The larger context shows that anti-Chinese organizations were not motivated solely by mere prejudice; they were also driven by an imperative to create a public sphere and invent a racial logic of postrevolutionary reconstruction. Attending to anti-Chinese organizations offers a different way to examine how the Constitutionalist claim to victory balanced the ideological transformation of national identity and the reconstruction of a modern state capable of overseeing economic development. The state acquired authority by promising citizenship and broad-based membership, but then it sought to reorganize, regulate, and discipline the populations of swelling urban centers, people inhabiting a scattered patchwork of rural agricultural zones, and rebellious or disinterested peasants and Indian people. Antichinismo served as a powerful critique of the status quo in the postrevolutionary order while expanding a regime of political subjection through mass experiments in racialized citizenship.

Mexico Rising

The expansion of individual and distinct anti-Chinese campaigns across Mexico led to a confluence of diverse political positions. As the targets of Mexican antichinismo evolved from disposable Porfirian motores de sangre to killable subjects of revolutionary discontent, so, too, did the political rationale for collective identity shift as the revolutionary state invented modes of subjection. More than an expression of discontent, antichinismo was an active outlet for discussing collective identity and new relations of state power—contested themes with uncertain consequences. The history of antichinismo illustrates that many conceptions of the nation competed for dominance.

The multiplication of anti-Chinese organizations and their growing membership base paralleled a larger trend in Mexico of the proliferation of civic societies, or *sociedades mutualistas*. These organizations testified to the loosening of categories of identity and to efforts to redraw their boundaries. These new collectives became a means to pressure local, state, and federal officials. For instance, the *página para todos* (page for all) section of *El Imparcial*, a Mexico City newspaper, shows that in 1913 the fraternal organizations El Fenix, Casa Mundial del Obrero, and the Baker's branch of the Unión y Amistad all announced social gatherings and agenda items for future meetings. Some of these societies organized entertainments like La Mixta's Gardenia, a family event with music and dancing, while other events were overtly political. On the same page was an announcement from the Sociedad Indigenista Mexicana (Mexican Indigenous Society) about membership drives, public meetings with expert speakers, and policy proposals for the "evolution of the Indian."[4] Civic organizations were cultural laboratories for the social life of citizenship, where people experimented with outreach and affiliation based on different visions of the nation—reflecting class interests, ethnic divisions, modernist aspirations, and expressive culture. Across the country, these organizations exhibited wide variation in organizational structure and concern. Among civic organizations, anti-Chinese organizations stood out because they openly engaged in ideological debates about the purpose of state power. The racial polemic they circulated drew together horizontally positioned allies while demanding specific types of government action. The pursuit of broad policy reform linked different actors in different states and made them among the first to establish a national network and effectively push a specific reform agenda into state and federal legislatures.

Socialist and fascist political parties were active during this time, but they were boxed in by their own narrow political commitments. Fascists sought a reversal of agrarian-reform measures, in addition to the racial exclusion of the indigenous peasantry from formal political and cultural life. The combination of an ideology of white supremacy and the absence of a populist agenda doomed the Fascist Party to failure. In 1922 the Partido Fascista Mexicano (Party of Mexican Fascists) formed as a reaction against populist agrarian reforms. Despite having support in many states and amassing 150,000 members, the platform negated any appeal to economic redistribution because it sought protection for the propertied class. In the 1930s political allies from Villa's Chihuahuan cabinet became founders of the Acción Revolucionario Mexicanista (Mexicans for Revolutionary Action) and the Camisas Doradas (Gold Shirts)—political organizations that directly borrowed German anti-Semitism and terrorized unsanctioned labor unions. These groups failed to gain political ground in part because their platform of reform was designed to insulate a narrow middle class, intrinsically alienating the vast indigenous peasantry.[5] These right-wing, authoritarian movements did not ideologically include the poor and browner masses mobilized by the revolt against Díaz, and so they failed to negotiate new terms of consent. The Socialist Party faced problems on the other side of the political spectrum because its challenge to the expansion of state capitalism made it an obstacle to the reconstruction programs of the revolutionary state. Furthermore, state-controlled unions, such as the Confederación Regional Obrero Mexicana (Regional Confederation of Mexican Workers) (CROM), formed in 1918, weakened the socialist influence. Antichinismo won out over other ideological positions because it became a compelling populist message that did not undermine the revolution's capitalists or the Constitutionalist government.

After Díaz's fall, the revolution's leaders tried to improvise new ways of understanding Mexico's past in order to chart a path toward a progressive national union. Through their continuous interplay, different actors shifted the grounds of political discourse, state formation, and the cultural sensibilities of state sovereignty. From Catholic people to Yaqui people and military coups to labor unions and even the rivalry between immigrant Chinese political factions, Mexican nationalism was a competition to solve the impossible puzzle of collective postcolonial identity. Discourses of national identity were historically important in this period because they provided different social coordinates by which Mexico's multifarious elements were thought to cohere in a unified whole. Antichinistas were particularly successful at this task.

Other than Gamio and Vasconcelos

Recent histories of twentieth-century Mexico claim that two figures, Manuel Gamio and José Vasconcelos, were the key architects of mestizo nationalism. Gamio, an anthropologist, believed that the revolution was more than just a political contest: it was the realization of a racial coming-of-age. His 1916 *Forjando Patria: Pro-Nacionalismo* (Forging a fatherland), in which he conceived of the revolution as a political movement, inspired a national race capable of industrial modernization. According to Gamio, centuries of Spanish colonization had led to the formation of diverse Mexican nationalities composed of Europeans, Indians, and mestizos. He argued for a nationalism that could provide for "the redemption of the indigenous class" by incorporating their cultural heritage into what he called "patriotic sentimentalism."[6] This redemption was, however, limited by a Eurocentrism that implicitly excluded Asian and African peoples from both his national imaginary and the benefits of the revolution.[7]

The intrepid philosopher and educator José Vasconcelos plotted a visionary path for the nation when he authored *La Raza Cósmica* (The cosmic race) in 1925. In contrast to Gamio, Vasconcelos interpreted the revolution as providing the ideal conditions for the emergence of a national mestizo race. This idea was controversial at the time because it exalted European miscegenation with Indian people. His proposals were not a rejection of biological notions of race but an articulation of good mixing, a positive eugenics.[8] Vasconcelos's ideas corresponded with prevailing notions of Lamarckian genetics, which emphasize that the culture and behavior of the parents could pass on acquired characteristics and, thus, shape what progeny inherit. This theory of genetic inheritance differed from one in the United States, where eugenicists preached a strict racial heredity that reinforced the supremacy and purity of whites.[9]

Even though Vasconcelos's appropriation of eugenics was not explicitly white supremacist, his nationalist prescriptions for good racial mixing disavowed Asian and African people from participating in mestizo racial progress.[10] Vasconcelos concluded that national policy should protect the purity of this mixed national race and harness its capacity for economic development through education.[11]

The thoughts of Gamio and Vasconcelos are represented in antichinista pro-raza discourse, but they were not the most important messengers, nor was their message the only source of racial ideology in the public sphere. Both intellectuals were actually absent from Mexico during this formative period. While holding the office of the secretary of education under Obregón, Vasconcelos led the national university system and helped initiate the use of schools as instruments of postrevolutionary nationalism.[12] However, he left Mexico in 1924 to live in the United States and returned in 1929 to run an unsuccessful bid for the presidency. Gamio left Mexico in 1925 and did not return until almost a decade later. Both men cited ideological differences and corruption in the Ministry of Education under the Calles administration as reasons for leaving. Even though they voiced yellow-peril racism in their writings, their ideas were rejected by Calles and his cronies. When Vasconcelos and Gamio returned to Mexico, they served in Cárdenas's administration, not because of their ideas but because they were political enemies of Calles and, thus, contributed to Cárdenas's political independence.

The historiography attributes importance to these two luminaries because doing so supports the idea that mestizo nationalism was a natural outcome of the revolution. Rather than casting them as central pillars of Mexican mestizo national ideology, it seems more appropriate to position them as parallel streams of thought with antichinismo, sometimes intersecting, sometimes not. Antichinista political campaigns tested a political process of advocating for an abstract mestizo public good and in so doing illustrated one way that certain strains of mestizophilia became articulated as a state ideology. The political class knew of Gamio's and Vasconcelos's ideas but did not canvass the nation for support and argue for the necessity of their agenda, as did the antichinista national campaign. In this regard, antichinismo had a separate and independent political life from the more well-known mestizophilia of Gamio and Vasconcelos; antichinismo coursed through the Mexican public sphere years before either individual would return to the Mexican bureaucracy. The overemphasis on Gamio and Vasconcelos in the formation of Mexican mestizo identity has served to obscure the history of antichinismo and limit the interrogation of Mexican national-identity formation.

Birth of a Movement

It is improbable that anyone in Mexico would have predicted that anti-Chinese organizations would be crucial building blocks for the first national political party. Modest, fractious beginnings did not portend national prominence. Yet, the political versatility of antichinismo began to convince many that anti-Chinese politics could be instrumental to postrevolutionary rule. When former President Obregón was assassinated in 1928, antichinistas already possessed a hierarchical organizational structure supported by popular discourses of racial unity. These political resources were accentuated by President Calles's call for political transformation and recovery from the national tragedy. From 1911 to 1924, anti-Chinese organizations had emerged heterogeneously and brought together different regional and class concerns. The antichinismo of the bartender and taxi union in Mexicali was independent from and advocated for different measures than Sonora's Commercial and Businessman's Group, which differed again from the Liga Nacionalista in Tamaulipas. Their visions of the nation all excluded the Chinese people. Class divisions among anti-Chinese organizations were directly related to the emerging status quo of the reconstruction, led by a nationalist bourgeoisie with sluggish plans for self-colonization. Unions, business leaders, and politicians looked to Sonora as the avant-garde of anti-Chinese measures.

In his days as governor of Sonora, one of the first state politicians to crack down on the Chinese people was Calles. Since 1915 his various decrees on segregation, expulsion, and discriminating taxes were crucial experiments in racial governance and helped him to ameliorate tensions with the state's unions. Calles later rescinded many of these orders, but they still illustrate a perennial challenge of balancing the popular fantasy of Chinese expulsion with the reality of dependence upon their commercial circuits, particularly in urban food supply. In 1919 he was nominated to become the secretary of industry, commerce, and labor. Months later, Calles joined Obregón in the Agua Prieta overthrow of Carranza, after which Calles became head of the Ministry of the Interior.

In 1916 José Maria Arana formed Pro-Patria, an anti-Chinese organization that was associated with his mayoral campaign in the Sonoran town of Magdalena. Pro-Patria became the most documented anti-Chinese organization of this era.[13] It had an open affiliation with and inclusion of women, and one instance from a Pro-Patria rally in 1917 illustrates how gendered narratives were integral to delivering anti-Chinese messages. On November 26, María de Jesús Váldez, a white, middle-class schoolteacher, gave a scathing public speech against the

Chinese people. She rehearsed common racial grievances and accused the Chinese population of ruining the soil and stealing the wealth of the people. As a schoolteacher, Váldez was a part of a white class of Mexican settlers that had colonized what had been and continued to be the site of indigenous Yaqui resistance to campaigns of pacification and extermination. Read in the context of an enduring Indian war, Váldez's characterization of the anti-Chinese campaign as "[a] work of light, of hope . . . to protect Mexican prosperity" shifted the focus of public discourse away from indigenous insurgency and Yaqui genocide and onto the Chinese threat to Mexican colonization. This rhetorical strategy obscured decades of concerted efforts to exterminate the Yaqui nation. Later in the speech, Váldez pleaded that the "voice of a Mexican woman . . . ensures the promise to the small, the humble, and the proletariat" in an effort to frame the anti-Chinese mission as a populist veil for ongoing Mexican occupation.[14] Efforts to build public support for Arana were not just about gaining consent to reconstitute state authority under the Constitutionalist revolution. They were fundamentally concerned with redrawing the categories of identity to suit new conditions of the ruling state and achieve the erasure of indigeneity. Váldez's claim drew on a gendered language of familial concern that invited men to castigate the Chinese people, affirm patriotic convictions, and vote. At the end of her speech, she signed off, "¡¡Abajo los Chinos!!" (Down with the Chinese). Her public diatribe was an example of how different actors gave shape to a nationalism structured by anti-Chinese politics. Feminized anti-Chinese discourse became an important tool for manufacturing a national "we" and a common idiom to reconceive politics and history.

The consolidation of anti-Chinese organizations in the 1920s addressed the two-pronged concern of political leaders: recrafting a national ideology and building a competent state. The array of concerns raised by antichinistas in this decade forced nearly every state of the republic to engage the conversation about national identity by discussing the Chinese racial threat to it. No other political party or political cause sought to organize ideological consistency and political discipline across state lines. At the time, larger political parties, such as the Partido Liberal Constitucionalista and the Partido Nacional Cooperatista, had no real commitments to liberal constitutional principles; they simply served the self-interest of their members.[15] Anti-Chinese groups had different objectives; they were polemic. Antichinistas were enthralled by a sense that Mexico was in a state of emergency that demanded an "urgent" and "genuine" nationalism to galvanize the people and drive the government to realize the radical potential of the revolution: not economic redistribution but the formation of a racial state.[16]

Shortly after Obregón took office in 1921, the Junta Nacionalista directors took to the chambers of Sinaloa's statehouse to enlist the officials' support in "adopting energetic means to restrict Chinese immigration . . . terminate the [1899] treaty . . . [and] expel the Asiatics from our territory." In their testimony, they argued that Chinese people made a mockery of Mexican citizenship because their degeneracy maligned the foundations of society. Furthermore, the junta summoned the specter of the 1911 Torreón massacre to contend that a more vigilant anti-Chinese posture would have prevented the violent expression of Mexicans' justifiable hatred of the so-called yellow race. In calling for the systematic expulsion of "these pernicious residents," the Junta Nacionalista pointed out the limitations of the Mexican government to act upon the basic principle of self-preservation because of the 1899 treaty.[17] Shortly thereafter, the Nayarit and Sinaloa branches of the junta sought out an alliance with Arana's Pro-Patria to advance his anti-Chinese platform and coordinate lobbying efforts "obliged by their national duty to defend our race."[18]

Obregón's annual public address to the national congress two months later signaled a two-sided approach of public determination and private deliberation. In the address, he announced his plan to revise the treaty with China to limit immigration in the interest of reducing competition with the more than twenty thousand Mexican workers repatriated from the United States—a speech that coded antichinismo as worker advocacy.[19] However, over the next several months, President Obregón and Calles, the secretary of the interior, exchanged private memos detailing seven points of Chinese-immigration reform. In what amounts to a revision of the Mariscal formula, the memos stipulated preference for Chinese immigration that contributed to agricultural colonization. They discussed a restriction on laborers in manufacturing, as well as open immigration for males with investment capital or merchants with explicit conditions: They were to obey procedures of documentation, they were to collaborate with Mexican business interests, they were to conform to health laws, and immigration was to be allowed only through Colima, Tamaulipas, and Veracruz.[20] Despite these special provisions, Chinese migrants were still relegated to a nonsettler class of immigrants, which maintained a graduated structure of citizenship rights. These guidelines illustrate the place from which Obregón sought to negotiate the terms of the treaty with Chinese officials. The terms of the treaty were always contentious, but the contrast between Obregón's public and private transcripts illustrates the level to which antichinismo sat at the intersection of racial nationalism, state authority, and economic reform. Yet, the junta's actions went beyond populism, because its message was directed at those in power. It interjected a racial imperative to command government action—a categorically different form of political instigation than that of calls for land reform or of power grabs to capture the reins of the state.

The 1899 China-Mexico Treaty

The China-Mexico treaty was a perennial issue during the Porfiriato and continued to be controversial throughout the revolution. As the previous chapter demonstrates, the 1899 accord between China and Mexico was never without trouble or without calls for its abrogation. The treaty came into being enigmatically, and its transformation would be equally obfuscated. After his state of the union address in 1921, Obregón hosted the Chinese legation to discuss the treaty's terms. The Chinese nationalist government was the first to recognize Obregón as the legitimate victor of the revolution and wanted to secure their international credentials in the aftermath of their own revolution across the Pacific. President Obregón had a tense meeting with Chancellor Quang Ki-Teng at the Palacio Nacional (National Palace) in Mexico City (figure 8). What resulted was a modus vivendi, or a new arrangement to agree to disagree on how to amend the treaty. Mexico wanted to retain trade relations but limit Chinese immigration, while China wanted both to preserve Mexico as a viable destination for immigration and to sustain access to the country's mineral wealth. Alberto Pani, Mexico's secretary of foreign relations, persuaded the Chinese minister to accept restrictions on the flow of Chinese laborers to Mexico and leave the remaining articles of the treaty open for negotiation at a later date.[21] The provisional modification allowed everyone to claim victory: Obregón could take credit for limiting the immigration of laborers, Quang succeeded in keeping the treaty alive, and antichinistas cheered, though they felt that the limitations did not go far enough. Immigration to Mexico did slow, but Chinese people increasingly used U.S. border-crossing cards to circulate between Mexico and the United States in this period.[22] From 1922 to 1931, almost ten thousand Chinese people crisscrossed the border in both directions, leaving Mexican officials in doubt about who were legitimate merchants and whether such crossings should be regarded as immigration.[23] Meanwhile, antichinistas decried the survival of the 1899 treaty with China and continued to argue that it prevented the government from taking stronger measures against the Chinese population.

Without a doubt, the federal government could have taken stronger action against the Chinese people, but the treaty certainly did not tie its hands. Had antichinistas been aware of the autonomous activity of state governments and

FIGURE 8. President Álvaro Obregón and Chancellor Ki-Teng at the Palacio Nacional in Mexico City, February 19, 1921. Photo by Underwood and Underwood, U.S. Library of Congress.

the quiet, targeted detention and expulsion of the Chinese, they might not have been so critical. In November 1922, the state of Oaxaca deported forty-one Chinese mariners and port workers at Salina Cruz on the USS *Newport*. The passenger list included fifteen others from Tapachula who were leaving voluntarily. The passenger log included working-age Chinese men, mostly single; however, families were deported, as well. The record includes Francisco Chang, a merchant; his wife, San Shang; and their one-year-old son, Rafael. The ship's manifest also includes a sixteen-year-old Arcadia Blanco, the "White" Mexican wife of one of the Chinese deportees.[24]

Antichinista pressure to raise the Chinese question to the national stage gave greater life to a racial polemic, but it also forced uneasy compromises, particularly, in regards to the unresolved problems of the revolution and the dependence upon Chinese people for the operation of national colonization projects. In 1923 President Obregón advised Secretary Pani that regular immigration of Chinese laborers to Mexicali was vital to the continued colonization of that region.[25] The same day, Obregón wrote to Lew Chun, Lee Wing, and Wong Charm, all prominent general managers for agricultural and mercantile Chinese operations in Mexicali, to assure them that their requests to introduce two thousand Chinese workers would be approved as long as those individuals conformed to Mexican law.[26] Baja California was a federal territory and not a formal state of the republic, so it was under direct administration of the president's cabinet. Obregón postured toward a pro-Mexican labor stance via the treaty, likely to mask a policy of measured integration, which played out against the backdrop of continuous insurrection and competing visions of what change the revolution would bring. The enduring perception that Chinese people were necessary in remote sites of colonization signaled the persistence of Indian condemnation and the Mariscal formula. The 1921 modus vivendi appears to have been more of a private gentleman's agreement to sustain Mexican national colonization than a hard-lined countermand. These compromises fueled the animosity of antichinistas because continued Chinese immigration gave the appearance of inept government regulation, or worse, the contemptible neglect of race traitors.

Tong Wars, Informants, and the "Pernicious" Chinese

Often excluded from accounts of Mexico's budding postrevolutionary political life are the Chinese immigrants who participated in the growth of the country's civic organizations. The proliferation of anti-Chinese organizations encouraged a wide range of countermeasures by the Chinese people. Chinese residents frequently challenged discrimination against them in courts and sought adjudication. The first mass social organization of Chinese Mexicans occurred at the Fraternal Union in Sonora. It used pooled resources to defend the Chinese community in the courts and lobby for favorable treatment from local functionaries. Similarly, the Liga de Trabajadores de la Colonia China en la Península, formed in 1911 in Mérida, Yucatán, advocated for its workers and even helped its members fight opium addiction. Despite the good legal standing of the Yucatán Chinese union, the head of the worker's organization was arrested for assaulting another Chinese resident. Ultimately, the larger social and political needs of the union's members and the wider Chinese community led to the formation of the Chinese Association of Yucatán in 1916 and a reorganization of the union the following year.[27] Like the Yucatecan league, the

Fraternal Union was a registered Mexican association, abiding by the bylaws of a state-sanctioned civic organization; it was not a political association with origins in China. The Fraternal Union gradually evolved to reflect the political divisions that emerged from the 1911 Chinese revolution. The most influential voluntary association among Chinese people in diaspora was the Chee Kung Tong (CKT), or Justice Society, also known as the Chinese Freemasons. The CKT advocated for the overthrow of the Qing monarchy and the restoration of Ming rule. During the 1911 Chinese revolution, Sun Yat Sen joined the CKT briefly in hopes of swaying the association and its members to the cause of his Nationalist Political Party, called the Kuomingtang (KMT). Membership in the Fraternal Union faded as the CKT and KMT split became more important to Chinese diaspora politics. By the 1920s harsh divisions emerged between these two factions. Their conflicts helped shape the structure of antichinismo because they provided key illustrations of the purported danger represented by the Chinese race. Although not explored here, historian Fredy González offers a detailed analysis of the transpacific diplomatic tensions between China and Mexico over tong conflicts.[28]

These organizations were not merely institutions that sustained transnational ties; they also served to articulate Chinese expressions of Mexican nationalism where they imagined themselves as legitimate liberal citizens, not motores de sangre or vile abarroteros. Political divisions among Chinese people in Mexico fomented violent conflicts. Their clashes were driven by China's own revolutionary politics. While Mexico's KMT had official government representation as the leading political party in China, the CKT was less a political party than it was a mutual-aid society of laborers and small-business owners. The CKT objected to KMT-driven economic policies in China and the monopoly of opportunities in Mexico by KMT members. These tensions boiled over in turf battles on the streets of Hermosillo, Sonora, in the summer of 1922, leaving several Chinese people dead and creating a perception of uncontrollable, violent Chinese passions. Their public shoot-outs and casino brawls became flash points for the discursive management of the representation of the Chinese racial threat.

The KMT-CKT conflict ignited government attention, popular discontent, and condemnation by antichinistas. In the weeks following the initial battle, Obregón ordered an investigation into the leaders of both groups and ordered their expulsion as "pernicious individuals."[29] Under pressure to control Chinese violence, restore order, and appease antichinistas, Obregón invoked article 33 of the 1917 Constitution to apprehend, detain, and deport Mexico's rowdy Chinese people. Sonoran judges protested what they saw as flagrant abuse of presidential authority, arguing that article 33 could not be used on naturalized Chinese,[30] but the judges were hindered by popular outrage over Chinese violence and perceived public endangerment. Obregón's decision to carry out deportations despite judicial contest was influenced by mass public protest against the Chinese people and the judges who protected them. These gatherings did not become grotesque assemblies, as described in the previous chapter. The protests flowed from a desire to be involved in governance. Rather than looting and killing, the participants, mostly members of area labor unions, local politicians, and other Hermosillo residents, took their protest to a meeting hall to discuss what should be done about the crisis of pernicious Chinese.[31] Sonora's governor, President Calles's son, telegrammed Obregón, asking for instructions on how to support the expulsion effort. The president responded with orders to relay back to him public reactions to the Chinese people.[32] Days later, the Sonoran legislature issued a statement attesting to the perniciousness of the Chinese racial threat, reasoning that individual pernicious behavior was indicative of the entire race. Sonoran state congressman Manuel Montoya wrote to Obregón that the "mysterious form" of murder in an assassination of a Chinese man in Cananea established broad conditions to suspect all Chinese people with political affiliations as members of pernicious Chinese mafias.[33] The president of the Comité Pro-Raza, José Angel Espinoza, wrote to Obregón about the same incident, pleading for action against all Chinese people.[34] According to protests by the court, it was vital for Obregón to document public petitions of grievances against Chinese individuals in order to establish the "pernicious" grounds for expulsion. It appears that Obregón's orders to the younger Calles were designed to produce enough evidence to overturn the court's obstruction. Free of judicial limitations, both KMT and CKT members were apprehended by police.

The detention of Francisco Yuen, president of Mexico's KMT, initiated an unlikely partnership with the Obregón administration. Obregón's earlier investigation into the Chinese rivalry identified Yuen as an important leader and target for expulsion. Yuen and his Mexican lawyer, Juan Sanchez Azcona, skillfully portrayed the CKT as violent peasant thugs and the KMT as civil capitalist victims—characterizations not unlike those that divided Conventionists and Constitutionalists in the previous decade. Yuen's apprehension and monthlong detention led to a relationship with the Obregón administration. The tone of Yuen's correspondence and open condemnation of the CKT indicate that he was not under duress, or pressured to become an informant. It is likely that he identified his vulnerable position as an opportunity to pick sides. Unremarked upon in the existing scholarly literature is that fact that Yuen and other KMT members went to great lengths to retell the political history of the KMT, aligning it with the liberal ideals of Constitutionalist revolutionaries.[35] Upon Yuen's release, he and his lawyer began to feed vital information about the CKT to Obregón and further corroborated the pernicious qualities of their adversaries, referring to them as a "mafia."[36] A striking series of memos from Yuen, his lawyer, and other KMT members to the Obregón administration documents how top KMT members became informants for a campaign to expel the CKT from Mexico. Just days after informants remitted letters and dossiers on CKT rivals to the president's office, Obregón would hand down orders to his cabinet to carry out deportations of the leaders the informants named. Based on KMT memos, the Mexican government deported groups of CKT members from Sonora, Sinaloa, San Luis Potosi, Durango, and Baja California.

Yuen was a prominent businessman and important political leader. He became a naturalized Mexican citizen in 1898 as a merchant in Mazatlán, Sinaloa.[37] In 1916 he began to consolidate the Chinese people across Sonora in an effort to pool resources from a base of two thousand KMT members and counter Arana's Pro-Patria campaign.[38] By the following year, Yuen's leadership of the KMT grew it to more than ten thousand members from around the state. They began to express Mexican belonging based on economic participation, philanthropy, and demands to uphold constitutional liberalism.[39] For them, the struggle for a democratic republic in China shaped ideas about liberal constitutional citizenship in Mexico. Most important, the KMT sought to portray themselves as rightful Mexican citizens through their condemnation of the CKT. This political strategy is most clearly observed in an October 22, 1921, public circular the KMT published. In it, they discuss their name change to El Partido Nacionalista Chino (the Chinese Nationalist Party), in conformity with Mexican political norms. The pamphlet consisted of four newsprint pages describing the immoral, uneducated, unsanitary, violent, and irrational character of the CKT's members. The circular states that CKT members formed the criminal element of all Chinatowns throughout the diaspora.[40] Within this political framework, anti-Chinese politics became a tactical mode of expressing nationalism, even for Chinese residents.

Despite political divisions among the Chinese people, irrigated colonization still utilized labor and capital of the Chinese diaspora. By 1922 Yuen had amassed great support among the Chinese population in Mexico and remained a vital functionary to the commercial and agricultural growth of the state. During Yuen's detention, at least six of his Mexican partners wrote to Obregón, vouching for Yuen's credentials as "an honorable merchant and hard-working agriculturalist."[41] Yuen was an unlikely ally for the Obregón administration because of the mounting popularity of anti-Chinese politics, but Yuen and his KMT compatriots were well positioned in the north's political economy and sustained close ties to China's ruling party. Secretly collaborating with the KMT to expel the CKT allowed Obregón to buoy the economy with Chinese capitalists and foster diplomatic friendship with the Republic of China while catering to antichinistas.

Yet, the partnership was only as durable as Obregón's power and the perceived necessity of Chinese functionaries—both of which would expire by decade's end. By the end of 1922, KMT members armed the Mexican government with a staggering array of information on their rivals, leading to the deportation of hundreds from several states. While Yuen and his KMT associates seemed to have safeguarded their position as silent partners to irrigated colonization, they sowed the seeds of their own demise by legitimating the racialization of Chinese people and by escalating conflict with the CKT through government complicity. By pursuing the narrow objective to expel the CKT leadership and cripple the organization, the KMT conformed to Mexican racializations of the Chinese people as threats to the revolutionary order. In order to expel CKT thugs legally, Obregón required the documentation of pernicious behavior to legitimize the use of article 33 expulsions. Historian Elliot Young, using other sources, shows government reporting that article 33 expulsions before 1927 were rare and after that date involved few Chinese people, indicating that deportations may have become extralegal after that time.[42] Because local, state, and federal authorities all claimed expulsion powers under this constitutional authority, records of the practice and reporting of actual deportations are not clear.[43] Like the Oaxacan deportation mentioned above, local and federal officials followed statutes when convenient, and extralegal action was not always curbed. Regardless of implementation, the use of article 33 as a tool of antichinismo produced an important racial logic and public perception of the government's legitimacy to act on notions of race. Because this power was limited to the expulsion of individuals, it established the grounds for individual removals based upon the recognition of the Chinese population as racially pernicious and, thus, individually removable. When doubts about adequate documentation surfaced, Obregón turned to grassroots anti-Chinese organizations, such as Comité Pro-Raza and Liga Anti-China.[44] These organizations were oblivious to the Obregón-KMT partnership but were encouraged by the CKT roundups to broaden and intensify their anti-Chinese activities.

Although the government campaign to punish the Chinese people for tong violence centered on the CKT, the KMT's partnership with those in power did not prevent its members from being harassed by ordinary people or local police. Many Chinese people unaffiliated with either group were also apprehended and deported. In the first group of more than five hundred deported in June 1922, only a quarter were apprehended for tong violence.[45] Others, like Lorenzo Wong of Navajoa, Sonora, who had lived in the country for more than a decade, were deported under the auspice of clearing out CKT thugs. He left behind his Mexican wife and their five children.[46] For Mexican officials and antichinistas, the grounds by which the Chinese people could be considered pernicious grew ever wider. The impact of KMT informants on the campaign to expel pernicious Chinese led to another round of CKT-KMT violence in 1924. This second war was set off in October by Yuen's public assassination at a Sonoran train station by Ramon Ley and Luis Huy, known members of the CKT.[47] The CKT leadership had likely discovered that Yuen was acting as an informant and gunned him down for his complicity, an act that confirmed to everyone else how dangerous the Chinese population had become. Despite the loss of Yuen, the KMT continued to supply the government with information on the CKT, and a new round of wide-reaching apprehensions and deportations followed. In this phase of escalation, Obregón formalized article 33 expulsion procedures through a judicial review.[48] It is unclear if this resolution increased protection of Chinese people from deportation or quieted local officials' reporting of expulsions.

The CKT-KMT rivalry did not define the political landscape for all Chinese immigrants in Mexico. Between 1922 and 1928 CKT protests of deportations were the most numerous legal disputes by Chinese people. Beyond this conflict, Chinese immigrants regularly fought for their rights in state and federal courts, albeit in an extremely hostile environment. For instance, in 1917 a Sonoran newspaper reported, "The Chinese are laughing" at "patriotic nationalists" whose discriminatory policies were blocked by a state court injunction to protect the legal equality of the right of Chinese people to inhabit the state and conduct business. Antichinistas critiqued the protection Mexican courts offered that had, in their words, allowed the nation's racial denigration to continue unchallenged.[49] The historical record contains many other successful Chinese suits against discrimination from individuals as well as municipal and state governments. From 1917 to 1931 naturalized Chinese people brought twenty-five cases to the Mexican supreme court.[50] These victories incensed antichinistas and drove them to increase their efforts and draw harsher contrasts for Chinese racial exception to the revolution's constitution.

Rather than think of these momentary flashes of victory of Mexican democracy at work, we ought to attend to the logic of the postrevolutionary state and the larger social and political context. One consequence of the revolution was the extension of constitutional protection to those the constitution had previously ignored. While this change corresponded with the populist redemption of Indian people, it was underwritten by a new set of juridical-racial discourses being articulated around anti-Chinese politics. That criticism of anti-Chinese politics as merely illiberal hides a more uncertain process of state- and national-identity formation. Such an ambivalent gesture, with regard to both the CKT-KMT rivalry and jurisprudence, could not stem from nationalist xenophobia, as much of the scholarly literature claims. Government action was driven by a blend of strategies to maintain political legitimacy, instill a postrevolutionary climate of law and order, and sustain the viability of irrigated colonization projects. In other words, mestizo nationalism was not yet hegemonic.

Antichinista Consolidation and Pro-Raza Ideology

The revolutionary government's continued dependence upon Chinese people in irrigated colonization fueled the indignation of antichinistas. The racial polemic of anti-Chinese campaigns reveals the discursive coordination between fantasies of restriction and expulsion with the enfranchisement and uplift of an imagined modern polity. Paralleling the escalation of the CKT-KMT conflict, antichinista activism grew bolder, gained greater legitimacy, and converged into a national campaign. In 1924, at the height of the tong wars, Sinaloa's chief antichinista, Augustin Larios Z., wrote to Obregón's office, notifying him of the newly elected board of directors and extended list of advisers and supporters of Comité Anti-Chino (Anti-Chinese Committee). In his letter, Z. included a public notice announcing the purpose and activities of the committee, which called for collective action to usurp Chinese commerce and engage in "patriotic colonization."[51] Sinaloa's Comité Anti-Chino later spawned a youth club whose goal was to practice citizenship such that its "work might have some good effect upon our race."[52] Similarly, a public health committee from San Pedro, Coahuila, wrote to Luis Morones, secretary of commerce, industry, and labor, asking for his support for an eight-point reform plan, which did not mention the CKT-KMT rivalry, and focused, instead, on a racial ideology of eugenics and ethical governance.[53] Antichinistas became among the first groups to disseminate an ideology of racial unification that had been bubbling at the surface of national politics. Antichinismo provided a new outlet for discussing postrevolutionary governance.

The concern for ethical governance was directly tied to the new constitution. As the first national constitution to articulate the state's obligation to guarantee the basic rights and subordinate private property to the dictates of the nation, Mexican officials were experimenting with alternative rationalities of authority. Most interpretations of the 1917 constitution center upon the powers of the state to act against foreign intrusion, such as nationalist expropriations; less attention has been paid to the ways that the constitution's social rights authorized the state to expand its subjection of the indigenous and peasant population, which constituted the ultimate realization of the self-colonization imperative. In other words, the 1917 constitution invented both the public good and the authority of the revolutionary state to safeguard it. This condition made the discussion of the public good a debate about ethical governance and about the balance between the ideal society and the state's method of achieving that ideal. The social rights of the 1917 constitution fundamentally altered the cultural sensibility of state sovereignty from an inherited colonial imperative to the defender of the people. By the 1920s the contests of state power began to illustrate that defense of the people meant domination of the people. The authoritarian impulse of revolutionary victors might lead to interpretation of these juridical practices as the mode of consolidating power during reconstruction. Yet, the emergence of antichinismo from popular violence to social organizations reflects the ways that racial discourse intervened and gave meaning to the revolution's social rights.

In contrast to the grotesque assemblies described in the previous chapter, antichinista campaigns demonstrate both a remarkable political self-discipline and unprecedented rush to participate in political institutions. Acts of physical violence did not halt, but violent sentiments ascended to the formal plane of political institutions. In this regard, antichinismo encouraged political domestication. These racist campaigns pushed state legislatures and national political figures to confront questions of race and state power openly as obligations of their office. The story of Mexican antichinista consolidation of a national campaign is also the story of the political discovery of mestizo nationalism. The campaign to reproduce anti-Chinese state laws across the republic taught both officials and the wider public to view antichinismo as a way to construct a mestizo good in a nationalistic public sphere.

Antichinista issues of public health, worker protection, economic restructuring along race lines, and denigrating race mixture became persuasive means of discursively managing a mestizo racial imagination among diverse classes in different regions. The state of Sonora was the pioneer of postrevolutionary anti-Chinese legislation. In December 1923, appalled by the first CKT-KMT battle, the Sonoran legislature passed two anti-Chinese laws: law 27, which authorized municipalities to segregate Chinese people from the rest of the population, and law 31, which prohibited Chinese and Mexican intermarriage.[54] Even though enforcement of laws 27 and 31 was inconsistent, the issues of racialized urban space and antimiscegenation became ways of expressing the necessity of racial governance in everyday life. However, like Obregón's Baja California caveat to the modus vivendi and KMT partnership, the jurisdiction for law 27 in Sonora was limited to cities. It did not extend to rural zones, where thousands of Chinese lived and worked in irrigated colonization. This statutory limitation illustrates an emerging racial order where urban spaces became privileged sites of state intervention.[55] The passage of these policies as the first anti-Chinese state laws made Sonoran antichinista leaders crucial political brokers while they linked to others across state lines. They would soon discover that states did not need Chinese residents in order for anti-Chinese politics to be mobilized.

Coordination across state lines was organized by promotion of the Sonoran platform of antimiscegenation, segregation, and abrogation of the 1899 treaty. The first instance of this campaign occurred in September 1924 when the Chihuahuan congress circulated an anti-Chinese referendum issued from neighboring Sonora. This strategy would require greater coordination than previous efforts from several years earlier to break the treaty.[56] Feeling the momentum of the campaign to expel the CKT, antichinistas established new regional alliances, and they saw new hope in the election of Calles to the presidency in December 1924. Antichinistas knew Calles as a Sonoran governor who had advanced their cause almost a decade previously. However, his commitment to antichinismo would be diminished by his inheritance of Obregón's fragmented and contradictory patterns of negotiated administration.

Two months after Calles's inauguration, founders of the Sonoran Liga Nacionalista Anti-Chino petitioned President Calles for thirty thousand pesos to fund an expansion of their efforts and host a "Grand Anti-Chinese Convention." These funds supported the gathering of more than thirty organizations from Sonora, Sinaloa, and Baja California.[57] Among the delegates of these organizations were individuals who had lost political races and sought alternative political careers. For example, Alejandro Lacy Jr., son of a staunch Porfirian colonist of Yaqui lands, made important contributions to shaping the discussion at the convention. In the 1911 Sonora governor's race, Lacy Jr. became a Constitutionalist candidate known for his harsh criticism of, in his words, "Científico Jews."[58] Left out of the postrevolutionary scramble for political office, the anti-Chinese movement allowed Lacy Jr. and other men of high position to reenter the public sphere as antichinista nationalists. With Lacy Jr.'s help, those attending the convention collectively articulated a coordinated vision to expand their grassroots campaign. Others, like convention coordinator Espinoza, were state legislators who contributed valuable information on parliamentary procedure, thus shaping a discourse of public interest. Both men later played significant roles in the ascendance of antichinismo to state ideology.

The convention was the first time antichinistas from different regions had gathered to discuss a way forward. They worked out a cultural and political logic of social change that did not follow the tradition of factional military politics (like Victoriano Huerta or Francisco Serrano and Arnulfo Gomez) or rely upon a charismatic leader (like Francisco Madero). Rather, they mobilized racial discourse to shape the public sphere more powerfully than ever before. Racially charged claims for ethical governance created a different, less-militaristic rationale for political legitimacy than that the revolution's generals practiced.

The convention tackled several goals: Take stock of Chinese financial resources, coordinate action between groups, establish identical bylaws to govern separate groups, find appropriate measures to redirect the desires of Chinese-loving Mexican women, concentrate legal and economic action on the network of Chinese cooperatives, and eliminate any expectation of governmental aid for Chinese people.[59] The proposal envisioned a broad-based popular movement to undermine the economic basis of Chinese communities and shame Mexican women, known as *chineras,* who married Chinese men. These anti-Chinese organizations signaled an important shift toward the popularization of a national racial ideal. They saw themselves as bearers of a new national culture and positioned themselves as racial stewards—policy-minded nationalists who had surpassed Porfirian technocrats and corrupt revolutionary generals as authentic patriots. These organizations did not possess a tinge of romanticism for redemption of Indian people; their goal was the protection of a racial future through state intervention in sexual and economic reproduction.

A central feature of antichinista cultural logic was to designate an active role for women. The antichinista organizations consciously promoted women's participation, like Váldez's involvement eight years earlier in Arana's Pro-Patria campaign. By December 1925 members of the Sonoran Comité Pro-Raza Femenino (Women's Pro-Race Committee of Sonora) had been to Aguascalientes, Durango, as well as Tamaulipas and Tlaxcala twice, each time pleading with the officials to prohibit Mexican women from marrying Chinese men. The committee distributed pamphlets and asked the officials to consider their ethical duty to prevent racial degeneration by expelling Chinese people in the country illegally, enforcing segregation, blocking further immigration, and breaking the 1899 treaty.[60] The issue of miscegenation remained a lynchpin of antichinismo because it invented the conceptual boundaries of the Mexican mestizo racial form as a thing to be protected, supported, and strengthened. The representation of women as the biological instrument of a race's capacity for reproduction and of female sexuality as the biological technology for racial refinement led to construction of a hypervisible female subject of political concern. Mexican antichinismo privileged the Mexican woman as an emblem, subject, and mechanism by which mestizo nationalism could be discussed and acted upon.

Gendered Antimiscegenation

By the 1920s women had become integral to the growth of the antichinista movement as both actors and objects. As with Váldez's speech, antichinista discourse used gender difference to mobilize civic action and structure an emergent mestizo racial imaginary. As women in Mexico ventured out of traditional gender roles and sought greater political influence, they frequently performed through antichinismo a fuller citizenship otherwise denied to them. Within antichinismo, the racial polemic of Chinese race mixing became an entry point for women to enter the public sphere and make claims for state action based upon this racial logic. Gendered anti-Chinese activism could be found in rural pueblos, white middle-class households, and working-class cities, illustrating a number of ways that women's gendered claims to a racialized public good shaped mestizo ideology. Women's accusations against the Chinese population relied on dominant gender roles to animate their concerns for household integrity, including procuring food, caring for children, participating in wage labor, and sexual reproduction. An instrumental interpretation might suggest women saw they could make more aggressive claims for their welfare when situated within a frame of antichinismo. Indeed, when they couched their arguments in these terms, they might have been more effective at gaining male support because they reinforced gendered domesticity and sexual discipline that favored masculine desires. While some women may have benefited from adopting antichinismo, the political appropriation of women's voices also served the architects of the national anti-Chinese campaign. Sonora's Comité Pro-Raza Femenino would become one of the most well-traveled antichinista organizations as they lobbied state legislatures across the country.

However, women did not acquire new political or economic rights because of anti-Chinese measures. While women were a focal point and a public voice, men were clearly the ideological architects and beneficiaries. The most prolific was Espinoza, Sonoran antichinista and key organizer for the anti-Chinese conventions. After the national campaign's apex, Espinoza authored two influential books circulated to other antichinistas, politicians, and literate urbanites. *El Problema Chino de Mexico* (The Chinese Problem of Mexico) (1931) and *El Ejemplo de Sonora* (The Example of Sonora) (1932) spelled out the antichinista platform, provided a history of their social movement, and provided a detailed outline of the political, economic, and biological consequences of not passing the entire slate of proposed anti-Chinese measures. These texts reflect the political curriculum that had developed over the course of the 1920s. It was a decade of drafting political messages and tuning a racial discourse through a national campaign built upon interstate collaborations and regional conventions. These texts most clearly document the formation of pro-raza mestizo nationalism through anti-Chinese politics. *El Ejemplo* argued, "Chinese mestizos do not yield even a drop of Indo-Latina blood," and *El Problema* called the anti-Chinese campaign an "urgent nationalism."[61] These texts compiled much of what the national campaign had developed over the previous decade. What was new about these texts were the images, which conveyed racial constructions of the Chinese people as well as a visual lexicon of the antichinista pro-raza imagination. With the assistance of these images, antichinista ideology constructed Mexican subjects of racial nationalism through a politics of the feminine.

Although other racial and political discourses were in circulation at the time, antichinismo was distinct in the particular attention it gave to the representation and participation of Mexican women. This was not a strategy of placating suffragettes or stuffing ballots for elections (women were not granted federal suffrage until 1953), but an acknowledgment that women occupied a vital position in the biopolitics of racial ideology.

One of Espinoza's most famous illustrations is a comparison of racial composites "La Mestización" (Miscegenation; figure 9). It is difficult to say which figure in the cartoon is more dramatic: the twelve-year-old mestizo Boy Scout on the left or the fourteen-year-old frail Chinese Mexican youth. To audiences in the 1930s, the opposition to the Chinese degenerate creates a play of differences essential to producing the representation of an Indian mestizo as a white Boy Scout. In symbolic terms, this portrayal uses the Chinese people to buttress the desired Eurocentric whiteness of an imaginary Mexican mestizo. Yet, naming this figure as a mestizo was not just a bold appropriation of a modern figure of whiteness. It was a message that a racial transformation of the country required the exclusion of the Chinese people. At the root of

4. *La Mestización*

mestizo indolatino de   Producto de la mezcla chino-
12 años.   mexicana de 14 años.

FIGURE 9. "La Mestización" (Miscegenation), José Angel
Espinoza's comparison of racial composites, 1932. The panels
translate as, "Twelve-year-old mixed Euro-Indian" (left) and
"Fourteen-year-old product of Chinese-Mexican mixture" (right).
Espinoza, *El Ejemplo de Sonora*.

this racial logic was a foundational parable of Mexican mestizaje—that there
were good and bad forms of miscegenation. Taken together with women's
antimiscegenation activism, the image implies that the development of a
superior national mestizo race depends upon the heterosexual choices made
by women. The racialization of the Chinese people as exterior to the ideal
mestizo national composite was simultaneously a disavowal of the Chinese
people and an effort to join diverse ethnic indigenous identities through an
appropriation of female sexuality. The sexual fantasy of national unity both
allowed antichinistas to render a national race of mestizos legible and implied
a very powerful biopolitics of female desire and reproduction.

   Espinoza's texts zero in on the ideological function of women in the depiction of the marriage between a Chinese man and a Mexican woman in a cartoon

FIGURE 10. "El Matrimonio" (Marriage), José Angel Espinoza's depiction of women's function, 1932. The panels translate as "The night of the wedding" (left) "and five years later." Espinoza, *El Ejemplo de Sonora* (Mexico City, 1932).

"El Matrimonio" (Marriage; figure 10). The left panel shows a smiling woman being watched by her perverted, drooling Chinese husband from behind a folding screen on their wedding night. Her posture, smile, and short hair mark her as a woman who had begun to shed normative gender and sexual behavior. The woman's haircut, known as a bob, signaled a controversial undoing of Mexican gendered expectations. The right panel shows the same couple five years later. She is haggard, frail, and caring for three disfigured children while her husband's pose signals disinterest as he speaks Chinese. Interestingly, in the left panel, the woman's gaze centers on the reader. The woman stands in front of a mirror but does not look at herself, nor is she looking at the man who looks on with lust. Rather than depict the woman's desire, the image reflects masculine fear. The cause-and-effect illustration was meant to convey that men's perception of women making nontraditional sexual choices threatened the viability of a national race and the hope for a prosperous Mexico. This racial logic relied upon a scientific and notably secular understanding of biological reproduction. The gendered nature of race for Mexican eugenicists defined sex as a racial technology that could be molded by policy. The emphasis placed by antichinista pro-raza ideologues on procreative sex further underscores deep-seated homophobia among elites and uncertainty about male and female

sexuality in the countryside. Antichinista pro-raza ideology asserted normative sexual expectations through anti-Chinese politics. The crucial role for
women in anti-Chinese politics allowed them to claim a political high ground
on racial terms by virtue of their compliance to patriarchal norms. Ultimately,
antichinismo helped make nationalism a cage for women after the revolution.

The mestizo Boy Scout figure that antichinistas such as Espinoza imagined
reflected both prevailing anti-Indian politics and the growing popularity of
the actual Boy Scouts program in Mexico, called Exploradores. Their official
state-sponsored handbook called upon new recruits to become a part of the
Tequihua tribe, a make-believe group that imagined all Mexican males to be
fit, rational, moral subjects who should exchange ethnicity and indigeneity
for state nationalism.[62] While the bureaucratic state denied the indigeneity
of its citizens as unencumbered liberal subjects, the Exploradores promised
to make Indians into citizens by fictionalizing indigeneity itself. The work
of the Exploradores aligned with antichinismo because the Exploradores'
ideas validated and confirmed the concern for the racial improvement and
state loyalty. Although I did not find any explicit anti-Chinese discourse from
the Exploradores, their national board of directors included members of the
Comité Nacionalista Pro-Raza.

Race Patriots

The inflammatory polemic that the antichinistas spouted on the campaign
trail after the 1925 convention authorized a resurgent wave of anti-Chinese
violence.[63] By the mid-1920s action in the halls of congress spilled back onto the
streets when antichinista representatives arrived in Durango, Coahuila, and
Tamaulipas.[64] While the reform campaign was punctuated by street violence,
other practices of nonlethal harassment (like being pelted with stones from
pedestrians, being spit on, and being targeted for extortion) were common
experiences for Chinese people before and after the convention. One measure of how much antichinistas had turned up the heat on Mexico's Chinese
population was the raising frequency since 1924 of solicitations to the U.S.
consulate for protection.[65]

In response, President Calles issued a reprimand on September 23, 1925,
to the governors of eight states with large numbers of Chinese people. The
governors of Chiapas, Coahuila, the North District of Baja California, Nayarit,
Sinaloa, Sonora, Tamaulipas, and Yucatán all received instructions to honor the
guarantees afforded to the Chinese people by virtue of the 1899 treaty and the
liberal disposition of the 1917 constitution. In reference to recent escalations,

Calles wrote, "Such conflicts caused by individuals and anti-Chinese groups . . . have come to constitute a serious danger to the internal peace of the country, threatening a massacre of the Chinese. There are international consequences that such excesses can lead to that would threaten our good name to the rest of the world."[66] He also called attention to the "termination" of Chinese immigration through the 1921 modus vivendi, yet he intentionally misrepresented the current state of Chinese immigration in the country in order to focus on the policing duty of the governors and the importance of maintaining order and control over anti-Chinese groups. He went further, asking that anti-Chinese groups be restricted to taking legal action against the Chinese people, not direct violence. Antichinistas from Ciudad Victoria, Tamaulipas, were outraged by the president's effort to dampen their campaign. They intended to embarrass Calles by reprinting and distributing his memo, arguing that he stifled the "energetic cries of protest by the Mexican people" to protect their communities from the ill effects of Chinese racial degeneracy. Calles's effort to maintain the tacit terms of the KMT partnership had cost him some measure of political legitimacy on racial grounds.

The lack of support from Calles motivated antichinistas from the Comité Pro-Raza in Torreón to call for another convention in November. Inspired by the notion that Chinese people were a mortal racial danger to the country, the antichinistas amplified Obregón's concern about the pernicious behavior of the Chinese population during the tong wars and added new grievances to their list. The second convention focused on the Chinese effect on racial degeneracy. This political discourse was incredibly successful in orienting public priorities and capturing the attention of a number of groups from anticlerics to economic reformers to labor leaders. In the invitation to the second convention, T. Q. Solomón, president of the Comité Pro-Raza, announced, "Attention, day in and day out, the struggle against the exotic yellow octopuses safeguards the future for our children and prosperity of our FATHERLAND. . . . We're fighting with courage and honor because WE ARE MEXICANS."[67] Anti-Chinese politics became a way to merge regionally fragmented spaces and people into the idea of a mestizo nation—a project of collective imagining.

Whereas the first convention focused on its own internal organization, the second was decidedly more ambitious, accepting delegates from a larger number of states. Espinoza identified four new objectives for this convention: Pressure the president through direct solicitation, lobby for reforms at the Bank of Mexico to increase credit for national commerce, increase action in state legislatures, and coordinate with organized labor.[68] Through the antichinista conventions, organizers gave life to a social and political movement to organize self-colonization along new racial lines. Antichinistas worked in a number of political arenas to characterize the project of self-colonization as mortally threatened by the Chinese presence. Through the conventions, antichinistas created a political platform that reached down into pueblos and cities to reconstitute relations of state authority by working against the Chinese people. Meanwhile, anti-Chinese protests and grassroots organizations reached up toward state officials. The simultaneous top-down and bottom-up antichinista political action constituted a dispersed traffic in racial discourse but one that played with the meaning of the public good, the obligation of the revolutionary state, and the ideal society. Antichinismo was instrumental to ambitious mid-level politicians as well as to peasants and workers as they all maneuvered through the reconstruction of the state. The relationship between the government and the governed was the subject of dialogues whose surface topics were race and the Mexican nation. The terms of rule and consent were being openly discussed vis-à-vis anti-Chinese politics.

After 1925 antichinistas appeared in nearly every state of the republic to agitate across a number of issues. This strategy expanded the relevancy and visibility of their political platform. The public records of numerous state legislatures and presidential papers attest to vigorous antichinista lobbying for a variety of concerns. More than simply an effort to proselytize antichinista views, the national campaign became attached to other political and economic problems. It was a readily available political discourse, rationale, and policy prescription that fit a variety of reconstruction issues.

Conquering Regionalism, Constructing Racial Nationalism

The proliferation of organized anti-Chinese politics, from 1911 to 1925, and its consolidation into a national movement, from 1925 to 1929, reflected the regional mosaic of Mexican political and cultural spaces. The staggered advance of the antichinista movement shows that the different political conditions and distinctive crises shaped how locals interpreted antichinismo. Their national campaign privileged formal institutions of the public sphere, such as state legislatures, but also encouraged local sponsorship, frequently setting off episodic street violence and boycotts. This strategy combined grassroots outreach and membership drives along with an effort to shore up votes for a national anti-Chinese referendum at the federal level. In doing so, antichinistas discovered the utility of anti-Chinese politics in the larger project of reconstructing state authority—a particularly influential strategy for civilian leaders vying for

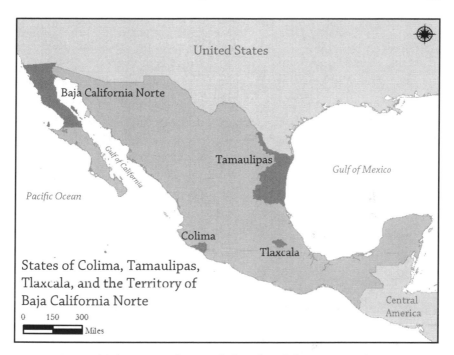

States of Colima, Tamaulipas,
Tlaxcala, and the Territory of
Baja California Norte

0   150   300
▬▬▬▬▬ Miles

MAP 7. States of Colima, Tamaulipas, and Tlaxcala and the Territory of Baja California North

power with the revolution's Constitutionalist generals. Antichinismo acquired national prominence because it facilitated the infusion of a pro-raza ideology in four key areas: agricultural expansion in Baja California, Coahuila, Durango, Nuevo Leon, and Tamaulipas; economic restructuring in Oaxaca, Tlaxcala, and Yucatán; the *anticristiada* (a secular and anticlerical counterinsurgency against Catholics in rebellion) in Colima, Guanajuato, and Zacatecas; and capitalist consolidation in Sonora and San Luis Potosi (map 7). Antichinista pro-raza discourse had the remarkable ability to transform bourgeoisie nativists into revolutionary patriots, peasants into rightful citizens, Indians into Mexicans, agricultural capitalism into national colonization, and state subjection into secular revolutionary nationalism.

Agricultural Expansion in Tamaulipas

In 1926 Sonoran and Coahuilan antichinistas assisted compatriots in Tamaulipas who wanted to push the state's congress to adopt antimiscegenation laws and expel the Chinese people. The state had become home to more than two thousand Chinese in an era when local efforts to restructure the economy were being stymied by Mexico City leaders. Antichinismo became a means of satisfying popular discontent while accommodating the federal limitation upon redistributing land. Mindful of Calles's warning to the governors, they couched their arguments in the terms of the constitution's article 11, which established the right to regulate immigration and immigrants.[69] Despite giving a law-abiding political performance on the congressional floor, antichinistas from Torreón harassed, vandalized, and intimidated members of Tampico's Chinese association.[70] Jesus Sujo Loek of the association wrote to President Obregón, calling out Torreón's Comité Anti-Chino: "They are the pernicious ones."[71] Nevertheless, the campaign's proposal was met with support because it corresponded with political needs that had been generated by new projects to expand irrigated agriculture under Governor Emilio Portes Gil. While federal officials stalled agricultural expansion, Portes Gil sympathized with campesinos of the Liga Agraria (the Agrarian League) in an effort to manage their political demands.[72] Antichinista activity in Tamaulipas distracted agrarians from the previous federal snub with propaganda to expel the Chinese people. Sonora's Comité Pro-Raza Femenino traveled to Tamaulipas to add further pressure on the legislature. In this case, their gendered antimiscegenation discourse became linked to agrarian reform. Some Tamaulipans could justify their anti-Chinese concerns because the Chinese people had been crucial functionaries to the expansion of irrigated agriculture since the Porfiriato (a fact that made them important targets for assassination during the revolution) and were identified as obstacles to national integrity by antichinistas.

Furthermore, up until this period, Tamaulipas had been an important state that connected clandestine migration from the Caribbean and the Pacific to the Texas-Mexico borderlands. Caribbean Chinese migrants traveling west or north frequently stopped in Tampico on the way north to the U.S. border. The following year, the Comité Anti-Chino of Torreón accompanied Tampico's Liga Nacional Pro-Raza on that state's congressional floor to press again for bans on intermarriage and orders to segregate the Chinese people. C. Sandoval, head of the Tampico Pro-Raza, congratulated his state's legislature for their patriotic work in taking up the antichinista petition.[73] However, real success would not come until the following year.

When the Liga Nacional Pro-Raza returned to the State of Tamaulipas congressional floor in July 1928, they were cheered by the officials as they celebrated the intensification of the anti-Chinese campaigns and their collaboration with unions. Realizing the constraints put on the state-level reforms by Mexico City, the congress replied enthusiastically. They moved to fund the league's publication of propaganda pamphlets and encouraged coordination with Secretary Morones, who also served as chief of the CROM worker's assembly, which at the time organized more than two million members.[74] The state's interim governor, Juan Rincón, supported the coalition between antichinistas and the CROM; he hoped it would build support for local political leadership, shift blame for sluggish agrarian reforms from Mexico City to the Chinese people, and counter the presence of the Partido Socialista Fronterizo (Borderlands Socialists), a leftist workers party.[75] By September a new round of expulsions was underway. It started with the apprehension of twelve Chinese men slated for deportation. Two of them, Antonio Esteban Chiu and Ramón Lee Roc, pleaded to President Calles that expulsion was "almost a death sentence." All twelve were longtime resident farmers or agricultural merchants; most had married Mexican women and had children with them.[76] The roundup was encouraged by pro-raza affiliates, petitioned for by members of the state legislature, and carried out by the local police. The removal of the twelve Chinese people, vilified as obstacles to the progress of self-colonization, helped build a benevolent image of industrial agricultural expansion even as reforms remained limited. The path of antichinismo showed how Tamaulipas leaders fostered consent for the mediated governance of the region through a benevolent concern for the preservation of the mestizo race. Other states, such as Coahuila, Durango, and Nuevo Leon, signed onto the national campaign to adopt anti-Chinese measures for similar reasons.[77] In Yucatán the state legislature moved to adopt the three-point platform illustrating the agricultural reform agenda of the peninsula's Constitutionalists, rather than the regional demands of Mayans.[78] Baja California shared some characteristics with these states but constituted a special case, as explored below.

The Anticristiada in Colima

When the Liga Anti-China of Torreón entered Colima's public assembly in 1926, they encountered a provincial government in the midst of a well-organized rebellion of Catholic people. After several months of violent exchanges between Cristiadas (Catholic rebels fighting to reinstate their religious freedoms) and the government, congressman Laureano Cervantes, soon to be governor, became extremely hostile toward the rebels and led a military campaign against them. Cervantes, as head of the state's legislature, recognized the Liga Anti-China on the congressional floor and allowed them to provide testimony and deliver their usual three-point agenda. They also characterized the Chinese Mexican race mixture as a mortal threat to Mexican prosperity. The liga also submitted a petition and pamphlets for the officials' consideration. In light of the liga's testimony, Cervantes moved to consider the petition immediately. After some debate, Cervantes charged the Committee on Constitutional Matters to review the state's civil registry, a docket of pending civil marriages. The committee was to enforce requirements for medical exams and blood testing of Chinese people, exams they would surely fail, and to ensure that all marriages had undergone review. Three other representatives supported Cervantes's measure, adding the provision that a group of backers be organized to push for a constitutional amendment at the national congress.[79]

The anticristiadas promoted revolutionary marriage as scientific, rational, and healthy and positioned it as antithetical to the Catholic sacramental union.[80] Conflict over this vision of marriage in Colima determined the reception of Torreón's antichinista petition. The Chinese population in Colima remained small and transient. However, when antichinistas raised the issue of antimiscegenation, Colima's officials recognized a compelling secular rationale for claiming the government's exclusive authority to regulate marriage. The day that antichinistas brought their petition to Colima, the officials focused their debates on the scientific basis of health and the medical concerns that arose because of Chinese Mexican marriage. The antichinista characterization of Chinese Mexican race mixture as a mortal threat to Mexican prosperity provided a racial logic that would reinforce the government's secular claims to state authority. An antimiscegenation statute would transform civil unions into a governing mechanism for regulating race, wrestling marriage away from priests who anticristiadas claimed were unconcerned with modernization. Anticlerical and antimiscegenation discourse became intertwined with the fear of the sacramental union of degenerates. Independent (that is, Catholic) sacramental unions provided the potential for a disastrous race mixture, but antimiscegenation provided a racial justification for a sovereign secular state in matters of marriage and sexual reproduction.

Whether enough Chinese Mexican marriage proposals existed to justify the measure, the antichinista political logic captured public attention of anticristiadas in Guanajuato and Zacatecas.[81] The antichinista polemic against a racial threat provided a compelling new rationale for secular state authority and overlapped with the issue of deportation. Antichinista calls for article 33 expulsion of pernicious tong members reinforced anticristiada strategies of deporting rebellious priests, such as Monseigneur Ernesto Phillippi during the Pénjamo insurrection in Guanajuato.[82] Antichinista pro-raza ideology also built new political images of women as particular racial subjects due to their capacity for biological reproduction and reinforced secular notions of a procreative duty for women.

Economic Restructuring in Tlaxcala

Torreón's Liga Anti-China launched a similar campaign in Tlaxcala in 1922, although the legislature there was persuaded to take up their platform for completely different issues than those found in Colima or Tamaulipas.[83] The return of antichinistas to Tlaxcala signaled a renewal of political pressure to inject anti-Chinese politics into the state's effort to limit the intrusion of the central government and restructure the economy.[84] Like in Tamaulipas, Tlaxcalan civilian political chiefs struggled to maintain their autonomy as Calles expanded the power of the central government. Instead of racializing the distribution of limited agricultural resources, though, as in Tamaulipas, antichinistas in Tlaxcala entered into the contest over collective identity in the consolidation of labor in fields and factories. On one side, Governor Ignacio Mendoza partnered with the Comité Pro-Raza to build his own authority over the racial identity of the state. On the other, federal reformers tried to sway residents from the influence of the local political chief by distributing land and pushing education reforms.[85] However, the reorganization of the state's economy was hampered by problems like those in Apizaco, where agricultural laborers and agrarians abandoned their lands to work in the town's factories.[86] Mendoza's socialist political ideology won popular support, but he lacked the authority to allocate lands to his constituency. This was the purview of the National Agrarian Commission and secretary of agriculture and development. The governor's populist appeal aided the secretary's efforts to resettle factory workers on newly formed ejidos and work through a five-year backlog of ejido restitutions.[87] Although many Tlaxcalans favored the redistribution of agricultural land, this transformation was hampered by indifference in places like Apizcao, where many workers lacked an agricultural background, or like Santa Cruz, where tensions simmered over the ownership of land with reliable water and road access.

Implementing a new regime of self-colonization required ideological commitments to keep individuals and families invested in difficult projects of agricultural production. Granting ejidos was more than a mechanism of resource redistribution. It was also a mechanism of political control. Agrarian citizenship tied a limited set of rights and privileges to obligations to cultivation and sustain crop production. Tlaxcalans were justifiably indifferent, if not resistant, to redistribution under the National Agrarian Commission. Yet, they faced no competition from Chinese functionaries, nor was there concern about intermarriage, as Tlaxcala had no Chinese residents. Nevertheless, the antichinista national campaign received a warm reception in the state. In Tlaxcala, antichinismo accented postrevolutionary state formations with a pro-raza ideology that leaders hoped would marshal collective action.

Antichinismo was also present in the state-federal conflict over public education programs to expand secondary and agrarian schools. Secretary of Education Puig Casauranc attended an important session of Tlaxcala's congress to pronounce the intent of the education law. For him the effort to combat illiteracy was instrumental to a state pedagogy that aimed to "awaken and enhance the civic and moral sentiments of the population." Puig Casuaranc emphasized that public education was designed to "prepare the educated to best exercise their rights as citizens and compliment their social duties." Yet, he argued that training in citizenship was intended to inspire a commitment to the "improvement of people's economic condition."[88] Antichinistas hoped that invoking the racial fear of the Chinese people would galvanize a fragmented polity. In Tlaxcala, a place with a Chinese population of zero, antichinismo managed to facilitate consent for projects of state capitalism. The slogan printed at the bottom of Torreón's Comité Anti-Chino letterhead reads, "Success in this cause requires the cooperation of good Mexicans."[89] Even in the absence of Chinese residents, antichinismo corresponded with the political need to inculcate a collective identity based on racial nationalism.

Like Tlaxcala, Oaxaca's state legislature signed onto the anti-Chinese campaign for strikingly similar reasons, and antichinismo joined the standard tripartite reforms in agriculture, education, and urban space as part of a nationalist ideology. Unlike Tlaxcala, Oaxaca had registered a considerable Chinese population since the 1880s, but both adopted antichinismo in similar ways, with the hopes of motivating unengaged Indian people to cooperate with the state.

Self-Colonization in Baja California

By the 1920s the Baja peninsula was still a federal territory and was not a part of the campaign to muster a national referendum. Still, Baja California was important for different reasons. It was home to the largest concentration of Chinese people since the revolution and was the only part of the republic where foreign-born individuals outnumbered domestic-born nationals. Much of the collective violence against Chinese people during the first decade of the revolution drove them from the interior to seek refuge in this peripheral territory. Still, Baja California was the site of a growing bonanza of irrigated cotton cultivation the CRLC organized. By 1925 thousands of new acres were under cultivation, primarily by Chinese cooperative shareholding partnerships. In Mexicali, the urban hub of the irrigated delta, Chinese people constituted a majority, numbering between ten thousand and fifteen thousand in the region by 1927. Mexicans who grew up in Mexicali knew the Chinese people as business partners, neighbors, and local storeowners.[90]

Baja was also important because it became the proving ground for Mexico's most important antichinista, the future interim president, Constitutionalist General Abelardo Rodríguez. In 1923, at the peak of Sonora's tong wars, President Obregón appointed General Rodríguez as governor of the territory. Rodríguez's predecessors acted as lenient stewards, shielding the territory's nascent Chinese colony from the turmoil of the country at large. Only after Rodríguez became governor did any systematic discrimination and state-sponsored violence organize around disabling the Chinese settlement. Rodríguez would later reflect on his time in Mexicali: "I had taken all reasonable steps to rid this country of the tainted elements that sought refuge in the prosperity of the region, bringing with them undesirable activities, promoting trouble and threatening public health."[91] He took decisive action to undermine the Chinese business community in an effort to build what he considered to be a racially pure Mexican working class. As governor, Rodríguez was able to exercise new authorities brought into force by President Calles. In April 1926, the president signed into law a Porfirian-styled colonization law that revived the imperative for national colonization. Chapter 2, article 17, provided the right of the government to dictate racial preferences for colonos, be they foreigners or the sons and daughters of Mexico.[92]

By 1927 the Mexicali–Imperial Valley region of the U.S.-Mexico border was the most intensively irrigated place in North America. However, the Mexican side was completely dependent upon Chinese labor as well as their transborder and transpacific business connections. Rodríguez interpreted this dependence as a criminal divergence from what he called "genuine Mexican colonization." He also reasoned that Chinese settlers were anathema to the Mexican nation and that their large concentration in Baja California undermined sovereign claims to the international waters of the Colorado River.[93]

Over his seven years as governor, Rodríguez advanced a plan to replace the Chinese people with domestic labor and buy out the CRLC's original colonization contract while keeping the irrigated colony unbroken. This ambitious and treacherous undertaking relied on three strategies: taxes and fees imposed exclusively on the Chinese population, the operation of Chinese-contracted casinos, and selective detention and deportation of key individuals. First, Chinese taxes and fees were extracted by specially assigned, brutal collectors. The taxes and fees, as well as the collectors, were intended to intimidate the Chinese community and, more important, to increase the cost of production for Chinese people while providing subsidies for domestically owned businesses. Second, special concessions for Chinese casinos catered to Chinese demands for legal places to gamble, but contracts for their operation included dubious licensing terms, which led to their extortion by local officials. While Rodríguez openly despised the Chinese casinos, he had large investments in their operation. He had supported and facilitated their expansion in Mexicali, which helped make him the peninsula's wealthiest individual. The numerous Chinese casinos also contributed to the racial image of the Chinese as agents of vice and immorality. In concert with the CKT-KMT violence unfolding in neighboring Sonora, Rodríguez adopted the racial discourse of the "pernicious" Chinese. While Obregón had used it to target CKT leaders, Rodríguez used it to disrupt and cripple Chinese cotton-growing cooperatives, whether or not they had a political affiliation.[94] In 1928 CKT-KMT violence emerged over casino conflicts, resulting in the deportation of thirty-two Chinese residents—half of whom were leaders of agricultural cooperatives. By removing the community's leaders, this selective deportation scheme crippled day-to-day business for Mexicali's Chinese people.

As a territorial governor, Rodríguez became a valuable partner in the national anti-Chinese campaign. He supplied antichinistas with news of the conditions in the peninsula. At anti-Chinese conventions, Baja California delegates from nacionalista and pro-raza groups provided colorful examples of what an unchecked Chinese invasion of the rest of the country would look like. Rodríguez also courted antichinista support for his administration of the territory. Particularly important was the work of the CROM and other antichinista agitators, such as the Liga Nacionalista Anti-Chino of Sonora, as they helped mediate criticism by Mexican laborers of working conditions in Mexicali by serving public endorsements of the progovernment agenda. The Mexican cotton-growing operations that Rodríguez established lacked the transnational infrastructure and shared profit motives of Chinese agricultural collectives, thus making them less stable and more exploitative. While Rodríguez deliberately increased the Mexican population of the region, he did little to protect workers from mistreatment or to prosecute violations of labor laws, unless the Chinese people were accused.[95] By the late 1920s, General Rodríguez was widely recognized as a respectable antichinista. More important, his local crusade against the Chinese population gave him the reputation of a trusted patriot and populist leader by virtue of his race politics alone.

The National Referendum

By 1928 the antichinista campaign was poised for a national referendum. In the spring, Tampico's Liga Nacional Pro-Raza and Guanajuato's governor,

Agustín Arroyo, joined Sonoran officials in Mexico City to propose a consti-tutional amendment to restrict Chinese immigration. Their proposal cited the support of twenty-one state legislatures and sought to fast track the vote by referencing constitutional articles that allowed the congress to pass laws without judicial review or presidential consent (articles 71 and 83). The refer-endum was tabled for the discussion, pending votes on related constitutional amendments.[96]

In three years the national campaign had achieved what no other political party in Mexico ever had: it created a broad coalition for national action based on a collective racial identity. However, the antichinista campaign conflicted with the agenda of the Obregón-Calles administration and was defeated in the following session. Head of congress and longtime Obregón loyalist Ricardo Topete ultimately squashed debate on the proposal through parliamentary procedures.[97] The failure of the campaign brings to light a fundamental conflict between the political utility of antichinista ideology to foster consent and the fear of economic and political repercussions of adopting the anti-Chinese platform. This conflict would begin to dissipate the following month when Obregón was assassinated, initiating a number of changes that will be taken up in the next chapter. Although the national referendum failed, antichinistas were not left empty-handed. Concurrent with debate on antichinista consti-tutional reforms, legislators passed a new migration law that temporarily banned foreign workers. The law did not specify the Chinese immigrant, but the congressional record noted that support had been provided by those who had previously championed the antichinista referendum.

Conclusion

Racism helped Mexico in its search for national and economic unity, and the anti-Chinese movement became an important means to rearrange public pri-orities and construct a façade of virtuous governance. Anti-Chinese organiza-tions used a number of political issues to build a national public sphere that was pro-raza, from the international treaty to the definition of citizenship and naturalization, to the administrative procedures of deportation, to the designs of national colonization and secular modernization. The internal architec-ture of antichinista pro-raza ideology was organized by a biopolitics that cast women as bearers of the nation's racial future. Anti-Chinese organizations drew diverse multitudes into the circle of people who were to be protected from the so-called yellow octopus. In other words, antichinistas redirected the authority of scientific biological racism against the Chinese population to implement a wider program of mestizo racial nationalism.

The racial polemic of antichinismo constituted a versatile nationalistic ideology that offered rationales for state power and tamed the revolution's populist impulses by channeling debate into a nationalistic public sphere. Popular civic participation in the anti-Chinese movement across the country brought people together to debate the public good through racial discourse. Antichinistas had also constructed a multistate political network that systematically pressured the executive and legislative branches, pushed for fiscal reforms, and sought out alliances with organized labor—all without sanction by more powerful caudillos like Calles or Obregón. No other racial discourse or political ideology was more effective at capturing the attention of public institutions with popular support. Antichinistas were not a political party of bureaucrats like the Porfirian científicos or of military strongmen like the Constitutionalist victors of the revolution; antichinistas were a multistate organization with grassroots affiliates organized by state-level elected politicians. They balanced constructions of national identity and state-formation through a discourse of Chinese expulsion, antimiscegenation, loyalties to a national race, and support for self-colonization. The political work of antichinistas from 1925 to 1928 positioned many of the movement's leaders to fill key official positions at a pivotal moment of crisis: Obregón's assassination in July 1928. Anti-Chinese politics was the last issue to have widespread support before Obregón's death and helped produce consent to national party politics thereafter.

Because anti-Chinese politics gave voice to debates about collective identity and structural change of the economy, it became incredibly useful to the formation of a national ideology. In the 1920s to be anti-Chinese was to be pro-raza. Mexican antichinismo occupied a specific political space that simultaneously reinforced elite legitimacy, recognized peasant discontent, mobilized labor unions, and demonstrated modern credentials to an international audience. These features of the campaign for juridical reform illustrate how anti-Chinese politics grew from a violent imaginary of revolution into a racial state replete with an institutional apparatus. The evolution of Mexican Orientalism from the battlefield to the legislature is an important distinction from the U.S. experience. This difference illustrates the centrality of the postrevolutionary state's quest for legitimacy through racial governance. The political aspirations of antichinistas echoed the calls from nineteenth-century liberals to "elevate the Indian to civilized life" through the governments intervention in everyday life.[98] The next chapter will discuss how impersonal bureaucracy came to mediate anti-Chinese violence and the ways that the revolutionary state depended upon racialized national discourse to manufacture consent and organize coercive rule.

5

Forging a Racial Contract

In May 1931 Rafael Melgar, the Oaxacan congressman and leader of a powerful congressional faction called the Bloque Nacional Revolucionario (Revolutionary National Block) (BNR), traveled to Tamaulipas to lobby the state congress in support of a nationwide campaign to strengthen the country's economy through a boycott of foreign goods, and to join antichinistas in bringing "racial fortitude" to the national economy.[1] Later that month Melgar stood with thirty-seven colleagues in the national congressional chambers to announce a policy and propaganda initiative, the Campaña Nacionalista (Nationalist Campaign). The campaign sought to shift public opinion about "the relationship between government and the governed" in the process of industrialization.[2] Although formally Melgar and his close associates shied away from xenophobic discourse, they also did little to stop the acts of violence and expulsion conducted in the name of the campaign—one of the core concepts of which was to protect the country from "foreigners who imported vice and extorted workers."[3] This government-sponsored campaign became the national call for antichinistas in the 1930s because the Campaña Nacionalista went beyond yellow-peril polemics to foment a racialized understanding of the wider political economy; the national economy was seen as an expression of mestizo racial strength. The campaña became an institutionalized space where antichinista ideology informed the official idea of a racialized public good. Local and regional branches of the campaign lashed out against the Chinese people, culminating in a mass expulsion of thousands of Chinese people and their Mexican families in the states of Sonora and Sinaloa in 1931 and 1932.

In addition, the campaign sought to shape national policy, and in so doing it merged antichinista ideology with other scientific and political discourses and distilled them into an administrative logic of mestizo racialization. While the actual implementation of the state's policies remained uneven and fragmented, Mexico's political elite were empowered by the revolution's social-rights mandate to legislate as if the government's hegemony were complete. This stage of antichinismo corresponds with what scholar Mara Loveman has referred to as the primitive accumulation of symbolic capital, or the process by which modernizing states invent new areas of expertise and become recognized as the sole legitimate authority.[4]

The Campaña Nacionalista gave structure and voice to the growing political urgency of national unification and responded to the deepening effects of the Great Depression. Obregón's assassination caused immediate political chaos but provided the opportunity for President Calles to usher in a series of rapid political changes, leading to the first national political party, Partido Nacional Revolucionario (PNR). The global economic downturn had exacerbated the weaknesses within Mexico's economy. Economic recessions scaled back demand for manufacturing and agricultural goods, leading to rising unemployment in some places and worsening work conditions in others. Government statistics showed that after a low point in worker strikes in 1928—only 7 strikes involving 498 strikers—every year thereafter, the number of strikes and the participants nearly doubled. In 1936 the state recorded 674 strikes involving 113,885 workers.[5] In this context, antichinistas, such as Alejandro Lacy Jr., Antonio Alanis, Alfredo Echeverria, and Mario Negrón Pérez, who had built their political careers in the 1920s, made bold moves to push antichinismo as a panacea to the country's ailments while they ascended to high-ranking positions.

In the wake of Obregón's assassination, the creation of new political structures like the PNR provided institutionalized discipline and political stability to reimagine state authority through the constitution's social-rights mandate. Antichinistas were well positioned to answer President Calles's call for an end to caudillo rule in favor of the supremacy of impersonal laws and institutions. Antichinista criticism was neither about the overbearing military nor sluggish land redistribution. Their primary criticism was the conservative and restrained, if not pragmatic, hand of the revolutionary leaders' political calculus. According to antichinistas, Obregón and Calles favored political power and profit over the well-being of the national race. The cultural logic of Mexican antichinismo was based on the necessity of the state as a benevolent aspect of everyday life, thus masking its other faces as the client of industrial capitalism and military arm of criollo Mexican elites. Antichinismo became an instrumental ideology for constructing the public charge to care for and improve Mexican people as mestizo racial subjects. This ideology helps to explain why antichinismo helped Mexicans rework the unwritten racial contract of the postrevolutionary order.

This chapter tells the story of how antichinista racial ideology from several different quarters coalesced in the Campaña Nacionalista. The resulting violence and displacement were combined with broad policy measures to govern Mexican populations through racialized notions of the public good. This chapter follows the articulation of official discourses of state-based mestizaje through the 1929 presidential campaign, the formation of a powerful clique in the national congress, and the return of organized eugenicists. The 1929 presidential campaigns of Pascual Ortiz Rubio and José Vasconcelos reflected the PNR's articulation of a state-administered mestizaje. These articulations of race in the public sphere were echoed by the formation of the BNR in the national congress. The BNR whipped up enough votes to pass PNR-backed legislation, and the BNR leader, Rafael Melgar, became the chief architect of the Campaña Nacionalista. The transformation of popular violence to state-endorsed discrimination made small communities of Chinese people the targets of popular persecution and expulsion. Political stability and education reform allowed eugenic scientists to contribute to the state's racial projects, primarily through the scientific discussion of race in terms of sex and sexuality.

The next section explores the intersection of the 1930 census, federal labor reform, and the creation of the National Registry of Foreigners. These three articulations of government action demonstrate the growing racial competency of the state. In this climate of juridical concern for race, the next section examines the maverick decisions of the Sonoran and Sinaloan governors to expel thousands of Chinese men and their multi-ethnic Mexican families.

Chinese people across Mexico experienced the Campaña Nacionalista through unsettling insecurity, violent removal, and utter disavowal. However, the adoption of an Asian Americanist interpretation requires attention not just to their treatment and subjectivity but also to the political function of this racialization and its relationship to other populations. If the analysis of anti-Chinese politics ends with how the Chinese people were treated, then it will have missed the most important and interesting transformation of Mexican society in the twentieth century—the revolution's racial contract. Mexican historiography in the conceptual turn toward the local and regional articulations of the revolution and postrevolutionary reconstruction has led to a relative abandonment of histories of federal-level institutions, such as the PNR, the national congress, and the politics and outcomes of the legislative process. The Asian Americanist line of critique addresses these areas as crucial sites for the construction of racialized citizenship. For more than twenty years, Mexicanists have been writing local and regional histories staking out the origins of influential social movements, the contests and mediations of state power, and the particular manner that the revolution played out in local contexts.[6] While recognizing the necessary, invaluable, and foundational quality of this enormous body of literature, I also recognize its limitations, particularly, with respect to an analysis of racial formations, especially the racial transformation of the Chinese population.

By shifting the analytical focus to racial formations, the history of anti-Chinese politics from the Porfiriato through the revolution offers a different perspective to long-standing debates about the nature of the revolutionary Mexican state. Debate about the revolution and the state apparatus of the 1917 government covers a spectrum of the state's characterizations. On the one hand, some historians favor a definitive political break with the Porfirian regime; on the other hand, other historians argue that the revolution's ruling ideology was used to bring about and stabilize a restoration of the Porfirian economic system. These differing interpretations led to further questions about the nature of the revolution, whether it was more deeply radical and liberatory or more intensely repressive than the state had been during the Porfiriato. These interpretive differences reveal a multifaceted political reality where Constitutionalists preserved the Porfirian regime within the revolutionary state (repressive continuity) at the same time that the authoritarian revolutionary state enacted deep structural transformation (repressive rupture). At other times we observe the triumph of a Mexican liberal tradition of individualization (radical continuity) as well as its socialist opposite of mass political enfranchisement and social reform (radical rupture). Each of these characterizations was true for different regions or states, but none of these characterizations was ever true for the country as a whole.[7] Whatever the interpretation of distinctive political characteristics of postrevolutionary Mexico, antichinismo was a common thread. Antichinismo evolved as popular and state-sponsored actors used it and, thus, became embedded in regional configurations of popular culture and state power. This chapter departs from recent histories of Mexico's Chinese population in order to attend to the transformation of the Chinese racial form and the ways that antichinismo influenced the construction of mestizo racial citizenship.

Much of the historiography on the PNR and national congress remains constrained by attention to the political careers of several presidents and their cabinet members. This has led to a common interpretation of the PNR as a continuation of Calles's rule and to this period's being labeled the era of "el Maximato" (Calles's political reign from 1924 to 1934, from his nickname "el jefe maximo," the highest chief)—signaling that Calles himself retained power as the PNR eliminated challengers. Although this is true, the rush to return to regional histories has led to a narrow interpretation of the PNR's obvious political function. The prevailing interpretation has led to a misguided assumption that mestizo nationalism was a self-evident, unifying force in this period. A closer examination of this period, though, reveals how mestizo hegemony came into being with the help of antichinismo's ascension to the level of state ideology. The long shadow of the caudillo system has hidden the study of racial ideology in driving public interest in national institutions. Antichinistas have shown that charismatic leaders were not necessary for national unification or a discourse of ethical governance. Rather, the Chinese racial threat invited multiple identifications with diverse facets of a bureaucratic state. In particular, concern for women's sexual relationships with Chinese men prompted many antichinistas to build a sense of national integrity through a popular discourse of fear about antimiscegenation.

Mestizo nationalism was never inevitable for Mexico. It was the result of complex and contingent historical power relations where contentious discourses of race, indigeneity, and sovereignty vied for hegemony. This chapter discusses the institutional context for postrevolutionary statecraft to illustrate how antichinismo intersected and supported the articulation of an ideal mestizo as the disciplined and enhanced racial subject of postrevolutionary self-colonization. The chapter pays special attention to the state's version of mestizo racial ideology, not because it referred to a transcendental collective identity but because it relied upon racialized sex and a moral economy—one that established new criteria for writing the revolution's racial contract. In other words, antichinismo gave rise to a mestizo hegemony that enframed politics and history. Mestizo hegemony conceded to popular demands through the creation of racial forms that circumscribed these demands' inclusion in ways that were convenient for the reproduction of the state. To arrive at this conclusion, we must begin with the formation of the PNR.

The State's Political Party

Antichinistas likely harbored ambivalent feelings upon hearing the news of ex-President Obregón's assassination in July 1928. The assassination was not just a political crisis but also an indication that reconstruction was incomplete. If a consolidation of the country could not be achieved, the multiple sovereignties of the revolution would plague the state with instability. The lynchpin of this structural pathology was the caudillo. In this system, state power was a function of the caudillo's assets and political skill to juggle multiple sovereignties. However, the application of revolutionary mandates and authoritarian efforts at reconstruction by both Obregón and Calles had led to an expansion of the governmental state. By 1928 it had grown more capable and more organized than ever before. Obregón's death provided a rare opportunity to reset national politics and broker political alignment among the republic's rival sovereignties. As new functionaries rose up to stake out positions within the new political order, antichinistas stood out. Those from the antichinista campaigns earlier in the decade held valuable experience and political capital that became useful as the state redefined legitimate authority in the wake of an assassination and global economic contraction.

As the news of Obregón's death spread, his pragmatic assemblage of political players and government functionaries began to unravel. President Calles mobilized to quicken the process of political disintegration. He astutely called for a turn toward control by institutions, rather than personally taking the helm as captain of the revolution. Obregón's skillful arrangement of loyal Constitutionalist generals and influential civilian leaders during the 1920s had allowed him to establish order by satisfying political demands throughout the country by redistributing government-owned land. By 1930 only 10 percent of post-1917 allocated lands were ejido titles. The 90 percent was still large-tract colonization contracts, continuing the Porfirian program of national colonization and a preservation of the large-estate plantation system.[8] The highest-quality lands were still concentrated in private hands, and ejidos were frequently located in poorer-quality tracts. Distributing government-owned land bought political loyalty, and Calles risked losing those bonds after Obregón's assassination. Despite the relative success of land concessions, the postrevolutionary state was dependent upon military violence to solve other political problems, with the Cristero (Catholic dissidents) rebellion as the prime example. However, the stability of the postrevolutionary state still depended primarily upon the political loyalties bought with land donations, either from armed peasants or wealthy, local power brokers.

To construct a more stable governmental state and secure his own seat of power, Calles called for the country to move to a "higher and more respectful and more productive and more peaceful and more civilized condition, to be a people of institutions and of laws," rather than one of caudillos. To this end, he called for the formation of a national political party to bring the competing choruses of the revolution into harmony. Even as the republic's president, Calles depended on the maintenance of Obregón's alliances and the assurance of military loyalty. By creating new lines of authority and establishing an institutional basis for sovereign rule, Calles was able to alter the terms of old alliances and invite the participation of representatives who desired to be part of the process. Within weeks of Obregón's death, Calles had negotiated peace with the Cristeros, divided Obregón loyalists, and dismantled Morones's hold on organized labor. The formation of the PNR in 1929 attempted to formalize the implicit political loyalties that agrarians and workers had made with the political class over the last decade. Calles hoped that the PNR party structure would hold the metaphorical ship together as they entered the Great Depression. No one thought this effort to institutionalize the Norteño (Northerner, criollo elites from the northern border states, particularly those in Sonora) grip on the country would become the most successful national political party in modern history or that the PNR would become the state's sole political party.

The PNR first existed only on paper, a hollow structure quickly filled by those eager to be a part of the new political class, if only to avoid being left out by the receding tide. Congressmen and senators that were previously at odds or committed to other parties, like the Liberal Constitucionalista (Liberal Constitutionalist) and Nacional Cooperatista (National Cooperationists), both regional parties that vied for national influence yet changed allegiance and joined together in the PNR, looked for chances to be on what promised to be the winning side. They put renewed political allegiance in the PNR as a good-faith bet that they would be included in the reorganization of a political institution of the state. In February, just weeks before the party's formal inauguration, the congress held an open debate about Calles's call for institutionalization. When the issue of PNR party affiliation was brought to the national congress, 51 congressmen opposed the party, and 221 of the remaining 227 joined it. In this climate of new beginnings, antichinistas reorganized to ensure the PNR took what it thought to be responsible action. During the antichinista campaign, its activists had become regular figures in the national congress, and now their political skills were in high demand. The importance of prior antichinista organizing can be seen in the decision to locate the first headquarters of the PNR in the office of Mexico City's liga antichina.[9] While new political lines were being drawn, antichinistas not only signed onto the PNR ticket but also formed their own power blocks, such as the Comité Directivo de la Campaña Nacionalista Antichino de la Cámara de Diputados (Executive Committee of the Anti-Chino National Campaign of Congress) to collect votes and push for legislation. Later, Lacy Jr. would become the PNR's secretary of public relations. As economic conditions worsened around the country, other antichinistas coalesced in 1931 to form the Comité Nacionalista de la Costa Occidental (Nationalist Committee of the East Coast). These congressional cliques signaled PNR's strength and the durability of the interstate networks of antichinistas.

While Calles's initiation of the PNR did not amount to broad democratization, it did lend importance to institution building as a means to introduce greater stability, more effective political management, and coordinated administration. Political discipline descended downward from the federal to state to municipal levels and promised well-crafted policy with consistent administration, but everyone knew this was a tall order. Antichinistas shared these ideals of modern statecraft. Yet, antichinista racial fantasies did not match the institutional realities of a highly mediated state apparatus—a dynamic that they never seemed to understand. Calles's reforms were not just about power; they were organized by ideologies that had demonstrated their usefulness to secure popular consent, support capitalist restructuring, and sway political opposition.

Although frustrated by the failure to pass the national referendum in congress in 1928, some antichinistas continued their campaign in predictable directions. The Liga Nacional Pro-Raza (National Pro-Race League) returned to Tamaulipas, Tlaxcala, and Zacatecas in 1929 in an effort to lobby states to issue expulsion orders and place permanent bans on Chinese immigration.[10] By the mid-1930s these efforts would have appeared rather prosaic—leftover strategies being played out as bolder action from rogue actors, such as Lacy Jr. and Sonoran governor Rudolfo Elías Calles. The state-by-state campaign failed in its national referendum, but it had succeeded in catapulting members into national leadership positions and fostering a robust grassroots following. The afterlives of the national anti-Chinese campaign of the 1920s show how antichinismo transformed into a state ideology and helped define the racial dimensions of the revolutionary "public good." This transformation both engendered the banalization of anti-Chinese race politics and marked an official articulation of the mestizo racial state.

The PNR helped create the political structure whereby Mexicans revised an implicit political contract between the revolutionary government and the governed masses. Antichinismo contributed to this political formation by emphasizing a racially defined mestizo public good, undergirded by the constitution's social-rights mandate, and along with that a race-based rationale for legitimate state authority. This racial transformation of the Chinese people simultaneously marked them as racial degenerates and signified others as mestizo subjects of Mexicanization and revolutionary improvement. As a political discourse, antichinismo created an unrestrained forum about the use of state power to intervene in the interest of the public good and helped the state rework consent to racial rule. Throughout the 1930s this contract would be articulated through policy and state propaganda to exchange state loyalty and subjection to a normative disciplinary regime for basic economic guarantees. Ejidos bought a degree of loyalty, but they were limited in their own right. The racial contract of mestizo nationalism conscripted a broad spectrum of people to occupy a new category of state subjection—the agrarian citizen. In the absence of the state fulfilling its obligation for basic economic guarantees, anti-Chinese violence appropriated the state's authority to threaten, displace, and kill Chinese for a perceived mestizo public good. It is helpful to follow the parallel developments in national electoral races, the formation of the BNR, eugenic science, and popular violence against the Chinese people to understand the emergence of this racial contract.

Racial Strength and a Disciplined Mestizaje

An important test of the PNR's political power was the presidential election of 1929. Ortiz was the presidential candidate, handpicked by Calles to go up against José Vasconcelos, an *anticallista* (anti-Calles, those against Calles and his policies), a spiritualist, and the revolution's first secretary of education, There is no doubt among historians that the election was rigged—Ortiz won by a dubious landslide—but both campaigns served as a crucial source of conflict by which the PNR articulated a populist mestizo ideology that would shape the character of a state-sponsored mestizo and the racial contract of the revolutionary state.

Vasconcelos's failed presidential bid explicitly promoted a metaphysical mestizo nationalism and illustrated the variations in racial discourse at the time. More important, it showed that a condition for mestizo hegemony would be the institutionalized capacity to build state authority, not the popularity of a transcendental collective identity. Mexican racial nationalism at this point had less to do with collectivist commitments and more to do with state constructions of the racial subject through the institutions of the revolution. The postrevolutionary government still practiced much of the positivist ideologies of their Porfirian predecessors, privileging technocratic solutions. Until the 1929 election few officials espoused a unified vision for the improvement and protection of the population en masse.

The PNR's criticism of Vasconcelos provides an important example of how the 1929 election articulated a racial logic of rule. During the campaign, Samuel Vásquez published *Las locuras de Vasconcelos* (The follies of Vasconcelos). He claimed no political allegiance, but the text still paid tribute to the PNR and served up a character assassination of Vasconcelos. Vasquez's text helped provide popular opinion of the *antireeleccionista* (antireelectionists, those against consecutive presidential terms) candidate at a crucial moment when public discourses about legitimate state power were being reshaped. One chapter, "The Height of Flirtation," mocked Vasconcelos as a Don Quixote of racial politics, insulting his notions of *la raza cósmica* (the cosmic race), his pacifist politics, and his childish allusions to Quetzalcoatl, an Aztec god of renewal. Vásquez insinuated that Aztec gods would not put land in peasant hands or magically persuade political challengers to put down their arms and painted Vasconcelos as a charming romantic with whimsical ambitions for national leadership. Vásquez dismissed Vasconcelos's notion of la raza cósmica not because mestizaje was a political distraction from the very real and material challenges of poverty, rural development, and modernization but because la raza cósmica was an undisciplined mestizaje. Vásquez approvingly notes that Vasconcelos abhorred African and Asian people, but the author's casual dismissal of la raza cósmica suggests a judgment structured by a particular notion of state-sanctioned racial formations replete with an administrative apparatus.[11] The PNR furthered this criticism of Vasconcelos in the widely circulated party newsletter, *El Nacional Revolucionario*, first published in the middle of the campaign in May 1929. It was important for the PNR to provide criticism of this concept because it was popular in some quarters. Writers for the periodical pushed an interpretation of the election as a choice between revolutionary institutions or a return to *caudillismo* (warlordism).[12] In other words, racial nationalism without mechanisms of racial discipline was merely populist pandering (a characteristic of caudillos); true revolutionary action was the construction of an administrative racial state.

Ortiz won the November election by 1,825,732 to 110,979, though, as noted above, these numbers are questionable. In symbolic terms, the PNR victory meant that discourses of racial fitness and racial administration were more important than a prophetic cosmic race. Because the PNR's postelection propaganda was ubiquitous, it mattered little that the vote represented less than 10 percent of the country (mostly a narrow sliver of urbanites). Even Mexico's Protestant publication, *El Abogado Cristiano Ilustrado* (The illustrated Christian lawyer), which supported Vasconcelos, described the PNR's victory as the first step toward justice, fraternity, and true democracy.[13] When Vasconcelos left Mexican politics, he was defeated, bitter, and increasingly reactionary, all of which further secured PNR claims against him as an impractical romantic. However, he remained active and contributed to Mexican political life until his death in 1959. In the 1940s he adopted a peculiar fascination with German fascism and eventually aligned with a strong vision of state intervention and disciplinary ideology of mestizaje.[14]

The 1929 election crystalized the PNR's political supremacy in the Mexican public sphere; paradoxically, its partisan control afforded greater entry for antichinistas. The party's structure was designed to accelerate the legislative process of crafting and passing new legislation by way of a PNR-sanctioned reform agenda. The party held great influence over the political process, but congressional debates still had bearing on the character of new legislation. Antichinista stalwarts like Miguel Salavar and Walterio Pesqueira formed the Comité Directivo de la Campaña Nacionalista Antichino de la Cámara de Diputados to collect votes and push for legislation. Later, Lacy Jr. would be appointed deputy of the national congress and would occasionally lead policy debates. Antichinista organizations were the only political groups, beyond unions and agrarians, to form regional political blocks within the PNR, signaling their political strength.[15] Other voices competed for attention in the national congress, but antichinistas spoke directly to the party officials' concern for transforming rationales of state authority and fostering national unity. Antichinismo supplied a useful racial logic of the state that corresponded to an imperative to ascribe government action with symbolic power.

The BNR and the Campaña Nacional

The PNR was formed amid rapid economic contractions, for which many around the country blamed the Chinese people. As U.S. and European trade with Mexico rapidly declined, inventories of agricultural and manufacturing exports accumulated. Production halted and unemployment grew. While Mexican businesses tied to European and U.S. trade contracted, Chinese businesses sustained productivity due to the economic support of the Chinese commercial diaspora and ties to import markets in China. The durability of Chinese businesses was interpreted as a yet another expression of their unnatural depravity and potential for their disastrous expansion into the hemorrhaging country. In these declining conditions, antichinistas initiated a resurgent wave of violence against the Chinese population, this time with the ardor of national salvation and a rescue of the proletariat.

"[T]he Chinese, have inundated every part of our country with their 'cheap merchandise,' with their unsanitary ways, and their vegetable crops irrigated with stagnant and stinking waters, meanwhile our government doesn't allow a campaign against these foreigners," complained labor leaders in the pages of *Pro-Patria*, the national periodical for the CROM.[16] The diatribe was reprinted from a circular written by CROM affiliates in Tapachula, Chiapas. According to them, Tapachula's abarroteros—like Juan Pon, Pablo Chang, and Angel Back and farmer José Chaufón, his wife, Anita, and their four children or the more than six hundred other Chinese people living in Chiapas—unjustly enjoyed the rights guaranteed to them by the ideals of Constitutionalist generals.[17] These concerns illuminated what was considered a central contradiction of the postrevolutionary status quo. Catering to these discontents helped build state authority around racial discrimination as a revolutionary measure. The passion with which workers fought to blame Chinese people for malaise made it easier for the ruling class to erect tighter controls around labor while satisfying anti-Chinese demands. Few were more successful at mobilizing support or creating the twin economic rationalities of racial disavowal and national unification than Melgar, the Constitutionalist general turned governor of Oaxaca and later a leading captain of the national congress.

In the PNR's reorganization of the national congress, Melgar led the formation of the BNR, a powerful faction of congressmen. By 1931 Melgar had become secretary of press and publicity in the Comité Ejecutivo Nacional (National Executive Committee) (CEN), teaming up with Lacy Jr. to fashion the party's public discourse of state authority.[18] With the PNR's support, Melgar used the BNR's congressional power to initiate the Campaña Nacionalista, a nationwide movement to respond to the economic depression. The campaign's public face was a plea to "Buy Mexican" so that domestic consumption would replace demand for export goods. While historians have considered the Campaña as a regular and predictable nationalist reaction to the economic crisis, few have considered its political affects and racial politics. Billed as a measure of worker protections, the dictate to bolster consumption remained a veiled effort to sustain the profitability of nearly every export industry. Going beyond this structural feature of the congressional campaign, the quotidian life of the program and its expansion followed in the footsteps of the anti-Chinese campaign of the previous decade. Melgar's BNR reinvigorated antichinista zeal through the Campaña Nacionalista, delivering the PNR-backed mandate to the state legislatures of Aguascalientes Chihuahua, Durango, Hidalgo, Morelos, Tlaxcala, and Zacatecas to "moralize commerce."[19] This time, antichinismo spread from Mexico City out to the states—the inverse dynamic of the previous decade.

This program became a widespread and popular campaign to "Mexicanize" the country's capitalist modes of production. In other words, the state sought to create its own controls on the reproduction of economic activity. The BNR's effort to moralize the political economy sought to create a popular image of the best type of capitalism—one defined in racial terms. The campaign was not uniformly antiforeign but promoted racial discrimination as a matter of good economic policy and moral patriotic duty. Through policy debates in the national congress, the Campaña Nacionalista defined Mexican self-colonization as the preparation of the population for rural modernity. In many parts of the country, placing peasants on state-owned land was a process predicated on the removal of Chinese people, sometimes real and sometimes imagined. This analysis of the campaign illustrates how seemingly mundane political slogans, such as "Buy Mexican" and "Mexico for Mexicans," reflected the subtle expansion of the Mexican racial state.

By 1933 the BNR's Campaña Nacionalista was a refined apparatus that provided widespread propaganda for PNR-backed reforms in the national congress.[20] Through these measures, legislators, politicians, and bureaucrats created a collectively constructed mestizo racial category supervised by state discipline. The revolution's mestizo economy would enable a more stable, efficient, and virtuous capitalism—free of vile abarroteros, factional rivalry, and armed revolt—an economy organized by scientific racial administration. Yet, to fully grasp the broader racial logic with which the PNR leadership, national congress, and bureaucracy operated, we must investigate the forceful return of eugenics to the Mexican public sphere. Before attending to the eugenic discourse of mestizaje, I return to an episode of violent displacement under these new conditions.

The surge of moralizing discourse from the Campaña Nacionalista and legal sanction from the legislature authorized a new round of anti-Chinese violence. These attacks were different from those of the previous decades because the racial polemic was no longer limited by factional alliance (such as KMT informants), an anxious authoritarian impulse (such as Calles's 1925 letter), or fear of economic collapse (such as Obregón's support of Chinese immigration to Baja California). The absence of the previous decade's constraints, combined with Depression-era federal campaigns of nationalist action, empowered locals to strike out against Chinese communities without fear of being charged by police authorities. Antichinismo, thus, expressed not just discrimination but also a voluntary identification with state-sponsored programs to Mexicanize the country. Whereas antichinistas in the 1920s behaved as beleaguered activists and vigilantes pleading for stronger government action, in the 1930s they moved with the confidence of an ordained crusade.

Local Removals: San Luis Potosi

The consequences of an official program to moralize commerce and Mexican-ize the political economy can be found in the state of San Luis Potosi, which in 1930 became a place where mestizo racial unity was bought with antichi-nismo. Antichinista networks had been in operation there since the mid-1920s, and the Comité Pro-Raza regularly petitioned the federal government for information on Chinese residents to intensify the agitation of Mexican resi-dents.[21] As the limitations of the past lifted, newspapers of the state began to circulate common racial discourses of the Chinese people as mafias. This sweeping racial polemic saturated public discourse with anxieties of Chinese miscegenation and vehement criticism of the rights of Chinese to naturalize. Claims for the "defense of local women" elevated nationalist justifications for federal intervention and authorization to expel the Chinese people. Pioneer-ing work by historian Saúl Hernández Juárez illustrates how these familiar public overtures against Mexico's Chinese population had new results in San Luis Potosi. The state legislature quickly passed a decree in September that year that ordered the Chinese residents of the state either to abandon their businesses and homes within five days or face expulsion. The decree set off hostile mobs marching through the streets, which encouraged the Chinese people to leave. Such decrees in the previous decade were frequently struck down by local courts or obstructed by federal officials, but thirty to forty Chinese residents in the hamlets of Ébano, Matehula, and Villa Guerro still left their homes within days of the announcement.[22] Among those who fled were Alfredo Chang, a young unmarried merchant from Canton, and an older established abarrotero named Benjamin Chow. Chow had a free union mar-riage to a local woman, Anastacia Galvan. They fled with their three young children De la Paz, Roberto, and Benjamin, all under the age of five.[23] Their displacement was understood through national frames of mestizo racial uplift.

The successful petition and execution of the removal order for a small population were the result of shifting tides, with popular endorsement from the BNR's campaign and the political alignment fostered by PNR dominance. *Acción*, a working-class local newspaper, popularized the incident, drawing connections to the Campaña Nacionalista as real progress toward a "genu-inely Mexican local economy." The popular identification with this national campaign further demonstrated the crucial linkages among race, sex, and economy in the making of the Mexican mestizo. Popular grassroots antichi-nista protests flourished in this era in places like Acaponeta, Nayarit; Apizaco, Tlaxcala; Guamúchil, Sinaloa; and Monclovia, Coahuila, taking the name of the

Campaña Nacionalista.[24] Across Mexico, antichinistas formed a paramilitary group called the Green Guard that picketed storefronts to enforce boycotts and agitate workers to protest for Chinese expulsions. The PNR supported the idea of mestizo futurity in need of protection because the PNR relied upon a bureaucratic state capable of racially ordering society.

The Eugenic Science of Mestizo Futurity

The 1930s was not the first time that Mexicans had considered the nexus of sex, race, and economy to ideologies of rule. In 1908 Manuel Velásquez Andrade, a Mexico City physician, organized Sociedad Mexicana de Profilaxis Sanitaria y Moral de las Enfermedades Venéreas (Mexican Society of Moral and Sanitary Profilaxis in Veneral Diseases) (SMPS), a group of doctors, lawyers, priests, soldiers, and teachers committed to "the progress of the country through the improvement of our race."[25] The following year, Mexican physicians considered a program of sex education for hygienic marriage.[26] In 1912 the Mexico City newspaper *El Correo Español* published a piece by Fidel Urbina reporting on the first international eugenics conference in London. Urbina asked, provocatively, "Do we know what we reproduce? Do we know how to raise our children?"[27] He asserted that eugenic science held answers to the questions that his readers were asking regarding the future of the country. Andrade returned to medical practice during the revolution to initiate a fledgling program to introduce sex education and other moral strictures as an intervention in the nation's Indian problem. The SMPS complained that a prudish middle class, peasant indifference, and religious dogma mired the realization of a serious eugenics program.

In September 1931 members of the university's medical faculty formed the Sociedad Mexicana de Eugenesia para el Mejoramiento de la Raza (Mexican Society of Eugenics for the Improvement of the Race) (SME). As obstacles dissolved and new conditions fostered opportunities, physicians and medical professionals found themselves at the center of a vivid public debate punctuated by government and popular interest in disciplining sex and creating better Mexicans. However, a scientific consensus was not possible until the political reforms discussed above had transpired. Medical professionals found that they were well positioned to weigh in on national debates. Notably, the 1929 election showed that the national university was among Vasconcelos's strongest supporters, and their protest of election fraud won them a greater measure of autonomy by President Ortiz. The reforms invigorated the Academia Nacional Medicina (National Medical Academy), the largest contingent within the national university, making them the most influential scientific voice in the country. Autonomy from oversight, political independence, and increased funding allowed Mexico's leading physicians and medical professionals the freedom and stability to conduct research, organize eugenics conferences, and find where their public charge met the institutionalization of the revolution.

On January 12, 1930, the Latin American Medical Congress held its seventh annual convention in Mexico City. One of the convention's highlights was the expert panel discussion on eugenics, puericulture, and pediatrics, which presented medical findings on the use of prenuptial health certificates, like those proposed in Zacatecas in the 1920s.[28] A Mexican physician in attendance associated the practical application of eugenics with the old Porfirian desire to improve the number and quality of people in the country. He noted that abortions and contraceptive use were poor tools for controlling or improving any population. Instead, sex education was the best method because it promised self-discipline and social consciousness: "Each individual learns to marry the idea of the economic responsibility you have for your home . . . to the wider collectivity . . . to bring about a noble and more effective social action. . . . This education is not a departure from the natural act of sex, but to elevate it beyond selfish pleasure to see the future; the coming of a new being that might give humanity comfort and joy."[29] For this doctor, as well as for many other eugenicists and government officials, sex education was a tool by which individuals were made into racial subject-citizens of a capitalist state. This method would help one to identify his or her own self-interests within the racial state—an ideology that would be amplified through agrarian reform.

The contributions of the SME to national debates in the 1930s were crucial because they reframed old debates about racial purity and Indian incorporation with racial improvement as a revolutionary ideal. They maintained the biological principles of racial preferences in immigration: "The natural selection that occurs among races demonstrates that in order to study the problem of mestizaje in Mexico we have to shape our immigration regulations. . . . Whether it is necessary for the Republic to intensify immigration to improve the population or its culture, we must limit it and be selective, for the opportunity to make a positive eugenics feasible . . . one that permits the improvement of the Mexican race." Eugenicists also claimed that the integration of Indian people into the civilized life of the nation was the principal biological problem of the republic.[30] By 1932 at least one state had institutionalized eugenics into the administration of public health. Anastasio García Toledo began his career as governor of Oaxaca by restructuring the state government to modernize his administration. Included in these reforms was special attention to public health through the creation of sanitation brigades, an anti-alcohol campaign,

and an office of eugenics.[31] Eugenicists provided a supportive scientific authority and moralizing discourse for the state's larger interests in organizing economic life through racial administration and disciplined mestizaje.

The discursive combination of sex, race, and economy would continue to
structure the government's expression of nationalism and the institutional
apparatus. Antichinistas facilitated the integration of eugenics ideology into
the nationalistic public sphere as a scientific discourse that complemented
and verified the scope of their concerns. Their fear of Chinese miscegenation
and obsession with the sexual discipline of Mexican women helped shape
federal legislation in profound ways. Antichinismo gained broad exposure,
as economic development, national unification, and political influence were
increasingly understood in racial terms. The congressional Campaña Nacionalista provided a highly charged meeting point for policy makers, officials,
and other influential groups to construct a state-based mestizaje.

Legislating a Racial State

By the 1930s the cultural sensibility of state sovereignty had shifted from the
military authority of Constitutionalist generals to the juridical mandates of
the constitution's revolutionary social rights. Antichinistas had pushed for
this form of ethical governance since the early 1920s, emphasizing the state's
obligation to protect all aspects of life from the Chinese racial threat. This
chapter section traces how the mandate of social rights operated in tandem
with ever-broader discourses of mestizo racial discipline, as well as the adaptation of governmental instruments and the invention of policy mechanisms
to implement, intensify, and evaluate the process of subjection to the state's
efforts to control and guide the country's social life.

The Mexican public sphere was inundated by a national concern for discipline. Popular discourse assisted in state formations in a reciprocal manner;
the administrative process produced official data authorizing racial discourses
that fed back into policy reform. The circular processes of the incipient racial
state can most clearly be found in the triangular formation of the 1930 census,
the Federal Labor Law (1931), and the National Registry of Foreigners (1931).
These policies and administrative instruments worked together to provide a
self-referencing index for the administration of the population. Population-
level interventions were thought to maximize economic utility across the
economy, not just for individual colonization projects. The policy instruments
created for this task (census, labor controls, and immigrant registry) were the
tools with which the government intended to build a virtuous racial order. The

desire for perfect administrative control reflects the responsibility that state actors assumed from a racialized interpretation of the state's social-rights mandate, ensuring the racial improvement of mestizos and the realization of rural modernity.

The 1930 Census

The census, mandated in 1929 by Calles's presidential decree, became an important symbolic marker for the imagination of a racially unified nationality. The consolidation of power and political discipline the PNR achieved after Obregón's death allowed the government to coordinate a comprehensive national census for the first time since 1910 (an attempt in 1921 was made but had a number of shortcomings).[32] This census purported to count nationality, not race, as a civil juridical construct. The fact that some Chinese people were left out of the census reflects racial exceptions to legal citizenship and naturalization.[33] Although never barred from naturalization outright, Chinese people who became naturalized Mexicans only periodically benefited from it.

Mexicali's recorded total population was 29,985; however, census figures indicate a deliberate undercounting of the surrounding rural area. Sources from the CRLC suggest the Chinese agricultural population fluctuated between 10,000 and 15,000, depending upon the cotton harvest, a number nearly equal to the number of Chinese people in all the other states combined.[34] Given Mexicali's population growth and the expansion of Chinese cotton-growing operations, a 42 percent decline in inhabited localities in Baja California's North District is not probable. The census ledger lists the disaggregated counts for the 540 previously recognized localities in 1921, but in 1930 the designation for 230 of the previously inhabited tracts was changed to "Does not exist," including places with ethnically suggestive names such as La Campo Chinesca, Ching Yeip, Kui Coo, Quong Sang, Rancho Chino de Tecalote, Tay Tosa, Wong Lung, and Yot Loy. Designating these tracts as nonexistent deliberately erased the Chinese population from the land.

The disavowal of the Chinese population was paired with an obligatory nationalization of the peasantry and Indian population. This census introduced language classifications for "indígenas monolingües" (monolingual speakers) and "bilingües" (bilingual speakers) as a catalog of indigeneity and an index of peasant integration in cultural nationalism.[35] Ostensibly, the census only counted Mexican people, but such a category elided the twinned mechanisms of disavowal and conscription. Indigenous conscription into national citizenship signified the state's quest for ethnic and indigenous erasure, which was also found in education and agrarian policy. The single category reflected an administrative fantasy of counting a homogenous population and formally excluding some racial pariahs and created the policy by which racial amalgamation, evaluation, and improvement were discussed.

The numerical tables and aggregates the census produced constructed demographic information that became political fact. Such information as population density, the number and location of indigenous language speakers, the age structure of children in different states, and the geographic distribution and concentration of foreigners became widely circulated. Educator Manuel Rousseau of Tlaxcala considered census statistics to be both a pedagogical and administrative instrument. The assumed dual function of statistics specified that individuals could identify themselves within the statistic and that the statistic made individuals known to the state. Rousseau commented, "The soul of the people is transformed by education; and one of the most educational social practices that has been used as guidance in this new era is without a doubt national statistics."[36] The census data fed back into the state's concern for development. By the 1930s the revolutionary mandate to deliver economic growth was interpreted as an imperative to improve the racial condition and reproductive capacity of the population such that development may arise naturally. This rationality represented in this racist policy debate assumed resources and rights were wasted on people without education or good racial stock. Statistics about monolingual Indians provoked questions about Spanish literacy and access to schools. Numbers of rural inhabitants triggered anxieties about access to health services and the inadequate supply of medical professionals.[37] When Chinese people were counted in the census, they became identified as problems and were targeted for state intervention and popular attacks. When the Chinese people were not counted, it paved the way for their physical erasure. Although each locality was made up of varying conditions and encapsulated endemic power relations, the census empowered federal officials to administer these diverse situations within a rubric of racial uplift. The Campaña Nacionalista also encouraged local and state actors to connect their particular grievance to the larger national platform, as in San Luis Potosi.

Labor Reform

The BNR supplied the Campaña Nacionalista with data from the 1930 census to emphasize in legislation the composition of the national workforce and the occupation and distribution of foreigners. This information became the basis for the sweeping Ley de Trabajo (Labor Law) and surveillance apparatus of the Registro Nacional del Extranjeros (National Registry of Foreigners), which were implemented in 1932. As the domestic economy contracted from the global depression, unemployment rose, strikes increased, and labor unrest spread. BNR members moved to strike out against the potential of an independent labor movement. The national congress sought to strengthen the government's ability to administer economic relief by pushing for reform of federal labor law and expanding a system of company- and state-controlled unions. Empowered by article 123 of the Constitution, which states that workers are guaranteed government protection from abuses, the BNR, with support from other company unions, crafted a labor plan to, in the words of President Ortiz, "give the worker's cries the force of law." However, the vast new set of regulations brought into existence by the labor law set into motion stronger government powers in three areas—areas that antichinistas had pioneered through a racialized discourse of ethical governance over the previous decade. First, the political bravado of the BNR's claim of worker advocacy helped produce political control of the revolution's meaning. Second, the state used its proclaimed responsibility to protect and induce economic development to create wider controls on the condition of labor with greater discretion to respond to industry needs. Third, the administration's new controls to allocate, distribute, and rearrange the composition of the national labor force reflected the imagined government capacity to manipulate the population's bio-economic power for the maximum expression of mestizo industrial muscle. In this way antichinista ideology strengthened the BNR's legitimacy and gave direction to national policy reforms.[38]

Although anti-Chinese discourse did not appear in the legislation's language, anti-Chinese politics helped sustain the political viability of this policy. In economic terms the law provided industry with the power to organize and induce the labor of workers at a minimum standard and created juridical uniformity for employment at the cost of worker autonomy.[39] By protecting the employment conditions while empowering sanctioned unions, the BNR ushered in a brutal era of corporatized unions. This legal framework became an effort to contain class conflict within the juridical limitations of the constitution.[40] According to the law, there could be no class struggle outside of authorized grievances. Unintentionally, one area that remained ferociously independent was union-backed anti-Chinese protests. The creation of more-rigid labor controls amplified anti-Chinese agitation as an area of discontent beyond state-mediated conflicts with employers. This outlet for aggression may have served as a safety valve to depressurize the broad dissatisfaction with the corporate-union system. For example, as organized labor spread in the Pacific northwest, workers and leaders intensified coordination among independent, corporate, and company unions to amplify anti-Chinese politics in Baja California, efforts that came to a head in 1936.[41]

The Registry of Foreigners

The federal labor law also provided new limitations on immigrants' rights. The law required that 80 percent of a business's employees be Mexican by birth or naturalization. Other industries, such as the railroad, were completely nationalized and required 100 percent Mexican labor.[42] Historians commonly remark on the dramatic turn against foreigners in this period; however, the 20 percent allowance reflected a subtle admission that foreigners would continue to play a role in the domestic economy. Yet, that role was more highly regulated than ever before. The registry retained information about immigrant labor, but it also satisfied the bureaucratic interest in racially indexing foreigners, their occupational positions, and their international ties. The application of the 80 percent minimum was unevenly applied across Mexico, and the highest incidence of regulation impacted small- to medium-sized Chinese businesses, which were also the favorite target of labor unions. The labor law represented yet another revision to the Mariscal formula, defined in the Porfirian period as the strategic infusion of labor, but this time it entailed absolute enforcement. The 1930 census revealed that the previous decade had incorporated more immigrants to Mexico than ever before, more than 160,000.[43] The overlapping concerns of demography and labor led to the creation of the Registro Nacional del Extranjeros, which the secretary of the interior created in 1931 and first began registration efforts in central offices in Guanajuato, Jalisco, Michoacán, San Luis Potosi, Tamaulipas, and Veracruz.

Officials crosschecked the registry with the migration department's records and the census to identify violations, such as a change in occupation, a relocation, or falsified information. Sonoran antichinistas were already monitoring Chinese immigrants in this manner. They maintained a catalog of Chinese people compiled from state records since the 1925 conventions. The federalization of this procedure widened the state's capacity to regulate foreigners and intervene in their lives and was unevenly applied. Individuals who registered were issued identification cards that verified their identities and registration numbers. These ID cards also became a site of enforcement, as exemplified by the detention of José Loo when he was found without his official identification. Loo, an established Tampico merchant, was picked up and held by officials for several days while his credentials were certified; ultimately, he was charged a fine for noncompliance.[44] The frequency with which such trivial infractions led to detention for Chinese people is unknown, but card-carrying rules were likely used to extort bribes from immigrants even when unreported.

These policy changes were clear steps taken by state actors who envisioned the potential for the administration of a nationwide mestizo racial project.

Questions of reliable implementation, local consent, an irregular capacity for enforcement, and uneven geographic distribution of federal power mattered little to members of the national congress, the PNR leadership, and the bureaucracy when they designed these instruments of racial governance. The enduring significance of ethnic and regional differences was not conceived as obstacles but as evidence of the necessity of the propaganda work of the BNR's Campaña Nacionalista. The political class was convinced that discipline and loyalty would result in national unity and economic strength. The elegance of their statecraft was needed in order to sculpt the meaning of the revolution and alter the terms of a racial contract that depended upon the consent— and, ideally, enthusiasm—of mestizo subjects as they were "cleansed" of their ethnicity and trained for productivity. In this period the national congress regularly reported on the deportation of expulsions of pernicious Chinese individuals, as defined under article 33, to affirm the government's commitment to maintaining a benevolent racial order.[45]

The postrevolutionary state would always be incomplete and uneven, but anti-Chinese policies affirmed the highest ideals of state power and a seemingly inexorable mestizo racial hegemony. The ability of the government to carry out its administration depended upon the ways that federal interests aligned with, clashed with, or complicated local power relations. The PNR promise that legislation crafted in the national congress would be recognizably translated through the nested sovereignties of the republic and achieve distinguishable local results was an old fantasy of the ruling class that was passed on to the postrevolutionary elite. What made anti-Chinese measures different is that they had been local phenomena before they were federal designs. Local anti-Chinese politics in the 1930s co-opted federal authority and armed local actors with a robust set of rationales and tools that were previously unavailable. The complexity of the Mexican political apparatus created the conditions for the unauthorized expulsion of thousands of Chinese people.

Maverick Expulsions

Political, legal, and economic conditions in the 1930s coalesced in the mass expulsion of Chinese people and their multi-ethnic Mexican families from the states of Sonora and Sinaloa in 1931 and 1932. The 1911 Torreón massacre and these expulsions are, by far, the most infamous in Chinese Mexican history; however, they were neither the first nor the last of these practices.[46]

Sonoran officials interpreted the boldness of the federal government's Campaña Nacionalista and the absence of presidential protections as an opportunity to realize the racial fantasy of expulsion—a dream twenty years in the making. A series of state-level edicts targeting Chinese and Mexican unions and Chinese business operations in the state escalated to a statewide scramble to apprehend, detain, and expel the Chinese residents and their mixed families. Official and popular punishment of women for choosing Chinese male sexual partners achieved its pinnacle in this movement. On October 7, 1930, Sonoran governor Francisco S. Elias ordered the elimination of current and future Chinese Mexican marriages in the state. The worsening condition of the state's economy led many back to the antichinista's racial polemic of the previous decade. As in San Luis Potosi, the impulse of Sonoran officials to drive out the apparition of Chinese mestización was linked to the Campaña Nacionalista ideal of building racial strength into the economy through "purification." However, Sonora was home to thousands of Chinese people, whose businesses were valued in tens of millions of dollars. Officials in each of the state's districts were to inspect households and businesses, fine perpetrators, and report them to the state's central office. The passage of the Federal Labor Law added fuel to the fire and armed the governor with the mandate to ensure the state's employment was "genuinely Mexican."[47]

A year later, Rudolfo Elías Calles, the enterprising son of ex-president Plutarco Elías Calles, was voted into office as a PNR candidate. Without authorization from President Ortiz or the PNR, the intrepid new governor issued immediate orders to enforce anti-Chinese measures to the fullest extent possible. No rural exemptions or favored political factions within the Chinese community were given, as in the previous decade; this was a program of ethnic cleansing. The governor's office ordered the closure of all Chinese businesses, the punishment of all Mexican wives of Chinese men, and the prohibition of Mexican women from occupying Chinese places of business or domiciles. Governor Calles also tried to annul current Chinese Mexican marriages through executive order. Months later, Sinaloa's governor, Macario Gaxiola, the Constitutionalist general who had tried to "cleanse" the state of Chinese people almost two decades earlier, got another chance and joined the "patriotic" effort to expel the Chinese people.

The focus on women as subjects of rogue racial enforcement reflected the discursive ubiquity of women's role in Mexican racial futurity. The harsh treatment received by Mexican partners of Chinese men communicated to other women the risks and consequences of deviation from patriarchy and revealed the misogyny that undergirded the popular mestizo racial imagination. For women, anti-Chinese politics was a tenuous bargain for security as a privileged object of men's concern. The disciplined mestizaje imagined by eugenicists, legislators, politicians, and bureaucrats relied upon women's subjection to state power as the prevailing condition for a "positive" mestizo synthesis. Antichinismo made this function of mestizo fascism appear natural and desirable.

The expulsions were neither spontaneous nor bureaucratically performed, yet they were the realization of more than a decade of anti-Chinese propaganda, and they occurred with broad consent. The actual removals were done by varied forms of large mobs, small vigilante groups, and state offices. Whereas the grotesque assemblies of the decade of revolutionary fighting were racialized scripts of anti-Porfirian rebellion, these mobs were the result of maverick orders of a state governor to execute a systematic expulsion. The cohesion of enforcement mobs allowed participants to perform citizenship through the expulsion of "racial contagions" and the "traitorous" women who bedded with them. Yet, a distinctive feature of Mexican antichinismo was the complementarity of formal policy and violent expressions of popular discontent. While many Chinese people hoped that the aggressive posture would be redacted as before, everyone quickly found the laws' enforcement to be swift and without reprieve. In 1931 and 1932, more than two thousand Chinese and their multiethnic families were expelled from the country, primarily by forcing them into the United States. Their entry to the United States was, of course, prohibited and forced the United States to adopt them as Mexican refugees and deport them to China. The situation for the Chinese people in Mexico had seemingly reached its lowest point, but conditions would get worse. A staunch antichinista was about to ascend to the highest office in the land.

Conclusion

Framers of the revolutionary constitution of 1917 created a radically different legal document that created social rights, which formalized the state's obligation to act in the interest of the majority Indian and peasant populations. While ejido land, a relic of colonialism and Liberal reform, was promulgated as a means to exchange land for political loyalty, antichinismo helped construct a political rationality for the revolution's racial contract. In this contract Mexicans exchanged their subjection to the state's normative regime and exploitation under a state-sponsored economy for political belonging and basic economic guarantees. By the 1930s agricultural-land donations were transformed into active recruitment to bind recipients to the institutional apparatus that guaranteed their plots. This postrevolutionary agrarian reform fulfilled the aims of self-colonization and mobilized the indigenous and non-Indian populations to become state-disciplined settlers.

The revolution's racial contract was an unwritten promise that the revolutionary state would govern in the interests of the indigenous peasantry. Unlike the preexisting, white population of scholar Charles W. Mills's original U.S. racial contract under white supremacy, the one established in Mexico invented the mestizo as a normative citizen-subject in a modernist mold, which the political class hoped the country would adopt. The state's repudiation of indigeneity, together with the mass political incorporation of Indians, sets Mexican anti-Chinese politics apart from that practiced in the United States. The history of finding Chinese culprits for Mexican problems illustrates how different classes, numerous ethnic groups, and a variety of institutions developed a widely circulated discourse of the public good that centered upon government support and protection of the Mexican mestizo race from the perceived Chinese racial threat. This nationalist ideology furthered integration and control of normative citizen-subjects and made the state appear necessary, even desirable.

This chapter aims to fundamentally shift the definition of social reforms from one of political economic reallocation and enfranchisement to the redefinition of membership within the capitalist state as a racial project of control and domination. Antichinistas envisioned the complete domination of Mexican life in order to protect it and safeguard its future. Even in different regions where state power was independently exercised and contested, the practice of antichinismo achieved similar ends—legitimization of the state and deeper institutionalization of the population. Anti-Chinese politics made the reproduction of state power and mestizo futurity synonymous. The racial polemic of anti-Chinese politics created a discourse of ethical governance that advanced a set of surveillance and disciplinary institutions to administer and coordinate biological (sex), social (identity), and economic (labor) reproduction during a global contraction and reorganization of the capitalist world system. These institutions allowed the Mexican ruling class to create a set of racial technologies that identified, measured, disciplined, and "improved" the national population as a mestizo race—as enhanced Indian people. The postrevolutionary state introduced policy designed to transform a polyglot, heterogeneous, indigenous population into a mestizo race fit for a state-administered program of agrarian industrialization. The interrelation of Chinese people and Mexico's indigenous racial formations reflected the terms of the revolution's racial contract. Antichinismo gave millions of nonwhite people permission to enact a state-endorsed identity of racial superiority. This act fulfilled important parts of the moral conditions of the racial contract, such as consent to the state's authority over race, sex, and land in exchange for services and the means of production.

The disavowal and eviction of the Chinese people and the conscription of Indian people were two sides of the same racial contract: a relational nexus of postcolonial sovereignty, national modernity, and racial citizenship. The state's vision of an enhanced and pliant mestizo achieved profound influence through the juridical formulation of agrarian citizenship. Agrarian reform by the Mexican state after the revolution created new ways of coordinating and mobilizing a previously fragmented peasant labor force. By defining beneficiaries of the Mexican Revolution as "agrarian-rights subjects,"[48] state officials accomplished three alterations to the relationships among race, citizenship, and indigeneity. First, state officials transformed all rights to land, including indigenous rights, into state-controlled social rights, which meant that rights to land could only be expressed and recognized as rights contained within legal statutes. Enacting these policies forced Mexicans to trade indigenous identity for access to state-allocated resources. Second, and related, state officials defined the terms of citizenship on the utilization of agrarian rights. This meant that citizenship was only expressed to authorities through the exercise of federally legislated rights—there were no concerns beyond those established by revolutionary doctrine. Third, state officials created new capacities to assess the biological and cultural traits of potential rights-bearing subjects to participate in the national economy. Attention to popular expressions of antichinismo reveals a mode of citizenship and belonging as well as a strategy of drawing government attention to local conditions. The disavowal of the Chinese people and their delimitation from the Mexican mestizo form must be included in the vast repertoire of popular national identifications—a bricolage of acquiescence, self-preservation, and strategic essentialism built into the revolution's racial contract.

In order to more fully understand the logic of rule that state agents employed, as well as the nationalist discourses with which people invented new associations, the current volume concludes by following the career of antichinista Abelardo Rodríguez as he ascended to the presidency and by examining the slate of reforms he and the PNR crafted through the mid-1930s.

Conclusion

The first cemetery in Mexicali was an informal site near the main canal in what is now the downtown district. In 1919 the municipality created the Panteón Municipal Número 1 on land opposite the CRLC's cotton-processing facility, La Jabonera del Pacífico, which segregated the remains of Chinese residents to the south section. Municipal cemeteries expanded throughout the late twentieth century. The largest expansion was El Centinela, created in 1977 on the far outskirts of the city's west end.[1] In this expansion, Chinese graves were exhumed from the city center and collectively interred at El Centinela. In Mexicali, as in many other places throughout Mexico, mestizo nationalism has produced an obligation to forget the Chinese.

The municipal registry of burials at the Panteón Municipal Número 1 contains records of people no longer buried there. One of them, Lim Sing, died as a cotton worker at the height of the turmoil before El Asalto, an agrarian raid on Chinese farms. At the age of forty, Sing widowed a wife in Canton; no local familial relations were recorded. He was buried on February 24, 1936, in the Chinese portion of the cemetery.[2] Forty-one years later, he was exhumed to make way for Unidad Deportiva Lopez Mateos, a municipal park and pool (figure 11). In 1977 Lim Sing's remains, along with more than a hundred other Chinese residents, were exhumed and transported to El Centinela (figure 12). The remains were supposedly consolidated according to their membership in the seventeen remaining Chinese fraternal and hometown associations in the city. The Chinese Association of Mexicali took responsibility for the unknown and unclaimed remains during their removal to El Centinela. For those Chinese people that stayed in Mexicali despite the Mexicanization campaigns and

FIGURE 11. Unidad Deportiva Lopez Mateos at the former burial site of cotton worker Lim Sing. Photo by author.

FIGURE 12. Headstones at El Centinela Cemetery, to which the remains of Chinese residents were transported from the Cementerio de los Pioneros. Photo by author.

harassment from unions, their burials in Mexicali's cemeteries were some of the last traces of their intentions to stay in Baja California. The deteriorating registry of municipal burials is the only record that Lim Sing and the other exhumed Chinese residents made Mexicali their final resting place.

This event is one episode in a series of systematic manipulations and reconfigurations of Mexicali's urban space, designed to erase the Chinese past in order to realize an idealized Mexican present. When the old site of the Jabonera was made into a popular consumer destination, the cemetery's proximity dictated that it also reflect a past imaged by proponents of Mexicanization. The municipal park's construction accomplished the cultural work of resignifying that location. In the eyes of city leaders, the alteration to the burial grounds enabled the renaming of the cemetery. In physical and symbolic terms, the cemetery could only become El Cementerio de los Pioneros after the Chinese section was erased from the grounds.[3] These choices reflect the role of antichinismo in Mexicanization.

Adding insult to injury, the headstones from the Chinese section of the renamed cemetery were demolished and used as backfill to reinforce a retaining wall on the cemetery's western flank (figure 13). Behind the rubble heap

FIGURE 13. Wall at the Cementerio de los Pioneros (Cemetery of the Pioneers) supported by Chan Sewo's headstone. Photo by author.

of smashed grave markers, Chan Sewo's headstone was carefully placed in the corner of the retaining wall to support a metal fence post along with poured concrete. Sewo, an agricultural worker, was buried in the cemetery in 1938 just after Cárdenas's expropriation. Sewo was evicted twice, once from the cotton ranches for agrarian reform and a second time from the cemetery to erase the trace of the first eviction.

The museum exhibition discussed at this book's introduction presented a false image of Mexicali's Chinese people. In Panteón Municipal Número 1, they were not misrepresented but completely removed. Both venues illustrate that authenticity in Mexican nationality involves an obligation to forget the Chinese. The organized forgetting of the Chinese people in Mexico is an imperfect mechanism to obfuscate the racist underpinnings of the postrevolutionary regime and its efforts to create and dominate a mestizo nation. It is imperfect because antichinismo remains an effective political resource, even in the absence of actual Chinese people, to support the fiction of a mestizo national well-being in the Mexican racial state. Despite acts of historical erasure, the figure of the Chinese people continually resurfaces in response to the crises of the mestizo state with racial, sexual, and economic alarm.

Racial Imperatives of Postrevolutionary Rule

In May 1933 members of the Alianza Nacionalista Chihuahuense (Alliance of Nationalist Chihuahuans) organized a mob lynching of three Chinese men in front of their place of business in Villa Aldama. The Alianza was a nationalist political group of middle-class Chihuahuans that traveled the country, pushed for protectionist reforms, and condemned the presence of the Chinese residents. Members of the pro-raza committee joined Vito Aguirre, the leader of the Alianza, to execute these Chinese men that the members claimed raped a young Mexican girl. The rape charge was accentuated as more than the violation of a minor but a racial crime that denigrated the mestizo nation. This event is explored in more depth later in the conclusion, but for now, this public and popular lynching of three Chinese men provides yet another gruesome example to analyze the local conditions of the racial contract in postrevolutionary Mexico. The popular support for the lynching reflected a profound measure of public consent to the violent enforcement of racial division. Furthermore, the enactment of the lynching at the men's place of business sought to signify Chinese death as a virtuous method of claiming a mestizo economic space. Not a single person associated with the killing of these Chinese men was charged with a crime. Not everyone expressed mestizo nationalism through lethal antichinismo, but this case is instructive because it illustrates an important element of the racial contract: antichinismo operated as a both popular discontent and state discipline. This combination of political functions reinforced each other; as aggression against actual or figurative Chinese people grew, the more popular state intervention became. Conversely, the more the state policed the Chinese people as a performance of benevolent care, the more readily Mexican people submitted to the state's ideological conditioning. The mechanism that makes this racial contract function in its various regional expressions was the populist rendering of a mestizo public good and the state's constitutional social-rights mandate. The 1917 constitution mandated the political integration of the republic's Indian people *"para su bien,"* or for their own good. The Mexican people when they killed, expelled, and evicted Chinese people in the 1930s acted out an idea of the public good, for which the state rewarded them with institutionalization and economic citizenship.

The previous chapters have traced the metamorphosis of the Chinese racial form from Porfirian motores de sangre to killable subjects of the revolution to the pernicious agents of defilement. The conclusion examines how anti-Chinese politics became eclipsed by its referent—the state's mestizo nation. The history of anti-Chinese politics, thus, mirrors the progressive articulation of Indian and state relations. Indian people were gradually transformed from being objects of eradication to being unruly insurgents and, ultimately, to being the recipients of care, discipline, and enhancement. Antichinistas contributed to the reformulation of the Mexican racial state—a state that took up the Porfirian mantle to increase the number and quality of the population. In fulfillment of this directive, the 1930s culminated in the simultaneous rejection of the Chinese people and articulation of self-colonization as a racial project to convert Indians into state-disciplined mestizo settlers. This chapter ends with the zenith of this transformation during the El Asalto a Las Tierras in Mexicali, Baja California, when thousands of Chinese farmers were usurped by relocated and desperate agrarians who were later granted title to state-organized collective agriculture across a massive, irrigated desert expanse. Through Chinese disavowal, Mexican people were conscripted as racialized agrarian subjects of the revolutionary state.

One legacy of these twinned racializations appears well into the 1940s, when eugenicists' fears of Chinese degeneracy collided with agrarian reform. These anxieties shaped the partnership between militant officials and eugenics organizations, such as Sociedad Eugenesia Mexicana, as they began to inculcate a program of self-colonization, a program that advertised a responsibility for disciplined mestizaje. In local agrarian offices, this eugenics organization posted regular panel displays with pamphlets, posters, and other printed materials that asked readers to think of agriculture as a metaphor for human improvement. As a farmer nurtures a tree to get the best fruit, the state nurtures good farmers to raise fit children.

This chapter follows the escalation of the state's racial authority through the substitute presidency of the antichinista governor of Baja California, Abelardo Rodríguez. With his help, the PNR articulated the political and judicial authority to build a bureaucratic state system out of the 1917 constitution's social-rights mandate. They envisioned a state that could discipline and coordinate the population to bring about the end of poverty, the redemption of the Indian population, and, most important, extinguish challenges to its authority. The creation of the Ministry of the National Economy, the Personal Identification Law, and the vicious mob lynchings of three Chinese men in Chihuahua demonstrate how President Rodríguez transformed antichinista ideology into an instrument of national racial rule. These trends were further entrenched in the 1933 PNR national convention and the passage of health reform (1933), agrarian reform (1933), sex education (1934), and the Law of Nationality and Naturalization (1934).

President Abelardo Rodríguez: Chief Antichinista

Motivated by the PNR's lack of confidence in the president, Pascual Ortiz Rubio resigned from the presidency on September 4, 1932. Upon the PNR's recommendation to nominate General Rodríguez as interim president, the congress unanimously voted him into the republic's highest office. In his meteoric rise to national power, his term as governor of Baja California Norte, from 1923 to 1930, was brought into the national spotlight. His political record and ardent antichinismo were displayed as evidence of his patriotism, his dedication to the institutionalization of the revolution, and his perseverance in cultivating "genuine Mexican colonization."[4] Two decades of military service, firm rule over federal territory, and open condemnation of Chinese settlements affirmed his revolutionary nationalist credentials. The American press speculated that his "enviable record" in Baja California put him ahead of his peers, and their Mexican sources cited his "administration of the Mexican Agrarian laws . . . and the effort to advance [Baja California Norte] as proof that he is of the caliber Mexico needs in its highest executive position."[5] Yet, for Rodríguez, antichinismo was not a political campaign or pet issue but a part of pragmatic administration of mestizo racial improvement. President Rodríguez's attitudes toward the Chinese population assure us that when Mexican people talked about the Chinese people, they were really talking about defining revolutionary state power through race, sex, and economy.

In a matter of weeks, Rodríguez, a confident and commanding bureaucrat, replaced Ortiz. Taking the oath of office, Rodríguez proclaimed a new Depression-era policy of "Work!—and no politics"; however, his brief administration was anything but apolitical.[6] His proclamation foreshowed the adoption of an explicitly fascist model of Mexicanization. The selection of Rodríguez as interim president reflected the PNR leadership's desire to intensify social transformation through policy. The majority of the national congress already thought of the state as the revolutionary instrument by which to "firmly organize and subject the masses to discipline."[7] With Rodríguez's help, the antichinista discourse of ethical governance would become the racial ideology that supported the state's domination of social life as a means of its preservation and improvement. The new juridical and administrative powers developed by the state apparatus in the previous year allowed many officials and politicians to envision even-greater state-centric methods of reconstruction. This section considers the significance of the Ministry of Development, Industry, and Labor, and the Personal Identification Law at the opening of the Rodríguez administration.

The clearest indication of the kind of governance President Rodríguez would practice was the bureaucratic transformation of the Ministry of Development, Industry, and Labor to the separate secretaries of labor and the national economy. Congressman Ezequiel Padilla swayed the national congress during debate on the measure, explicitly calling for the government's transition to a "fascist state apparatus," to which the congressional hall erupted in applause. Padilla argued that the revolution had failed if poverty was not eradicated. It was, therefore, the responsibility of the government to make that objective, guaranteed as a social right by the 1917 constitution, a reality. He reasoned that liberalism and socialism were not suited to the conditions of reconstruction but that a fascist hierarchical model of scientific administration of labor, land, and education would ensure the government was equipped with the supreme powers to mold the population into efficient economic forms and, thus, abolish poverty. The director of the Department of National Statistics offered testimony to verify that the government possessed a sufficient data-acquisition program—like the census and documentation from other programs like the Federal Labor Law—to knowledgeably direct and instruct the national economy.[8] The corporate structure of unions, achieved the previous year, would come under direct administration of the secretary of labor, who was charged with coordinating the government's obligation to supply work and coordinate profitable industrial production.

Padilla described the advantage of fascism was that individuals need not find "TRUST" among each other but only "TRUST" in the institutions of the revolutionary state. The popularity of this vision of the public sphere demonstrates the antidemocratic nature of Mexican state nationalism as well as mestizo racial identification. The ruling class never imagined Mexican nationalism as a fraternity; the diverse and fragmented aspects of the population were to be subjects who collectively identified with the state. Mestizo nationalism was never possible without the construction and maintenance of a racial state apparatus. Antichinismo supported and expanded this vision of the Mexican racial state. The congress passed the creation of the position of secretary of the national economy by a vote of 103-1, thus fulfilling popular desires for greater command over the social relations of economic production.[9]

Several months later, Interior Secretary Eduardo Vasconcelos moved the national congress to pass the Personal Identification Law to "provide order to the multiplicity of methods, means, motives and purposes created by the problem of identification." Rodríguez's cabinet reasoned that "the growth of the population, the social division of labor, specialization of functions of groups or individuals have made increasingly necessary that the state provide the legal capacity to respond to multiple and urgent needs of . . . mandatory, . . . scientifically verifiable . . . personal identification."[10] The registry of foreigners, land registries, employment, union membership, professional certifications, and dozens of other existing personal identifications complicated how the state carried out the administration of "individuals, associations, and authorities." The consolidation of these vehicles of recognition echoed aspirations for a centralized administration of the national population as a mestizo population. Verifiable identities were necessary for a centralized administration, but politically they could also confirm the morality of Mexicanization. What began with the registry of foreigners as a process of providing useful information to the state about individuals' physical, social, and economic characteristics became a vision for knowing the entire population. The surveillance of immigrants, one of the anxieties anti-Chinese politics most provoked, taught the state about legal domination and administration of the wider citizenry. These controls were useful political devices that went beyond the regulation of a Chinese threat to include the administration of states with high concentrations of unassimilated Indian people and peasants. The Personal Identification Law was first implemented in the states of Aguascalientes, Baja California, Morelos,

Oaxaca, and Yucatán. The rapid adoption of the Personal Identification Law likely fulfilled new needs to create, maintain, or deny access to the emerging political order as regional politics dictated.[11]

The evolution of executive powers and refinement of the administration created the bureaucratic capacity to direct the economy as if the population were composed of mestizo subjects of state discipline. To many, the state itself was the ultimate expression of the revolution because it derived its sovereign authority from the social-rights mandate. However, debate continued over the power of this state and the gravity of its influence. Other scholars have referred to development of postrevolutionary rule as the mimicry of European statism after World War I, a political formation that some argued eventually succumbed to a more authentic revolutionary nationalism.[12] Rather than characterize reconstruction as a transition to a supposedly more authentic domestic strain of revolutionary nationalism, I argue that Mexican history and politics have been subjected to mestizo hegemony that has shifted domestic racism onto foreign agents in order to produce the racial innocence of mestizo national identity. This ideological apparatus of the state was an important artifact of the transition of antichinismo from a grotesque assembly to a social organization to a state ideology. Where the bureaucracy was weak and policies were altered by local conditions and politics, the discourse of national identity remained a durable and vital source of state authority. Under Rodríguez's administration, these government powers would be used in the articulation of a program of self-colonization—one that relied upon the surgical removal of Chinese people from key areas of the political economy.

Mexicanization: The Material Effects of Antichinismo

President Rodríguez began his first address to the national congress in September 1933 by reveling in recent victories against Asian colonization at home and abroad. He congratulated the Ministry of Foreign Relations on its cooperation with the El Monte strike of Mexican workers against Japanese growers across the border in California.[13] The triumph over what they considered to be pestilent Asian agriculture carried over to Rodríguez's personal contributions toward the growth of Mexican agricultural colonies in Chinese-dominated Mexicali. His speech announced a five-point agenda for aggressive self-colonization: Finish colonization projects already underway, use repatriated workers for colonization projects, nationalize foreign-owned land, redistribute the population, and incorporate marginal lands. This agenda placed particular emphasis on Baja California. Rodríguez hoped to make an example of the government's capacity to create a virtuous racial order as the best expression of revolutionary reform—a process of simultaneous Chinese disavowal and mestizo conscription. The president considered Chinese immigration to be a "world danger" that threatened the state's project to improve the population and administer national colonization.[14] These issues supported a number of other measures that strengthened the postrevolutionary racial state.

Rodríguez's formal call to maximize self-colonization as a Depression-era policy marked the beginning of a centralized program to construct a rural modernity, the lynchpin of which was the racial formation of Indian people as state-disciplined mestizos. National colonization was not just an articulation of the distribution of laboring bodies and modes of production; it was a process of subjectification to a nationalist racial formation. The Campaña Nacionalista advanced this racial regime not only through the support of policies but also through particular characterizations of Rodríguez himself as a legitimate leader of Indian people. That year the BNR sponsored a commemoration of Rodríguez as a champion of the mestizo nation (figure 14). However, they did so by appropriating indigenous iconography as a visual marker of authenticity in what some have called "aesthetic statism."[15] Figure 14 is a photograph of a large deerskin painting that honors Rodríguez's role in the Campaña Nacionalista. The image is adorned with various icons from major indigenous groups and Indian republics along with icons of the state, like the tricolor flag and the monument to the revolution.[16] Here the nation's chief antichinista is in a banker's suit adorned with indigenous markings—a reflection of intimate symbolic bonds among antichinismo, indigenismo, industrial capitalism, and the postrevolutionary racial contract. However, Rodríguez carefully managed how anti-Chinese politics and mestizo nationalism were associated, particularly when it came to anti-Chinese violence.

To many observers, especially antichinistas, the Campaña Nacionalista seemed to be working. Heightened surveillance of foreigners, the mass expulsion of Chinese people from their Sonoran and Sinaloan strongholds, and the rise of a powerful antichinista to the presidency indicated that important steps had been made to racially fortify the nation's economy. Rodríguez's program of self-colonization implemented ideas that had been circulated for the last several years about the creation of a virtuous racial order. Nevertheless, Chinese immigration continued, and their communities persisted. Wherever the Chinese people lived, they became a privileged screen onto which people projected their political identity in alignment with the state's racial contract through violence.

FIGURE 14. Campaña Nacionalista commemoration for President Abelardo Rodríguez, 1933. Photo from pamphlet, Bloque Nacional Revolucionaria, Archive, Howard Tilton Memorial Library, Tulane University.

The Lynching at Villa Aldama

On May 24, 1933, the governor of Chihuahua, Rodrigo M. Quevado, sent an encrypted telegram to President Rodríguez about recent anti-Chinese activity in Villa Aldama. The previous day, three unnamed Chinese men had been taken from their cells in the municipal jail and lynched in the street.[17] The communiqué did not explain why the victims were jailed—only that they were removed from their cells and murdered because the mob's leaders accused them of raping a young Mexican girl. Quevado's coded message explained that the mob lynched the men outside their business, where the alleged rape had occurred and that the Alianza Nacionalista Chihuahuense, the Liga Nacional Anti-China, and Anti-Judia de Mexico (National Anti-Chinese and Anti-Jewish League of

Mexico) had carried out the lynching. No further violence was reported after the lynching, and no record of arrests or even an investigation was found. By all accounts, the other non-Chinese townspeople, the governor, and the president accepted the lynching as racial justice.

From the choice to encrypt the message, to the accusation of rape, to the method of murder and the history of the executioners, this event reveals the popular intersections of race, gender, and sexuality within the formation of a cultural sensibility of a mestizo racial state. The Chinese men were never formally charged with rape, but the Alianza asserted that a rape by a Chinese man was a killable offense, and a rape by a Mexican man was not. According to the logic of racialized sex, a Mexican man would not threaten the biological futurity of the nation even as the rape is the assault of a Mexican woman. This difference underscores the importance of race, reproduction, and women's bodies in the political formulation of mestizo-state nationalism. The lynchings of three Chinese men for rape were both an expression of racial alterity and an active creation of the terms by which a mestizo national identity was mapped. Lynching the men in front of their own store marked Chinese establishments as places of sexual perversion and warned the rest of the Chinese people in town, about twenty in all. For the mob the lynching functioned as a projection of their mestizo racial authenticity.

Mexicanization and antichinismo went hand in hand in the 1930s. The Alianza had formed several years earlier to combat Chinese Mexican unions. In 1932 the organization began to publish *Raza*, a weekly periodical designed to draw attention to the preponderance of businesses owned by "the Mongolian race" in Chihuahua.[18] With the help of other organizations, the focus on economic concerns shifted to a focus on the sexual deviance of Mexico's women and the degenerate effects of Chinese race mixture. In this way, Vito Aguirre, Alianza president and *Raza* publisher, shaped the local character of Mexicanization while also racializing the broader public sphere. Conforming to expectations in the revolution's racial contract, Aguirre also become a major recipient of ejido lands in 1937.[19] Aguirre and the Alianza continued to pressure the government to revoke business licenses Chinese people held and to expel them from the country as late as 1938.[20] The Villa Aldama lynchings help illustrate how anti-Chinese violence was irrevocably linked to the making of mestizo subjects or citizens of the Mexican state.

The president's and governor's choices to encrypt the telegrams about Villa Aldama lynchings further expose the tender politics of mestizo nationalism. The use of encryption signaled the sensitive nature of the information and suggested that issues of popular national racial identity were delicate political matters. The governor took action to bring martial order to Aldama so the violence did not escalate; however, the meager measures were not about protecting Chinese people but about controlling violence without being seen as restricting or punishing the activities of racial nationalism. In his cryptic response to the governor, Rodríguez gave lip service to the constitutional rights guaranteed to the Chinese people and warned the governor to maintain control lest the state become another example of the rogue expulsions in Sonora and Sinaloa. Rodríguez would not publically discourage or punish the lynching, as President Calles might have in the 1920s. Yet, for Rodríguez, only the state had legitimate authority to carry out anti-Chinese measures. According to this racial logic, the lynchings at Villa Aldama only fulfilled half of the government's guarantee to remove racial threats. When the state practiced antichinismo, the result was not just Chinese expulsion but conscription of mestizo citizens or subjects.

Governing through Race

Under Rodríguez's administration, the federal government enrolled more rural citizens and became more integral to their lives than any previous administration. His administration helped shift the idea of agrarian reform to a procedure of active recruitment and institutional enlistment. Repatriated workers, internally displaced farmers, and landless peasants were political liabilities the Great Depression spawned. Their political demands for ejido land, colonization rights, and restitution of property conflicted with the aims of a centralized administration of the economy. Rodríguez's administration took advantage of the vulnerable state of these workers and families by using them as labor for his program of self-colonization. A major project within his program was the use of repatriated Mexican workers from the United States to oust the Chinese agricultural associations of Mexicali, associations that, according to Rodríguez, "constitute[d] a dangerous and absurd dismembering of national territory."[21]

Antichinistas were sprinkled throughout Rodríguez's administration. For several months in the autumn of 1932, Alejandro Lacy Jr. led an official Partido Nacional Revolucionario (PNR) propaganda campaign to advertise the nation's racial strength through sports. He and pro-raza affiliates moved to assemble municipal pro-raza athletic pageants with a PNR-sponsored grand spectacle in Mexico City. The athletic parades sought to "fortify the body and discipline the spirit for the racial improvement of our citizens."[22] Accompanying the invitations to the PNR's pro-raza athletic events were pleas for states to adopt anti-Chinese policies. Lacy's five years of running antichinista campaigns and courting high-ranking allies earned him the role of lead publicist for the PNR. As the party's publicist, he was charged with creating its public image and communicating its vision for the nation. Lacy's position in the PNR infrastructure reflects the instrumental value that many saw in antichinismo as an ideology of the state and serves as an illustration of one way that antichinista activists achieved greater influence within the state apparatus. Lacy's choice of athletic demonstrations used the themes of education, physical fitness, and cooperation in sports as allegories for statism, discipline, morality, and subjection to an administrative regime of racial amalgamation and improvement.[23] The promotion and institutionalization of sports in Mexican popular culture were ways that antichinistas helped give rise to a mestizo racial formation.[24]

The scope of antichinista influence went beyond a regional program of anti-Chinese self-colonization in Baja California. Antichinismo continued to shape policy debates in the PNR and national congress, from schools and sex education to agrarian reform and the redefinition of nationality. These issues took center stage in June in Queretaro at the PNR's 1933 convention, a major political event that drew delegates from every state of the republic. The most important outcome was the first party-backed policy agenda for the next presidential administration. The policy agenda, el Plan Sexenal (Six-Year Plan), covered the six years of a president's term in office. The CEN described the plan as the definitive political break with old traditions. The PNR discarded abstract statements in favor of clearly defined laws. This policy defined subsequent administrations and preserved the legacy of antichinismo for years.

The convention's second session discussed the articles of the Proyecto Plan de Sexenal (Proposal for the Six-Year Plan). Discussion of the party's policy agenda turned on every part of government action, from foreign relations to agrarian development. While some issues were more contested than others, the area of *gobernación*, or the interior ministry, perhaps the most central to the articulation of executive authority and the administrative logic of state sovereignty, evoked no debate—a surprising political turn given the multiple sovereignties of the revolution and its competing nationalisms. The Campaña Nacionalista and widespread consensus on the need for discipline and a state-directed mestizaje had laid vital groundwork for widespread agreement on such measures. Agreement was unanimous at the convention about the necessity of containing the revolution within the legal nature of institutions "so that legislation and all acts of public power be translated into the correct situations."[25] This common articulation of modern state power was expressed in Mexico by the eugenicists' conception of racial administration.

The convention's proceedings reported, "It is not enough that there is good administration of justice, but the government has the obligation to establish a moral standard and direct collective defense against certain social evils and to that end the government will be dictated by general principles of prevention and social prophylaxis."[26] The Ministry of the Interior was not merely an administrative logic of the state; it was a state logic of racial nationalism. This articulation of state logic illustrates again the critical intersection of race, sex, and economy. The focus on race and sex was thought to be a pragmatic guide to harnessing the bio-economic power of the population. The convention adopted measures to adjudicate delinquent youth, curb prostitution and alcoholism, discipline women's sexuality, and provide moral training for the working class. The final point of articulation was concerned with immigration and the correct "management and distribution" of the national population. The PNR outlined preferences for certain foreigners, agricultural functionaries, and those with technical expertise. Rodríguez's program of self-colonization and the PNR consensus on the Ministry of the Interior demonstrated a striking similarity to the Porfirian proposal for self-colonization nearly thirty years earlier. In this instance, the cultural sensibility of state sovereignty was captured by a conviction of the economic potential of mestizo racial futurity. The biopolitical designs of the postrevolutionary racial state connected the discipline of women within peasant and indigenous communities with the dismantling of Chinese communities.

The most contested subject was education. Debate on education ranged from the need for a socialist educational model to the lack of funding for rural schools to the insistence that rural schools were the most important mandate of the revolution. Yet, there was agreement that "where there are no rural schools, there is no revolution." The political class had intended for schools to embody "multiple vigilances" from the government to the family. However, the most applauded interjection in the education debate came from Ezequiel Padilla when he argued that rural schools have no use for "Agemenón and Aquiles, or the fine adventure of Ulysses in the Odyssey. . . . What we need is the school to prepare men to know the secrets of the cultivation of land; that they can live the life of a carpenter, a blacksmith, a mason or a useful trade for a practical life."[27] His speech reflected popular ideas about the disciplinary function of rural schools and provides a useful point of comparison for Rodríguez's self-colonization program. Padilla's notion that technical-skill training provided the necessary knowledge for industrial-agricultural production presumes that ejido donations in a self-colonization program constitute a regime of self-discipline. In other words, self-colonization sought to make the ejido the master of peasants, not the patron or the local agrarian commission. The legal status of ejidos as state-donated land transformed beneficiaries into guardians of the political order that guaranteed their titles. The ejido introduced both economic discipline and sociopolitical discipline since applicants applied for ejido donations as collectives. If the cohesion of rural communities fell apart, the applicants risked losing their ejido title. The rationale for technical training was that it would not only increase the skills of Mexican farmers but train them to respond to market pressures through agro-economic techniques. A key economic tool that accompanied mass ejido distributions was agricultural loans. Elites thought that once indebted to the agricultural bank, farmers would independently make decisions appropriate for commodity and financial markets. Indigenous and peasant farming populations possessed little experience with the economic abstraction of credit, yet they would, nevertheless, become subject to the nested consequences of agricultural loans and global commodity circulation.[28] Self-colonization experimented with citizenship and racial rule on an unprecedented scale. Rodríguez's administration continued to push aggressive new reforms so that the Mexican state apparatus would be completely changed by his brief occupation of the presidency.

Defining Racial Rule

After the PNR convention, in the fall of 1933 Rodríguez delivered his state of the union to the national congress. The address emphasized "the establishment of an agrarian class as the promise and guarantee of stability and strength for the nation," yet for him this agrarian class was not represented by the enfranchisement of the rural masses but their conscription into state institutions that organized and disciplined their bio-economic potential. Rodríguez reversed Calles's previous model of minimalist ejido donations and quickened the pace of allocation and recruitment. This model of governance, combined with the disciplinary vision of education, answered popular demands for agrarian reform by offering an agrarian citizenship circumscribed by juridical limitations and the necessities of agrarian modes of production. Rodríguez expanded eligibility criteria and access to ejido application procedures, although granting ejidos to more people would not by itself expand production, realize rural modernity, or enact a virtuous racial order. To achieve these ends, Rodríguez pitched a platform of legislative reforms and enlisted the government's civil engineers and the national military to guide rural development through efforts to organize, in his words, the national "intensification of labor."[29]

The scope of Rodríguez's state of the union reflected the swift movement of the first months of his administration, which was made possible by PNR's refined political agenda, the BNR's power in the national congress, and the popularity of antichinismo as a political logic of ethical governance and racial rule. What stands out most about his address is the emphasis on the expansion of institutions designed to act upon individuals as racial subjects. For example, under his administration, the number of *escuelas centrales agrícolas* (central agricultural schools) was doubled through the creation of more than seventy-five-hundred rural schools and the training of more than 10,300 "dedicated teachers with true care for the important work of elevating the culture of Indians and mestizos who live in the rural zones." In addition, sports were supported to provide for the physical improvement and discipline of the "Indian races" through the creation of an Oficina de Educacion Fisica (physical-education office), and in 1932 the bureau boasted enrollments of more than 12,500 children in the Distrito Federal (Mexico City, the federal district).[30] To appreciate the kind of change being implemented during Rodríguez's administration, we must understand the juridical redefinition of state power as a fascist mestizo state.

This juridical redefinition can be found in the congressional debate on Rodríguez's legislative agenda. On November 16, 1933, the national congress continued debate on amendments to the constitution's article 4, which guaranteed rights to health for all men, women, and children. The debate was not led by concern over access to health services or adequate nutrition; it was led by antichinistas concerned with the legal constructions of a national race. The benevolent ideal behind a constitutional guarantee for health and well-being was used to expand the articulation of a national mestizo race: national health became a platform for racial formation. The debate considered information about nutritional diets and the needs of the Huasteco people displaced from a hurricane in Veracruz, but it also considered state governors' power to act upon the guarantees stimulated in article 4—particularly, those actions the Sonoran governor took to expel Chinese residents. This debate was punctuated by a familiar cadre of antichinistas, including the BNR; the Liga Mexicana Antichina of Tapachula, Chiapas; the murderous Alianza Nacionalista Chihuahuense; and Sinaloa's Comité Nacionalista Pro-Raza, that defined national welfare through antichinismo. Rather than argue for a pointed constitutional amendment to block Chinese immigration, antichinista legislative activism sought to authorize stronger state action to create the conditions where a national race might be cultivated, cared for, and subjected to improvement.[31] The continued presence of these groups in the formal public sphere illustrates how anti-Chinese violence was predicated on social advocacy for the protection of women and children. This line of reasoning put racial policing at the heart of a constitutional right to health.

An often-forgotten aspect of Rodríguez's administration is his initiation of massive agrarian reforms. He and his secretary of education, Narciso Bassols, initiated a major amendment that introduced the eligibility of hacienda laborers to apply for ejido lands. To quicken the process of distribution, Rodríguez created an independent agrarian department that removed judicial review, articulated a new agrarian code, and created powers to allocate new lands, making a hundred million acres available for distribution. The agrarian department also became a way to rectify the national census and determine eligibility for ejido lands. These reforms gradually trickled down to the local agrarian commissions, which administered donations, and states with high concentrations of Chinese farmers were targeted for Mexicanization. Initially, the agrarian department's reforms focused on Baja California, Coahuila, Guerrero, Jalisco, Lake of Texcoco, Nayarit, Sonora, and Tamaulipas. However, the larger effect was a popular political investment in the government to award land. This change to the terms of agrarian citizenship and the nature of membership in the postrevolutionary racial state was also represented in a major reform to the juridical redefinition of nationality.

In January 1934 the national congress made sweeping changes to the Law of Nationality and Naturalization with several important alterations to the criteria of race, gender, sexuality, ethnicity, and indigeneity in national identification. The most important change was in Mexican women's relationships with foreign-born men and emphasized jus sanguinis rather than external notions of purity. Instead of punishing women who married outside of Mexican nationality, the state sought to incorporate them in order to include them in the state's vigilance. This change was ultimately motivated by the conception of racial futurity through female biopower, a juridical form that understood women as progenitors of nationality.[32] To make this legal category pragmatic, the state created a third form of recognition beyond jus soli and jus sanguinis. Jus domicili was introduced as a juridical concept that emphasized individuals' participation in a home rather than their civil or biological relations. The legal vagueness of what constituted a home relied upon heterosexual and patriarchal norms for the family unit even as it recognized complexity. The law accommodated the redefinition of belonging so that the state could more fully subject society to its sovereign power to intervene and instruct, not just to exclude. This juridical reform theorized the home as the site of important nutritional, behavioral, and sexual decisions—decisions that eugenicists thought would influence racial outcomes. The state's effort to redefine nationalism reflected larger aims to erect government institutions across the spectrum of social life. This law identified the home as the primary site of biological and social reproduction of labor, and control over the definition of home and its inhabitants became an instrument of settlement and self-colonization. The state governments of Baja California Norte, Hidalgo, Oaxaca, Puebla, Sinaloa, and Sonora were the first to use the new legislation. These states were active in the antichinista campaigns of the 1920s and were already familiar with the racialized regulation of sex and domestic space.

The more that officials were driven by racial polemics of ethical governance and understood the ideological function of racial nationalism, the more that sex and sexual education became an explicit concern. While medical professionals were aware of sex education's potential to address wide-ranging social problems, antichinistas introduced the political urgency of government attention to sex and mestizaje as a national concern. In 1934 Bassols announced plans for sweeping education reform that included a robust sex-education program to introduce eugenics in primary school. The announcement set off a firestorm of controversy, leading to the appointment of a congressional commission to evaluate Bassols's proposal. The PNR leadership agreed with Bassols that the purpose of education was to "mold the spirit and mind" of the masses, but an obsession with mestizaje sex became the central node around which race and the economy intersected. One supporter of the reform, in an *El Nacional* editorial, "The Ethics of Sex Education," questions whether it was better for children to lose their innocence or suffer the societal denigration of their uneducated decisions.[33] Meanwhile, detractors cited the perversity of teaching sex instruction to children, even when Bassols's proposal said that sex education did not conflict with religious dogma.[34] The congressional commission supported Bassols's proposal, but the controversy ended his career in the department.

The Ministry of Education and the National Medical Academy rushed to Bassols's defense, stating the government's responsibility to implement a program of sexual hygiene to achieve the greatest "bio-economic" potential from the population. Alfonso Pruneda, a prominent public-health specialist, issued a medical endorsement of the nation's sex-education curriculum in a 1935 edition of the *Gaceta Medica de Mexico*. He reasoned that for a robust racial policy of state-disciplined mestizaje to be effective, the government must conduct regular surveys to ascertain the "Mexican sexual reality." Although the federal sex-education program stalled politically, some states were motivated to implement such a program. That Baja California Norte was among the first to convene education experts to discuss the introduction of sex education in the territory's secondary schools reflects the importance that officials gave to sexual discipline in the realization of a virtuous mestizo racial order—particularly in a region heavily populated by racial "degenerates."[35]

Rodríguez failed to change Baja California as he wished during his brief administration; however, his successor, the populist candidate General Lazaro Cárdenas from Michoacán, who was handpicked by Calles, did fulfill the promise of racial transformation. Cárdenas did much more, but wrestling with this complicated figure's history is beyond the scope of this book. However, three points of his policies relevant here are: first, much of the bureaucratic structure that Cárdenas used to broaden the ejido system was developed under the aegis of his predecessor Rodríguez. Second, even as Cárdenas distanced Calles from power and remade the PNR into a new political party, the Partido de la Revolución Mexicana, the ruling ideology became more refined and the racial contract more entrenched. Third, Cárdenas's expansion of the agrarian program of ejido distribution was a part of the national colonization tradition and marks the most successful period of self-colonization, not for its economic productivity but for the number of people it institutionalized.[36] Cárdenas became president in 1934 and has overshadowed Rodríguez's influence on reconstruction. Cárdenas's actions in Baja California further demonstrate the important link between antichinismo and agrarian reform in Mexico's racial contract. I interpret ejido donations not as the rewards of activism but as enlistment into state dependency. Table 2 shows the growth of ejido donations from the Díaz to the Cárdenas administrations.

In December 1935 Cárdenas moved the national congress to reform the migration law to be inclusive of the entire population. He argued, "It is essential to provide the Department of Population the statutory power to regulate, plan and implement a population policy that is beneficial for the country, especially for the peasant and working classes who most directly suffer the consequences of abandonment to the natural contingencies of the poor

TABLE 2. Ejido donations, 1894–1940

Years	Administration	Land (hectares)	Beneficiaries
1894–1900	Díaz	66,478	5,822
1901–9	Díaz	114,180	8,418
1917–20	Carranza	132,639	59,846
1920	De La Huerta	33,695	17,355
1920–24	Obregón	971,627	158,204
1924–28	Calles	3,088,071	302,432
1928–30	Portes Gil	1,173,118	155,826
1930–32	Ortiz Rubio	1,468,745	84,009
1932–34	Rodríguez	798,982	161,327
1934–40	Cárdenas	20,074,704	771,640

Sources: Lazcano Armienta, *La política agraria*; Secretaría de Desarrollo Agrario, "Las transformaciones."

distribution of the population, the imbalance between economic means and population density, and the competition that arises between small industries, commerce and manual labor."[37] On New Year's Eve the national congress began to discuss a vote on the Ley General de Población (General Law of Population) and described it as an "urgent and obvious . . . necessity to improve the demographic laws."[38] The policy was framed as a means to address the "fundamental demographic problems" of the nation. It proposed to "increase the population, provide rational distribution within the territory, advance ethnic fusion of the nation's groups, increase national race-mixing through assimilation of foreign elements, protect nationals when they migrate, prepare Indians through physical, economic, and social improvement from a demographic point of view, protect the national race, and conserve and improve the species."[39] This law introduced broad new powers to index, monitor, manipulate, and instruct the republic's people according to ideas about health, fitness, biology, economic necessity, indigencity, and race. The broad scope of the law encompassed demographics, economics, education, health, and recreation to build the state's capacity to instill in the existing population the ideal agent of revolutionary change—the state-disciplined mestizo.

Making Mestizo Hegemony in Baja California

In the 1930s, the Comité Ejecutivo Antichino in Mexicali, Baja California, began to court support for the expulsion of the Chinese colony, pulling together labor unions, middle-class merchants, and supportive state legislators.[40] At the end of Rodríguez's term in 1934, union demands across the country spiked, especially in Baja California. The president feared that Baja California would suffer the same fate as Sonora if the anti-Chinese campaigns could not be satisfied with rapid reform. Fearing that the labor unions could no longer be controlled through the Council of Conciliation and Arbitration, the president ordered the governor to protect Chinese business operations from union activity.[41] Rodríguez did not want to risk the certain collapse of the region's economy if the Chinese citizens were removed, nor could he risk the political backlash for protecting the so-called yellow octopus.[42] Furthermore, the subsidies to small Mexican businesses came from taxes and fees collected from Chinese businesses. For all the debate and anguish over engineered policy and the administrative instruments of racial governance, their implementation proved difficult, at best. However, these measures did succeed in shifting public priorities to institutional growth and in framing public problems as the state's responsibility to provide for a mestizo racial well-being.

Anti-Chinese politics supported ideological elements of the regime, but the activists' interests frequently conflicted with the federal self-colonization scheme. Antichinistas in Baja California and Coahuila renewed petitions for the federal expulsion of Chinese people in the area, asking the government to follow through with the Campaña Nacionalista.[43] Both petitions failed to produce evictions but provoked local violence and harassment. The escalation of violence in the north motivated leaders from the Chinese communities in Ensenada, Mexicali, San Diego, and Tijuana to discuss their future in the region.[44] In the ensuing weeks, many Chinese storeowners and residents in Ensenada fled under cover of night to Mexicali and farther south to the states of Guanajuato, Jalisco, and Michoacán.[45] Mexicali's antichinistas were emboldened to intensify their local propaganda campaigns and posted public notices condemning the Chinese people and praising the Mexican people who followed their convictions to drive the Chinese residents out. The antichinistas cited the earlier success in Sonora, the El Monte agricultural workers in California, and an earlier campaign to expel black people from Mexicali.[46] Frustrated by the lack of work, the persistence of Chinese communities, and dithering government action, antichinistas forced new municipal regulations targeting Chinese residents and sought more direct collaboration with the CROM and PNR members. In an astute political gesture, Cárdenas met with the chief organizers of the nationalist leagues and CROM, promising action from his administration to settle tempers. Two months before his inauguration, Cárdenas came to an agreement with the anti-Chinese campaign leaders in Mexicali and the Sonora governor, promising support for the Chinese expulsion.[47]

At the outset of Cárdenas's administration, it appeared that Rodríguez's plan for self-colonization had become a Mexico City consensus. The year following his inauguration, Cárdenas gave a public address about the problem of the federal territories, which outlined his administration's plans to incorporate the territories of Baja California and Quintana Roo in order to "fight against isolation . . . to maintain this race of people, its cultural unity and economic relations."[48] The central outcome for this pledge was the New Project for Colonization of Landholdings of the Colorado River Land Company, the realization of four years' planning for the region's transition through aggressive self-colonization and subjugation of thousands of Chinese people.[49] The renegotiation of the colonization contract was the first legally binding agreement barring the Chinese people from leasing land from the CRLC. The contract prohibited any new leases to non-Mexican colonists, implicitly excluding Chinese people who had become naturalized.[50] To carry out these reforms, Cárdenas appointed General Gildardo Magaña (a decorated Conventionist who had served as Emiliano Zapata's secretary) as territorial governor.[51] In preparation for the colonization plan, Magaña set an aggressive quota for Mexican settlement in Mexicali: three repatriated Mexicans for every Chinese resident. The Mexican state's channeling of racial populism relied on the coordinated involvement of Mexican unions on both sides of the border and institutional methods of directing the settlement of a migrant citizenry.

Magaña's policy was a deliberate measure to escalate public hostility against the Chinese population.[52] In 1936 he repatriated from California three thousand Mexican workers to occupy new leases on CRLC lands.[53] In this shortsighted effort to inflate the Mexican resident population in Mexicali, the administration created volatile political conditions that were not easily contained by population law or company-sanctioned unions. As the Mexicali population swelled with repatriates, colonists, and agrarians, their interests began to diverge into two general camps: the colonists and the agrarians. These divisions illustrate the contentious nature of "genuine Mexican colonization" and widespread dissatisfaction with industrial agriculture, in general. Most of the repatriated people were agrarians. On the one hand, the colonists were already leasing farmlands and desired the security of private-property rights. On the other hand, the agrarians, who were much poorer, favored government-sponsored entitlements to ejidos.[54] In this regard, the Cárdenas administration was made into an enemy of both groups. Both believed that the federal government was either going to displace current Mexican settlements or deny poor farmers the benefits of agrarian reform.[55] This frustration led to several agrarian protests and revolts, all of which received harsh government repression from Magaña. Further complicating the self-colonization scheme, the CROM offered support to the colonists and threatened a general strike if they were displaced from their land. These contentious politics illustrate why the political class was attracted to fascism as a political philosophy and as a vision of the relationship between people and the state.

In an effort to control the political heat, Cárdenas terminated CRLC's colonization contract and forced it to sell its land directly to the Mexican government. The announcement produced a violent rampage by agrarians across the valley, and the rush to resolve the colonist-agrarian conflict reached a tipping point in January 1937. At the end of the month, Chinese farmers were caught off guard when, without provocation, hundreds of armed agrarians ransacked them. The governor issued a military proclamation prohibiting squatting and "unauthorized" acquisitions of Mexican lands, claiming that such actions went against the institutionalized nature of the Mexican revolution.[56] While there are few written records of the assault's immediate aftermath, it is likely that many Chinese people fled to Tijuana, and others took refuge in Mexicali's urban core. However, the popular belief spread that Mexican farmers had successfully driven out the Chinese people from the rich, irrigated desert colony. In the first two months of the official expropriation, forty ejidos were created with forty-eight hundred people covering more than two hundred thousand acres.[57] Raids on Chinese farming operations continued throughout the year; although physical violence was a certain outcome of the attacks, no deaths were reported.[58] In November, in a list of thirty-one demands petitioning reforms to the ejido system, Mexicali's Union of Agrarian Communities included the expulsion of the remaining Chinese people. Local anti-Chinese CROM members patrolled the countryside to agitate further for the agrarians' rural entitlements.[59] In October 1938 the last Chinese-operated cotton farm was turned over to Mexican hands; Rancho Tres de Lee was transformed into ejido Quintana Roo.[60] With this final eviction, the Chinese farmers were removed from Baja California agriculture. This event is famously known in Mexico as El Asalto a las Tierras because it was perceived that the Cárdenas administration was forced to perform the public spectacle of national expropriation because of spontaneous collective action.

The Chinese community in Mexicali, wedged in by exclusion from the United States, hostilities from Mexicans, and civil war in China, had few alternatives. Their search for a new life and belonging in Mexico had collided with the limits of the postrevolutionary racial order. In the months after El Asalto, the CROM issued a general demand that all foreigners leave Mexicali within sixty days.[61] Bands of organized workers systematically targeted Chinese stores, forcing each one to close down.[62] The CROM posted flyers all over Mexicali, blaming the Chinese people for poor economic conditions and using such racial metaphors as "these Asiatics have been a yellow octopus that sucks the blood of the Mexican people." The CROM flyer cited a familiar chronology of national racial ideology, starting with the Torreón massacre, the more recent expulsion of Chinese people from the state of Sonora, and the racial pride of Mexican workers in the United States. This antichinista historical imagination established the basis of mestizo racial ideology and political power in Baja California. The CROM further threatened to humiliate anyone who did not support the cause by calling them a "Chinese Mexican"—a race traitor.[63]

This exclusion of Chinese from elite notions of "genuine Mexican colonization" created two illuminating contradictions. First, state officials and political elites had to contend with scrutiny from numerous political factions for their revolutionary authenticity. Second, the legitimacy of the benefits of industrial capitalism had to fall within the rubric of a nationalist ideology.[64] The governmental efforts to shift the demographic balance of the region illustrate their adherence to the prescriptive racial limits of a nationalist ideology, even to the exclusion of the reality of economic conditions and the transnational relations of production. The perceived success of state intervention and the looming expropriation of CRLC lands, despite the deepening of the economic depression, show how valuable such racial motivations were for garnering political legitimacy. For all the statistical data, centralized governance, and new bureaucratic powers, the centrality of racial administration led to a myopic consideration of economic consequences and privileged symbolic objectives.

State-directed national colonization and popular protest for agrarian reform became key expressions of the revolution's racial contract. El Asalto and the new project for colonization plunged the entire region into a deeper economic depression and further strengthened the dependence on American corporate agribusiness. Ejido donations were not only used to enact the racial replacement of Chinese residents but were also used to negotiate new terms with rebellious Indian people. That same year as El Asalto, in neighboring Sonora, the state with the longest-running Indian rebellion against the Mexican republic, granted 2,159 agrarians 108,000 acres of the Yaqui valley Indian land and carved out a 1.2 million acre Yaqui reservation and ejido lands.[65]

When Manuel Gamio returned to Mexico, he became department head of the population office. He had written in 1935 that the lack of statistical knowledge about the Mexican population made federal policy ineffective and "delayed the evolution of the mestizo."[66] In 1939, as population department head, he issued orders to all of the republic's governors to gather vital demographic information to aid his administration of the General Population Law and the registry of foreigners to "more effectively direct workers."[67]

In anticipation of the population growth resulting from the colonization initiative, Cárdenas's cabinet recognized the need to expand the knowledge of the population and build the capacity to instruct them. In June, Cárdenas charged the secretary of agriculture and development to conduct "ethnodemographic" studies in hopes of devising appropriate means to enhance the bioeconomic potential of workers.[68] In September, Baja California implemented a vast expansion of the school system to ensure that the pedagogical apparatus of the state could instruct labor and influence rural sexualities. The new schools would teach federally approved curriculum for both rural and urban schools, provide teacher preparation, and create a school of eugenic hygiene.[69] Competing class interests and the desperation of displaced and repatriated workers diffused the racial designs of the state, but the tacit identification with the state as a mestizo subject remained.

Historian José Jorge Gómez Izquierdo and Guy Rozat Dupeyron have characterized Mexican racism during reconstruction as the political and cultural formation of nationalist ideals by the state, as part of an unavoidable necessity to invent a collective identity of unity and harmony, and as an indication of the consolidation of power by the national state.[70] The national ideology of mestizo identity as a mixed-race population certainly fulfilled a political need to project unity and harmony, but this characterization does not explain why such a racial project became popular and politically successful. An Asian Americanist critique of racial citizenship underscores the process by which discourses of Asian-ness assisted in the definition of a state-disciplined mestizo nation. These articulations of anti-Chinese politics converted Chinese death, dispossession, and displacement into political currency. Antichinismo is historically significant because it helped show that mestizo nationalism was not simply an oppositional alternative or a common denominator across indigenous and peasant regional cultures but that the state's ideological conditioning served to replace ethnic difference and indigeneity with a racial project of state loyalty. Tracing the evolution of the Chinese racial form from animals to corpses to defilers illustrates the dynamic notions of race during the reconstruction of the revolutionary state. The shifts in Chinese racialization illustrate its functional relationship to the state's broader Indian racial projects and attempts by elites to create legitimacy and expand state authority.

This book used an Asian Americanist critique of racial citizenship to illustrate the role that antichinismo played in the articulation of the postrevolutionary state and influence on the formation of mestizo national identity. The revolution's racial contract was articulated through the relationship between antichinismo and the domination of peasant and indigenous populations. Drawing from a legal analysis of the sovereign claim to state authority made in the 1917 constitution, the ways that anti-Chinese violence became a popular means of interpreting the social rights mandate of the revolutionary order were traced. Race was both a foundational philosophy of the constitution's authority, defining the good of the Indian population, and the means of reproducing sovereignty, through the care, discipline, and improvement of Indian people and peasants as mestizos. Although the figure of the Chinese people has been erased from the Mexican historical imagination, this national mythology, nevertheless, remains structured by the effects of antichinismo.

Notes

Introduction: Finding Mexico's Chinese, Encountering the Mestizo State

All translations are by the author, unless otherwise noted.

1. Wu, "Where Are You Really From?" 14; Ngai, *Impossible Subjects*.

2. "Telegram Received from Consul at Piedras Negras to Secretary of State, December 7, 1916," and "Telegram from Holis to Secretary of State, December 8, 1916," RG 59 312.93/162, Chinese Problem in Mexico, General Records of the U.S. Department of State, University of Arizona Main Library, Tucson (hereinafter referred to as Chinese Problem).

3. "Trail of Blood Follows Villa's Path in Parral," *Prescott (AZ) Journal Miner*, November 19, 1916, 1. Other foreigners included Americans, Germans, Jews, French, and Arabs. Although the newspaper under-reports the number of deaths, Chinese residents of Mexico were the most numerous foreign group and sustained the most casualties.

4. Raul Argudin, "El partido de las mentiras," *El Estado de Veracruz*, August 11, 1912, 1–2.

5. Espinoza, *El Problema Chino*.

6. González Navarro, *El Porfiriato*.

7. Evelyne Sánchez, "Una ciudadania experimental: La creación de colonias rurales desde el Porfiriato hasta los años 1940," *Naveg@mérica* 3 (2009), http://revistas.um.es/navegamerica/article/view/74941.

8. Hernández, *Mexican American Colonization*, 25–65.

9. Historians of human rights frequently refer to the 1917 Mexican constitution as a key legal document that established legal obligations to meet fundamental needs. However, such legal histories must contend with the shifting terms of power on the ground, not just the eloquence of the printed word.

10. Lomnitz-Adler, *Deep Mexico, Silent Mexico*.

11. Guidotti-Hernández, *Unspeakable Violence*, 204–5.

12. Rodríguez quoted in Jones, *War Has Brought Peace*, 1.

13. González Navarro, *La Colonización en México*.

14. Covarrubias, *La Trascendencia Política*, 13.

15. Saxton, *Indispensable Enemy*; Daniels, *Politics of Prejudice;* Lowe, *Immigrant Acts*; Chang, *Pacific Connections*; Chuh, *Imagine Otherwise*. Lye, *America's Asia*; Jung, *Coolies and Cane*.

16. Appadurai, *Modernity at Large*.

17. Investigations into these migration streams have generated a rich field of research of which the most covered subject has been the coolie trade (Chinese and Indian indenture, primarily in Trinidad, Cuba, and Peru) of the nineteenth century.

18. Day, "Lost in Transnation"; Yu, "Global Migrants."

19. Lee, "Orientalisms."

20. Lomnitz-Adler, *Modernidad indiana*, 12.

21. Hu-DeHart, "Immigrants to a developing society."

22. Puig Casauranc, *La cosheca y la siembra*.

23. Lipsitz, *Possessive Investment;* Quijano, "Coloniality of Power."

24. Sue, *Land of the Cosmic Race*.

25. Hernández, *Racial Subordination*.

26. See Loveman, *National Colors* (documents the development of this political condition in a comparative history of racial categories across Latin American national census programs).

27. Omi and Winant, *Racial Formation*; *Goldberg, Racial State*.

28. Ristow, "From Repression to Incorporation."

29. Habermas, Lennox, and Lennox, "Public Sphere."

30. Mills, *Racial Contract*.

31. Castellanos Guerrero, *Imágenes*; Castellanos Guerrero and Sandoval, *Nación, racismo, e identidad*.

32. Moreno Figueroa, "Distributed intensities."

33. Omi and Winant, *Racial Formation*.

Chapter 1. The Politics of Chinese Immigration in the Era of Mexican National Colonization

1. Manuel Zapata Vera, "Emigracion China," *El Monitor Republicano* (Mexico City), April 5, 1882, 1–2, http://www.hndm.unam.mx/index.php/es/.

2. Saxton, *Indispensable Enemy*.

3. Fitzgerald and Cook-Martín, *Culling the Masses*.

4. Basch, Glick-Schiller, and Szanton Blanc, *Nations Unbound*.

5. Vinson, "Racial Profile"; Vincent, "Blacks Who Freed Mexico."

6. "Esterior," *El Monitor Constitucional* (Mexico City), October 5, 1845, 1.

7. Hing, *Defining America*.

8. Craib, *Chinese Immigrants*; R. C. Romero, *Chinese in Mexico*.

9. Anderson, *Imagined Communities*.

10. Hale, *Transformation of Liberalism*.

11. For more information about Spanish colonial racial hatred, docility, and erasure, see Robins, *Native Insurgencies and the Genocidal Impulse*; Bennett, *Colonial Blackness*; Seijas, *Asian Slaves in Colonial Mexico*.

12. African Mexicans consisted of mostly a mix of *pardo* (Indian and African) and *mulatto* (European and African). Vinson and Restall, *Black Mexico*, 99.

13. Bennett, *Colonial Blackness*; Sue, *Land of the Cosmic Race*.

14. The indigeneity was due to African persons' integration into indigenous cultures, participation in independence from Spain, and subsequent recognition by the republic.

15. Azcárate y Lezama and Cháve, *Un Programa de Política Internacional*, 3.

16. Santiago, *Jar of Severed Hands*, 14–15.

17. Azcárate y Lezama and Cháve, *Un Programa de Política Internacional*, 13.

18. González Navarro, *La Colonización en México*.

19. Benjamin and Wasserman, *Provinces of the Revolution*; Vaughan, "Cultural Approaches."

20. Lomnitz-Adler, *Deep Mexico, Silent Mexico*.

21. Smith, *Nationalism*; Tilly, "Does Modernization Breed Revolution?"; Giddens, *Contemporary Critique*, 219.

22. Anderson, *Imagined Communities*.

23. Lomnitz-Adler, "Anti-Semitism," 2, 23.

24. Knight, *Mexican Revolution*, 1:3.

25. Annino, "Ciudadanía 'versus' Gobernabilidad Republicana"; Lomnitz-Adler, *Deep Mexico, Silent Mexico*.

26. Kourí, *Pueblo Divided*.

27. Hale, *Transformation of Liberalism*.

28. Borah, "Race and Class in Mexico," 341.

29. Hale, *Transformation of Liberalism*, 260.

30. Redfield, "Indian in Mexico," 138.

31. Hernández, *Racial Subordination*; Quijano, "Coloniality of Power."

32. See Slack, "Chino in New Spain"; Seijas, *Asian Slaves in Colonial Mexico*.

33. Alonso, *Thread of Blood*.

34. "Colonización Nacional," *La Lima de Vulcano* (Mexico City), May 26, 1836, 4.

35. De la Maza, *Código de Colonización*, 368.

36. Vance and Clagett, *Guide to the Law*.

37. Lafragua, *Memoria Que en Cumplimiento*, 108–9, original emphasis.

38. Utley, *Frontiersmen in Blue*.

39. Chan, *This Bittersweet Soil*.

40. "Parte Oficial," *Periódico Oficial del Estado de Yucatán*, August 31, 1857, 1.

41. Falcón, "Force and the Search for Consent."

42. "Maximilian, Emperor of Mexico," in *Estatutos de la Compañía de Colonización Asiatica* (Mexico City: J. M. Lara, 1866), Sterling Library, Yale University.

43. Cervera, *La Gloria de La Raza*, 43–45.

44. Hu-DeHart, *Yaqui Resistance*.

45. De la Maza, *Código de Colonización*, 5.

46. Ruiz Medrano, *Mexico's Indigenous Communities*.

47. Knowlton and Orensanz, "El ejido mexicano."

48. González Navarro, *El Porfiriato*, 194.

49. González Navarro, *La Colonización*.

50. Granados, "Inmigración de una 'raza prohibida.'"

51. Alfaro-Velcamp, *So Far from Allah*, 134.

52. Hale, *Transformation of Liberalism*, 21–23.

53. M. Romero, *Geographical and Statistical Notes*.

54. Hale, *Transformation of Liberalism*, 78.

55. Ibid.

56. E. Rodríguez, *Manual de Física General*, 15.

57. Justo Sierra quoted in González Navarro, *El Porfiriato*, 163.

58. Northrup, *Indentured Labor*, 109–12.

59. Jenkins, *Coolie*.

60. Yun, *Chinese Indentured Laborers*; Moon-Ho, *Coolies and Cane*.

61. See also Lee-Loy, "Chinese Are Preferred."

62. Peffer, *If They Don't*.

63. Bulnes, *Sobre el Hemisferio Norte*; Valdés Lakowsky, *Vinculaciones Sino-Mexicanas*, 87.

64. Lee, *At America's Gate*.

65. Ngai, *Impossible Subjects*.

66. Lee, *At America's Gate*.

67. Young, *Alien Nation*; McKeown, "Conceptualizing Chinese Diasporas"; Lee, *At America's Gate*; R. C. Romero, *Chinese in Mexico*.

68. Cott, "Mexican Diplomacy."

69. Young, *Alien Nation*.

70. Mexican Colonization and Land Law of 1883, chapter 2, article 5.

71. Ibid., chapter 3.

72. Craib, *Cartographic Mexico*.

73. Wilkie, "Primera reforma Agraria."

74. De la Maza, *Código de Colonización*, 1125.

75. M. Romero, *Geographical and Statistical Notes*, 212.

76. "Estados Unidos," *El Ferrocarril* (Mexico City), August 6, 1870, 2, http://www.hndm.unam.mx/index.php/es/.

77. "Cámara de Diputados," *La Nación* (Mexico City), May 11, 1886, 3, http://www.hndm.unam.mx/index.php/es/.

78. Holden, *Mexico*, 86.

79. Wilkie. "Primera reforma Agraria."

80. Ibid.

81. McBride, *Land Systems*, 175.

82. Kourí, "La invención."

Chapter 2. Motores de Sangre: They Do Not Think, or Assimilate, or Master

1. Richard Crawford, "Riot at Sea Brought 'Hell Ship' to San Diego Bay," *San Diego (CA) Union Tribune*, February 18, 2010, http://www.utsandiego.com/news/2010/feb/18/riot-sea-brought-hell-ship-san-diego-bay/; "Slave Ship," Star Collection, Special Col-

lections, Charles E. Young Library, University of California, Los Angeles (hereinafter referred to as Star Collection).

2. Hu-DeHart, "Immigrants to a Developing Society."

3. Young, *Alien Nation.*

4. Craib, *Chinese Immigrants*, 6.

5. Gardiner, "Early Diplomatic Relations"; Cott, "Mexican Diplomacy"; Valdés Lakowsky, *Vinculaciones sino-mexicanas.*

6. See Delgado, *Making the Chinese Mexican*, 35; R. C. Romero, *Chinese in Mexico*, 179.

7. Valdés Lakowsky, *Vinculaciones sino-mexicanas.*

8. Gonzalez Navarro, *La Colonización en México*, 23–24.

9. Much of what was exported from Mexico was shipped north via rail into the United States for reexport; developing ports and steamship lines also offered a way out from under U.S. dependence.

10. *Diario Oficial*, October 18, 1871, 3.

11. Alfred Bablot, "La Transformacion de Mexico: Colonizacion europea, asiatica, y africana," *El Federalista* (Mexico City), October 6, 1871, 1. For this article Bablot received a forceful critique from Jesus Casteñada in the pages of *El Siglo Diez y Nueve* (Mexico City), November 8, 1871.

12. *La Revista Universal* (Mexico City), May 30, 1874, 2.

13. *El Minero Mexicano* (Mexico City), November 12, 1874, 382; *El Minero Mexicano* (Mexico City), August 26, 1875, 240. For treatment of women as motores de sangre, see *La Patria* (Mexico City), May 24, 1883, 1.

14. "Exterior: Peru," *La Revista Universal* (Mexico City), September 7, 1873, 2.

15. Van Hoy, *Social History.*

16. Lee, *At America's Gate.*

17. Craib, *Chinese Immigrants*, 4. Article 27 of the company charter stipulated higher reimbursements for a "European immigrant" than for an "Asian worker," 75 and 35 pesos, respectively.

18. "From Malo to Whitehall," April 10, 1889, FO 50/546, Office of Foreign Affairs, British National Archives, Kew.

19. "From Edward Winyfield," April 18, 1889, FO 50/546, Office of Foreign Affairs, British National Archives, Kew.

20. David Midgley to Under Secretary of State for India, April 20, 1896, FO 50/546, Office of Foreign Affairs, British National Archives, Kew.

21. González Navarro, *La Colonización*, 81.

22. A. K. Corry, Mexican Consul in San Francisco to President Porfirio Díaz, 1886, Papeles de Porfirio Díaz, Instituto de Investigaciones Históricos, Universidad Autonóma de Baja California, Tijuana.

23. Cott, "Mexican Diplomacy"; Mandujano-López, "Transpacific Mexico." British scrutiny of Chinese departures stems primarily from the embarrassment revealed by the 1876 Cuba Commission Report that cites extreme abuses of contracted Chinese workers in the Spanish colony. *Cuba Commission Report.*

24. Woo Soo, Chinese Exclusion Act Case Files, 1922, 2295/3, RG 85, National Archives and Records Administration (NARA), Perris, California (formerly Laguna Niguel).

25. Gonzalez Navarro, *La Colonización*, 82.

26. *El Economista Mexicano, Semanario de Asuntos Económicos y Estadísticos* (Mexico City), 7, June 22, 1889, 242.

27. Ibid., emphasis added.

28. "Sir Pelham Warren v. the Owners and Parties Interested in the Str. *Maori King*," *North China Herald and Supreme Court and Consular Gazette* (Shanghai), January 17, 1908 (Shanghai: *North China Daily News and Herald*, 1908), 86:147–49. Two other Russian associates are named as James Markham Dow and Morris Ginsberg.

29. "Chinese Defy Orders," *Mexican Herald* (Mexico City), May 23, 1907, 3.

30. "Slave Ship," Star Collection.

31. "Sir Pelham Warren," 147–49.

32. Gilberto Valenzuela, "Charge of the Inspection of Immigration at Salina Cruz, 1919," Pacific Mail Steamship Company Papers, Huntington Library, San Marino, California (hereinafter referred to as Pacific Mail Papers).

33. *Memoria Presentado*, 195.

34. M. Romero, *Geographical and Statistical Notes*, 3. The completion of the Panama railway in 1855 gave support to the idea that the Tehuantepec railroad would be successful in attracting commerce.

35. González Navarro, *La Colonización*, 32.

36. "La Inmigración Asiatica," *El Siglo Diez y Nueve* (Mexico City), February 24, 1893, 1.

37. Van Hoy, *Social History*.

38. Ibid.

39. Ibid., 90, 127.

40. Valenzuela, "Charge," Pacific Mail Papers.

41. Cott, "Mexican Diplomacy." For On Wo Company details, see Delgado, *Making the Chinese Mexican*, 36.

42. *El Economista Mexicana* (Mexico City), August 1, 1903, 10.

43. Williams, *Isthmus*. See also Van Hoy, *Social History*, for many other such examples.

44. Craib, *Chinese Immigrants*.

45. J. M. Romero, *Comisión de Inmigración*, iv, Sterling Library, Yale University. Also see Cott, "Mexican Diplomacy," 70.

46. See Schiavone-Camacho, *Chinese Mexicans*, and Gómez Izquierdo, *El movimiento antichino*.

47. Lewis, *Iron Horse Imperialism*, 93–97.

48. "Rama de Guaymas a Guadalajara," *El Economista Mexicana* (Mexico City), July 27, 1907, 363.

49. Schiavone-Camacho, *Chinese Mexicans*; Castillo-Muñoz, *Divided Communities*; R. C. Romero, *Chinese in Mexico*.

50. Guidotti-Hernández, *Unspeakable Violence*.

51. Ibid., 216–33.

52. Herrera Barreda, *Inmigrantes Hispanocubanos*, 7–12.

53. Cervera, *La Gloria*, 51–52.

54. *El Tiempo* (Mexico City), April 22, 1892, 2.

55. Joseph, *Revolution from Without*.

56. Comandancia Principal del Cuartel de Peto, *Periódico Oficial del Estado de Yucatán*, March 11, 1850, 2, Biblioteca Nacional, Mexico City.

57. Cervera, *La Gloria*, 56–57; *El Siglo Diez y Nueve* (Mexico City), September 24, 1892, 3.

58. "Dodging from across the Frontier: Chinamen Coming from Cuba, via Mexico, Also from Vancouver, B.C.," *New York Times*, May 20, 1893, 1. The history of connections between the Yucatán and Cuba in the Chinese diaspora deserves more research, but it would be safe to assume that over the course of the late nineteenth century, Cuban coolie practices made their way to the Yucatán.

59. "Chinamen Bound for Yucatán," *Boston Evening Transcript*, June 3, 1897. Coolies were not a regular part of Chinese migration to the United States, save for a brief experiment in Louisiana, although Chinese coolies frequently traveled through the U.S. rail system as bonded passengers.

60. González Navarro, *El Porfiriato*, 4:124.

61. Ibid., 4:168.

62. Ibid., 4:226.

63. Joseph, *Revolution from Without*, 72.

64. The brutality of this system can be corroborated by accounts of Korean contract workers. See Patterson, "Early Years of Korean Immigration."

65. Turner, *Barbarous Mexico*, 45, 16.

66. Ibid., 62.

67. Zuleta, "La Secretaría de Fomento."

68. "Colonizacion: La Importacion de Trabajadores Chinos a Mexico," *El Economista Mexicana* (Mexico City), August 23, 1902, 12.

69. Bulnes, *Whole Truth*, 98.

70. Canudas, *Las Venas de Plata*, 2:998.

71. J. M. Romero, *Comisión de Inmigración*, Sterling Library, Yale University. Persons of Japanese descent were dropped from inspection in a revised draft of the commission in 1904 owing to Japan's ascendency after the Russo-Japanese War.

72. González Navarro, "El Porfiriato," 4:124.

73. Raigosa, *Desagüe De La Ciudad*.

74. Ibid.

75. González Navarro, *El Porfiriato*, 4:111.

76. Liceaga, "Bubonic Plague," 226–37.

77. González Navarro, *El Porfiriato*, 4:111.

78. Ibid., 4:123–30.

79. Craib, *Chinese Immigrants*, 2.

80. Ibid., 17.

81. Shah, *Contagious Divides*.

82. Molina, *Fit to Be Citizens*.

83. Craib, *Chinese Immigrants*, 16.

84. J. M. Romero, *Comisión de Inmigración*. Japanese immigrants were to be preferred over Chinese immigrants. It was also recommended that there be clarification between Chinese and Korean immigrants in matters of voluntary individual immigration and that contracted by companies.

85. Cott, "Mexican Diplomacy," 83.

86. González Navarro, *El Porfiriato*, 4:167, emphasis added.

87. J. M. Romero, *Comisión de Inmigración*, 97.

88. Ibid., 121.

89. Tejada, *National Camera*.

90. Sufficient evidence is lacking to make a direct link between Molina's appointment and the abeyance of the anti-Chinese report; however, speculation is shared with other historians. See Cott, "Mexican Diplomacy," 84.

91. Turner, *Barbarous Mexico*, 8.

92. Molina, *Mensaje leido*, 20–21.

93. Covarrubias, "La Inmigracion China."

94. "Nombramientos de Instruccion Publica," *El Imparcial* (Mexico City), February 25, 1908, 8.

95. J. M. Romero, *Comisión de Inmigración*.

96. González Navarro, quoted in Craib, *Chinese Immigrants*, 23–24.

97. Molina Enríquez and Córdova, *Los Grandes Problemas*.

98. Meyers, "Seasons of Rebellion."

99. Bulnes, *Whole Truth*, 96–98.

100. Cott, "Mexican Diplomacy."

101. Ramon Corona to Albert Owens, 1904, Correspondence, Owens Collection, Huntington Library, San Marino, California.

102. Butler Edward, "Fixed Value for the Peso," *Los Angeles Times*, November 27, 1904.

103. Kerig and Segovia, *El valle de Mexicali*.

104. Oscar Straus, Secretary of the Bureau of Immigration and Naturalization to the Secretary of State, December 22, 1909, Part 1: Asian Immigration and Exclusion 1906–13, series A: Subject Correspondence Files, Research Collections in American Immigration (hereinafter referred to as Part 1, RCAI), Records of the Immigration and Naturalization Service, Bethesda, Maryland, and Newspaper and Microfilm Collection, Doe Library, Berkeley, California (hereinafter referred to as Doe).

105. Stuart Fuller, Vice-Consul in Hong Kong to the Assistant Secretary of State and Commission General to Commissioner in San Francisco, April 21, 1909, Part 1, RCAI, and Doe.

106. The C-M Ranch was the Mexican subsidiary of the Colorado River Land Company (CRLC). Mexican law stipulated that no foreigner may own land in Mexico, so the CRLC simply created a new company with a Mexican lawyer who was a CRLC board member. For a more detailed company history, see Kerig, "Yankee Enclave."

107. Vice-Consul in Hong Kong to the Assistant Secretary of State.

108. This policy was a necessary step to encourage Chinese migrants to stay south of the border. See also Chan, *Bittersweet Soil*, for more regarding the migration of Chinese agricultural workers.

109. Samuel Backus, Immigration Commissioner of Angel Island to the Commissioner-General of Immigration, September 4, 1912, Part 1, RCAI, and Doe.

110. Boweker to Harry Chandler, June 18, 1908, Correspondence, CRLC, Sherman Library, Corona Del Mar, California (hereinafter referred to as CRLC correspondence).

111. Brant to Davis, June 21, 1908, CRLC correspondence.

112. Chang, "Outsider Crossings."

113. C. T. Wardlaw to Brant, October 9, 1915, Anderson Portfolios, CRLC correspondence.

114. R. P. Davie, "Review of Indenture Contract," February 1, 1911, Anderson Portfolios, CRLC correspondence.

115. Commission General to Commissioner in San Francisco, January 22, 1913, Part 1, RCAI, and Doe.

116. Topik, "Revolution, the State."

117. Rippy, "Negro Colonization Project."

118. Bulnes, "Las Tres Razas Humanas."

119. Lomnitz-Adler, *El Antisemitismo*.

Chapter 3. Violent Imaginaries and the Beginnings of a New State

1. Jose Díaz Zulueta, "La inmigración china para el fomento," *El Tiempo* (Mexico City), April 10, 1911, 2.

2. Li Chung Ping, Li Yuck Ling, Moy Hah Sing, Chion Ah Wan, Tam Tip Hong, and Chin See Yin, "En defense de la Colonia China," *El Tiempo* (Mexico City), April 21, 1911, 2.

3. "From Henry Wilson to Secretary Bryan, 13 July 1913," RG 59 7737, 812.00/8035, NARA, Washington, DC.

4. Garcia, *Looking like the Enemy*.

5. Notas Editorials, *El Tiempo* (Mexico City), January 5, 1911, 2. The editorial includes Chinese-immigration restrictions as a part of revolutionary platform. Although it was written in support of Madero, he did not pen the article himself.

6. "Porfirio Díaz, Poeta(?)," *Revolución* (Mexico City), November 23, 1911, 1.

7. Zertuche Muñoz, *Ricardo Flores Magón*, 97. For more on solidarity, see Young, *Alien Nation*, 239–40.

8. Gojman de Backal, *Camisas, Escudos, y Desfiles Militares*. For specific instances, see "Trail of Blood Follows Villa's Path in Parral," *Prescott (AZ) Journal Miner*, November 19, 1916, 1.

9. Fanon, *Black Skin, White Masks*, 145.

10. Schröder and Schmidt, introduction, 9.

11. Individuals acting alone did perpetrate violence against the Chinese, but these are not considered here.

12. Scholars studying the Mexican revolution include Womack, *Zapata*; Knight, *Mexican Revolution*; Cumberland, *Mexican Revolution*; and Benjamin and Wasserman, *Provinces of the Revolution*.

13. Kourí, "La invención del ejido."

14. Carlos Negrete, "Estudios Economicos," *El Tiempo* (Mexico City), November 11, 1911, 4.

15. Kourí, "La invención del ejido."

16. Dambourges, "Chinese Massacre."

17. Meyers, "Seasons of Rebellion."

18. Alonso, *Thread of Blood*.

19. All dollar amounts are U.S. dollars.

20. "Chinese Colony in Torreón Is Annihilated," *Mexican Herald* (Mexico City), May 23, 1911, 1.

21. George Carothers, "Report of Investigation of Chinese Massacre, 1911," microfilm, Chinese Question in Mexico, 1910–1930, decimal file RG 59, 312.93, 1910–29, 1930–39, and 704.9312, 1910–29, 1930–39, General Records of the Department of State, University of Arizona Main Library, Tucson (hereinafter referred to as Chinese Question).

22. Ibid.

23. Ibid.

24. Pérez Jiménez, "Raza, nación, y revolución."

25. "Declaración del Dr. Lim al Juez Martínez" (Declaration of Dr. Lim to Judge Martínez), May 16, 1911, exp. 13-2-34, folder 2, Archivo Genaro Estrada de la Secretaria de Relaciones Exteriores (Secretary of Foreign Relations, Genaro Estrada Archive) (SRE), Mexico City (hereinafter referred to as SRE).

26. Ibid.

27. Carothers, "Report of Investigation," Chinese Question.

28. Wilfley and Bassett, *Memorandum*.

29. "Declaración de Cunard Cummins a Ramos Pedrueza" (Declaration of Cunard Cummins to Ramos Pedrueza), exp. 13-2-34, folder 2, SRE.

30. Carothers, "Report of Investigation," Chinese Question.

31. Jamieson and Payne, *Tulitas of Torreón*.

32. Carothers, "Report of Investigation," Chinese Question.

33. Pérez Jiménez, "Raza, nación, y revolución."

34. "Las pérdidas de los chinos asciendan á $500,000," *El Tiempo* (Mexico City), June 9, 1911, 1.

35. Carothers, "Report of Investigation," Chinese Question.

36. For details of the comparison, see Pérez Jiménez, "Raza, nación, y revolución."

37. Carothers, "Report of Investigation," Chinese Question.

38. "Un Contraste," *El Imparcial* (Mexico City), June 5, 1911, 6.

39. "From Carothers to Department of State Regarding Protection of Chinese in Mexico, 23 May 1911," and "From Carothers to Department of State Regarding Protection of Chinese, 1 June, 1911," Chinese Question.

40. "From Carothers to Department of State Regarding Memorandum on Sheltering Chinese, 6 June 1911," Chinese Question.

41. Dambourges, "Chinese Massacre."

42. Wilfley and Bassett, *Memorandum*.

43. "Consideraciones sobre la muerte de chinos en Torreón," *El Diario del Hogar* (Mexico City), June 15, 1911, 1.

44. Wilfley and Bassett, *Memorandum*.

45. "Convocatoria," *Periodico Oficial del Estado de Coahuila*, December 18, 1909.

46. Root, *Charges*.

47. "Memoranda of Affairs in Mexico: Embassy Matters. July 9, 1913," RG 59 7737:812.00/8203, 23, NARA, Washington, DC.

48. "The Agrarian Problem and the Calles Regime," *Agricultural Studies* 1, no. 5 (1928): 38, Bancroft Library, University of California, Berkeley.

49. Dambourges, "Chinese Massacre."

50. Pérez Jiménez, "Raza, nación, y revolución."

51. "Agrarian Problem," 38.

52. "¿Han vendido los señores Maderos sus propiedades huleras?" *El Tiempo* (Mexico City), May 11, 1910, 8.

53. J. M. Romero, *Comisión de Inmigración*, viii.

54. See state-level accounts in following reports: "Dispatch from Chihuahua," 6 August 1919; "Dispatch from Monterrey," 6 August 1919; "Dispatch from Mazatlán," 8 August 1919; "Dispatch from Mexico City," 13 August 1919; "Dispatch from Piedras Negras," 16 August 1919, RG 59 312.93/177, all in Chinese Question.

55. This government correspondence of the U.S. State Department records found at NARA provides more detailed information than is available in Mexican archives. The fleeting and destructive nature of revolutionary fighting often prevented accurate accounting of the loss of life and property of Chinese people. Foreign reporting on domestic events of the revolution proved insightful for the watchful coverage of the revolution.

56. "Memoranda of Affairs in Mexico: Embassy Matters, July 9, 1913," RG 59 7737:812.00/8203, NARA, 10.

57. "Telegram from Mazatlan to Secretary of State, 16 March 1912," Chinese Question; "500 from Cananea Sent to Mazatlan," *Bisbee (AZ) Daily Review*, March 20, 1912, 1.

58. "Telegram from Wilson regarding Instructions to Protect Chinese Attacked at Cananea 29 April, 1912," RG 59 312.93/20, and "From Wiswall to Secretary of State, 27, April, 1912," Chinese Question.

59. "El Gran. Blanquet va á Durango," *El País* (Mexico City), May 31, 1912, 8; "Notes of the Passing Day," *Mexican Herald* (Mexico City), August 3, 1912, 8.

60. "Telegram from Mazatlan, 16 March, 1912," RG 59 312.93/18, and "From Carr to Secretary of State regarding the Prohibited Anti-Chinese Meeting, 1 April, 1912," RG 59 312.93/19, Chinese Question.

61. "Report to Secretary of State regarding the Failure of the Federal Troops from Mazatlan, 21 October, 1912," RG 59 312.93/17, Chinese Question.

62. "From Alger to Secretary of State regarding the 571 Chinese in Mazatlan, 10 December 1913," RG 59 312.93/55, Chinese Question; Knight, *Mexican Revolution*, 23.

63. "Telegram from U.S.S. Pittsburgh to Secretary of State, 10 July 1913," RG 59 312.93/36, Chinese Question; "Telegram Captain Cowles, U.S.S. Pittsburgh to Secretary of Navy, July 14, 1913," RG 59 812.00/8051, NARA, Washington, DC.

64. "Letter from Simpich to Secretary of State, August 11, 1915," RG 59 312.93/127, Chinese Question.

65. "From Simpich to Secretary of State regarding Women's Union Manifestation against Chinese, 24 February 1914," RG 59 312.93/61, Chinese Question.

66. "From Simpich to Secretary of State regarding Situation in Cananea, 26 February 1914," RG 59 312.93/62, and "Letter regarding Anti-Chinese Demonstrations at Cananea, 27 February 1914," RG 59 213.93/63, Chinese Question. The Chinese community approached the U.S. consulate and asked for protection, citing the Torreón massacre and the murder of a Chinese storeowner in Nogales by Constitutionalist forces.

67. I draw from Kwame Anthony Appiah and Amy Gutmann's notion of racial scripts that serve as collective narratives that "people can use in shaping their life plans and in telling their life stories." Appiah and Gutmann, *Color Conscious*, 97. Also see Molina, *How Race Is Made in America*.

68. "Report on the Murder of a Chinaman to Secretary of State, 20 January 1915," RG 59 312.93/84, Chinese Question.

69. "Case Report of Joe Wong, Chinaman, Murdered in Durango, Mexico, 19 April, 1915," RG 59 312.93/109, Chinese Question. Despite the complaints of the Chinese community and the U.S. State Department, Monico remained at liberty two months later.

70. "Telegram from Tampico to Secretary of State, 6 January 1914," RG 59 312.93/56, and "Telegram from Tampico to Secretary of State 12 January 1914," RG 59 312.93/57, Chinese Question.

71. "From the Captain J. H. Oliver of the U.S.S. New Hampshire to Commander, Fourth Division, 7 July 1913," RG 59 7737/185–12, NARA, College Park.

72. Hart, *Empire and Revolution*, 209.

73. "Telegram from El Paso to Secretary of State, 6 August 1913," RG 59 312.93/42, and "Letter to Immigration Service from El Paso Supervising Inspector, 20 May 1914," Chinese Question. For Booker's request, see file 53108/71-K.

74. Reed, *Insurgent Mexico*, 295.

75. "Telegram from El Paso to Secretary of State, 29 February 1916," RG 59 312.93/139; "Letter from G. Henderson to Secretary of State, 29 February 1916"; and "Report to Secretary of State Regarding the Death of Charlie Chee, 1916," Chinese Question.

76. "From Vice Consul Silliman Review of the Three Months ending June 30th to Secretary Bryan, Saltillo, 1 July 1913," American Consulate, 198, RG 59 7737 812.00/8074, NARA, College Park.

77. "Telegram from G. Carothers to Secretary of State regarding Villa's Treatment of the Chinese, 27 March 1915," RG 59 312.93/94, Chinese Question.

78. Hu-DeHart, *Yaqui Resistance*.

79. Alacrón, *José Maria Maytorena*; Hu-DeHart, *Yaqui Resistance*.

80. "Telegram from Nogales, Sonora to Secretary of State, 7 January 1915," RG 59 312.93/80, Chinese Question. Losses recorded in U.S. State Department correspondence measured against the listings in the 1913 Chinese International Business Directory suggest that looting wiped out almost all of the general stores in the Yaqui lowlands. Wong Kin, *International Chinese Business Directory*, 1580–88.

81. "Telegram from Nogales, Arizona to Secretary of State, 29 January 1915," RG 59 312.93/81, Chinese Question.

82. "Telegram from U.S. Vice Consul to Chinese Minister Shah, 18 March 1915," RG 59 312.93/88, Chinese Question.

83. "Telegram from Cochran to Secretary of State regarding Maytorena's Response to U.S. State Department Request, 26 March 1915," RG 59 312.93/93, Chinese Question.

84. "Letter from Simpich to American Consul regarding Chinese Merchants in Arizpe, 4 May 1915," RG 59 312.93/97, Chinese Question.

85. "Telegram from W. Pu to Chinese Legation in U.S., 21 March 1915," RG 59 312.93/97, Chinese Question.

86. "Letter regarding the Protection of the Chinese at Mazatlan, 30 March 1915," RG 59 312.93/105, Chinese Question.

87. "Letter from Simpich to Secretary of State regarding the Murder of Chinese by State Troops near Ojo de Agua, 15 April 1915," and "Letter to Secretary of State regarding Murder of Chinese by State Troops near Ojo de Agua, 21 April 1915," RG 59 312.93/108, Chinese Question.

88. The reported losses from burned-out buildings, vandalism, and theft amounted to more than half a million dollars. "Telegram from Chinese Minister K. Shah to Secretary of State, 24 July 1915," RG 59 312.93/124, and "Letter from Simpich to Secretary of State regarding Losses by Chinese during Riots at Cananea, 11 August 1915," RG 59 312.93/127, Chinese Question.

89. "Report from Simpich to Secretary of State regarding Losses of Chinese by Raids at Nogales, 24 September 1915," RG 59 312.93/130, Chinese Question.

90. "Telegram from Cananea, Sonora to Secretary of State, 1 October 1915," RG 59 312.93/131, Chinese Question.

91. "Letter from Simpich . . . at Cananea, 11 August 1915."

92. Alacrón, *José Maria Maytorena,* 353.

93. E. M. Lawton, "Viewpoint of Mexican Army Officers in Sonora on European War and Sidelights on Yaqui Situation, 1917," Records of the Department of State Relating to Political Relations between the United States and Mexico, 1910–1929, RG 59, Huntington Library, San Marino, California.

94. "Telegram from Blocker to Secretary of State regarding the Reports of Executions of Chinese, 13 November 1916," RG 59 312.93/159, and "Telegram from Carpenter to Secretary of State regarding Reports of Villa's Murder of Chinese, 4 December, 1916," RG 59 312.93/161, Chinese Question.

95. "Telegram from Cobb to Secretary of State regarding the Murder of Chinamen in Cusi, 4 October 1916," RG 59 312.93/157, and "Telegram from Edwards to Secretary of State regarding the State of Chinese in El Paso, 9 November 1916," RG 59 312.93/158, Chinese Question.

96. "Telegram from Nogales to Secretary of State, Complaint of Chinese against Calles Order, 20 June 1916," RG 59 312.93/155, Chinese Question.

97. "Calles to Campaign against Bandit Raids," October 3, 1919, 4; "Sonora Chinese Fear Mexicans," December 10, 1919, 2; "Juarez Alarmed by Anti-Chinese Pogrom," May 10, 1919, 3, all *Bisbee (AZ) Daily Review.*

98. Archivo General del Estado de Sinaloa, no. 89, 8 December 1919, reproduced in Guzmán, "Segregación racial," 133–37.

99. Duntley and Buss, "Homicide Adaptations."

100. Said, *Orientalism.*

101. Tilley, *Seeing Indians*; Lee-Loy, *Searching for Mr. Chin*; Lesser, *Negotiating National Identity.*

102. Fanon, *Black Skin, White Masks,* 154.

103. The term *wages of mestizaje* was suggested to me by Tanya Hernández during a panel presentation at the Latin American Studies Association annual meeting, San Juan, Puerto Rico, May 2015.

104. Roediger, *Wages of Whiteness.*

Chapter 4. Abajo Los Chinos: The Political Invention of Mestizo Nationalism

1. Mallon, *Peasant and Nation*; Skocpol, *States and Social Revolutions*. Gil and Nugent distinguish between process and outcome in interpreting the Mexican revolution; this chapter is about process.

2. Puig Casauranc, *La Cosecha y La Siembra*, 171.

3. Foucault, Ewald, and Fontana, *Birth of Biopolitics*.

4. "Pagina Para Todos," *El Imparcial* (Mexico City), July 26, 1913, 7.

5. Gojman de Backal, "Minorías" and *Camisas*.

6. Gojman de Backal, *Camisas*.

7. An interesting exception is when it comes to Japanese persons. Several times in *Forjando Patria*, Gamio exemplifies Japanese nationalism as a model for Mexico. Throughout the early twentieth century, Japanese immigrants were thought to be couriers of industrial modern culture as illustrated by the budding imperialism of the Japanese Empire. Japanese immigrants were more often than not lumped together with Chinese people in anti-Asian campaigns throughout the 1920s and 1930s. Gamio, *Forjando Patria*.

8. Stern, "Mestizofilia."

9. Stern, "Responsible Mothers."

10. Vasconcelos, *La Raza Cósmica*.

11. Ibid.

12. He crowned the institution of higher learning with the slogan "por mi raza hablará el espíritu" (for my race, the spirit will speak). The phrase reflects his ambitious vision for developing an educational system to inspire the almost limitless power of racial patriotism.

13. José Maria Arana, Papers, 1904–21, Arizona-Sonora Documents, Special Collections, University of Arizona Library, Tucson (hereinafter referred to as Arana Papers).

14. "Anti-Chinese Speech by Profa, Maria Jesus Valdez, Magdalena, Sonora, November 26, 1917," folder 1, Arana Papers.

15. Medina Peña, *Hacia el Nuevo Estado*. Also see Buchenau and Beezley, *State Governors*, for examples of regional articulations of party affiliations.

16. Espinoza, *El Ejemplo de Sonora*; Vasconcelos, *La Raza Cósmica*.

17. "Secretaría de Gobernación, Gobierno General," *Periódico Oficial del Estado de Sinaloa*, March 22, 1921, 1–3.

18. "Letter from Junta Central Nacionalista to Presidente de la Republica Mexicana, 25 October 1920," folder 5, Arana Papers; "Letter from Junta Central Nacionalista to Jose Maria Araña, 1921," folder 5, Arana Papers.

19. "Informe," *Periódico Oficial del Estado de Tamaulipas*, October 5, 1921, 1–2.

20. "Telegrama de la Secretaria de Relaciones Exteriores a el Presidente, 25 Julio 1921," 104-Ch-1 Legajo 1; "Telegrama de la Secretaria de Gobernacion a el Presidente, 25 Julio 1921," 104-Ch-1 Legajo 1; "Informe del Presidente a la Secretaria de Gobernacion, 21 Julio 1921," 104-Ch-1 Legajo 16, all Obregón-Calles Papers, Archivo General de la Nación (AGN), Mexico City (hereafter referred to as Obregón-Calles Papers).

21. *China and the United States of Mexico: Exchange of Notes embodying an Agreement for the Provisional Modification of the Sino-Mexican Treaty, 14 December 1899*, League

of Nation's Treaty Series, World Legal Information Institute, www.worldlii.org/int/other/LNTSer/1922/154.pdf.

22. See Delgado, *Making the Chinese Mexican*, for claims that Chinese immigration halted.

23. Border-crossing cards, 1895–1964, NARA, San Bruno, California; "Letter to the Secretary of Foreign Relations, 1921," 1:2, Obregón-Calles file, Instituto de Investigaciones Históricos, Universidad Autónoma de Baja California, Tijuana (hereinafter referred to as Obregón-Calles file).

24. Log Book #325, Pacific Mail Papers. The event was recorded in the USS *Newport* passenger log of the Pacific Mail Steamship Company, yet the lack of documentation in Mexican archives suggests the expulsion was likely a clandestine action by local or state officials.

25. "Letter from B., A G. in the Office of the President to the Secretary of Foreign Relations, 1923," Obregón-Calles file.

26. "Letter from S.S. in the Office of the President to Chun, Wing, and Charm, 1923," Obregón-Calles file.

27. Cervera, *La Gloria de la Raza*, 138; "Decreto 613," *Periódico Oficial del Estado de Yucatán*, November 11, 1916, 1.

28. González, "We won't be bullied anymore."

29. For more information on the investigation, see "Telegram from President Obregón to Secretary of the Interior, 15 June 1922," 104-Ch-1 Legajo 1, Obregón-Calles Papers. For expulsion orders, see "Telegram from President Obregón to Secretary of Foreign Relations, June 20, 1922," 104-Ch-1 Legajo 1, Obregón-Calles Papers.

30. "Telegram from Governor Calles to President Obregón, June 23, 1922," 104-Ch-1 Legajo 1, Obregón-Calles Papers.

31. "Telegram from Vice Consul to Secretary of State, 25 June, 1922," RG 59 312.93/218, Chinese Problem.

32. "Telegram from President Obregón to Governor Calles, 23 June 1922," 104-Ch-1 Legajo 1, Obregón-Calles Papers.

33. "Telegram from Montoya to President Calles, 5 November, 1924," 104-Ch-1 Legajo 16, Obregón-Calles Papers.

34. "Telegram from Espinoza to President Calles, 22 December, 1924," 104-Ch-1 Legajo 16, Obregón-Calles Papers.

35. Letters also provide lessons in Chinese naming conventions to distinguish Chinese first and last names in addition to adopted Spanish first names. This was particularly important for Francisco Yuen because he shared the same family name as the CKT leader, Ley Fon Yuen.

36. "Letter from Francisco Yuen to President Obregón, 20 September 1922," 104-Ch-1 1, Obregón-Calles Papers.

37. *Mexican Herald* (Mexico City), December 11, 1898, 1.

38. "Report from Vice Consul to Secretary of State Regarding the Chinese Located at Cananea, 28 November, 1916," RG 59 312.93/160, Chinese Question.

39. "From Vice Consul to Secretary of State, 21 September 1917," RG 59 312.93/165, Chinese Question.

40. "Informe El Partido Nacionalista Chino, October 22, 1922," 104-Ch-1 Legajo 4, Obregón-Calles Papers.

41. "Telegram from Harispuru and Others to President Obregón, 18 July, 1922," 104-Ch-1 Legajo 1, Obregón-Calles Papers.

42. Young, *Alien Nation*, 257.

43. Yankelevich, "Extranjeros indeseables."

44. "Telegram From Governor of Sinaloa to President Obregón, 28 July 1922," 104-Ch-1 Legajo 1, Obregón-Calles Papers.

45. "Letter from Vice Consul to Secretary of State regarding Interview with Mayor in Sonora, 26 June 1922," RG 59 312.93/220, Chinese Question; "Telegram from Vice Consul to Secretary of State regarding Hundreds of Chinese in Jails of Sonora, 16 July 1922," RG 59 312.93/222, Chinese Question.

46. "Telegram from Lorenzo Wong to President Obregón, 17 October, 1924," 104-Ch-1 Legajo 2, Obregón-Calles Papers.

47. "Telegram from Comité Pro-Raza de Naco to President Obregón, 4 October 1924," 104-Ch-1 Legajo 2, Obregón-Calles Papers.

48. "Telegram from Obregón to Castro, October 18, 1924," Obregón-Calles file.

49. "Los Chinos Estan Riendo, 1917," news clipping, Chinese Question.

50. R. C. Romero, *Chinese in Mexico*, 166.

51. "Letter from Comité Anti-Chino, Sinaloa to President Obregón, 16 April 1924," 104-Ch-1 Legajo 1, Obregón-Calles Papers.

52. "Letter from Sub-Comité Juvenil Anti-Chino, Sinaloa to President Obregón, 12 March 1925," 104-Ch-1 Legajo 2, Obregón-Calles Papers.

53. "Letter from Comite de Salud Publica to Secretary of Commerce, 5 December 1924," 104-Ch-1 Legajo 3, Obregón-Calles Papers.

54. Some states had municipal-level decrees to segregate Chinese residents, such as that of Mazatlán, Sinaloa, issued in May 1915. "Telegram from Vice Consul to Secretary of State regarding Continued Molestation of Chinese, 14 May 1915," RG 59 312.93/116, Chinese Question.

55. "Telegram from Vice Consul to Secretary of State regarding Chinese Citizens being Segregated in Towns of Sonora, 15 June 1923," RG 59 312.93/237, Chinese Question.

56. "Acuerdo," *Periódico Oficial del Estado de Chihuahua*, September 27, 1924, 3.

57. "Telegram from Secretary of Interior to President, 4 February 1925," 104-Ch-1 Legajo 1, Obregón-Calles Papers.

58. "Oposicion a la candidature de Lacy Para Gobernador de Sonora," *La Patria* (Mexico City), May 25, 1911, 2.

59. Espinoza, *El Ejemplo de Sonora*, 190–91.

60. "Avisos," *Periodico Oficial del Estado de Tamaulipas*, January 14, 1925, 4; "Avisos," *Periodico Oficial . . . Aguascalientes*, May 14, 1925, 3; *Periodico Oficial . . . Tlaxcala*, January 28, 1925: 9; *Periodico Oficial . . . Tlaxcala*, April 15, 1925, 2; *Periodico Oficial . . . Durango*, October 8, 1925, 13.

61. Espinoza, *El Ejemplo de Sonora*; Espinoza, *El Problema Chino*.

62. Escobar, *Las tribus*. See also Albarran, *Seen and Heard*.

63. This wave is also noted in Delgado, *Making the Chinese Mexican*.

64. "From Myers to Secretary of State on Behalf of Chinese Interests at Durango, 24 July 1924," and "Telegram from Yost to Secretary of State regarding the Protection of Chinese Interests, 25 August 1925," RG 59 704.913/23, Chinese Question.

65. "From Myers to Secretary of State."

66. "Letter from President Calles to the Governors of Yucatán, Chiapas, Tamaulipas, Coahuila, Sinaloa, Sonora, Nayarit, and Baja California," September 23, 1925, Obregón-Calles file.

67. T. Q. Solomón, "Excitativa de Nuestros Colaboradores," *El Nacionalista* (Sonora), November 22, 1925, 1, 1:6, Miscellaneous, Arana Papers (original emphasis).

68. Jose Angel Espinoza, *El Nacionalista* (Sonora), November 22, 1925, 1, 1:6, Miscellaneous, Arana Papers.

69. *Periodico Oficial del Estado de Tamaulipas*, December 30, 1925, 5; *Periodico Oficial . . . Tamaulipas*, January 16, 1926, 4.

70. "Telegram from Chinese Association, Tampico to President, 29 January 1926," 104-Ch-1 Legajo 2, Obregón-Calles Papers.

71. "Telegram from Jesus Sujo Loek to President, 25 June 1926," 104-Ch-1 Legajo 2, Obregón-Calles Papers.

72. "Dirección #91, Gobierno Federal: Poder Ejecutivo: Secretaria de Agricultura y Fomento," *Periodico Oficial . . . Tamaulipas*, January 30, 1926, 9.

73. *Periodico Oficial . . . Tamaulipas*, June 11, 1927, 6, 8.

74. *Periodico Oficial. . . Tamaulipas*, July 18, 1928, 9.

75. Piñera Ramírez, *Visión histórica*, 5:93–96.

76. "Telegram from Secretary of Interior to President, 21 September 1928," 104-Ch-1 Legajo 3, Obregón-Calles Papers. More research is needed to investigate the particular role that these Chinese men played in the Tamaulipas economy.

77. For Nuevo Leon, see "Telegram from Secretary of Interior to President, 4 January 1927," 104-Ch-1 Legajo 3, Obregón-Calles Papers; "Telegram from Secretary of Interior to President. 18 January 1927," 104-Ch-1 Legajo 3, Obregón-Calles Papers; *Periodico Oficial del Estado de Nuevo Leon*, February 5, 1927, 4. For Coahuila, see "Telegram from Comite Anti-Chino, Torreón to Secretary of Interior, 13 January 1927," 104-Ch-1 Legajo 3, Obregón-Calles Papers. For Durango, see "Telegram from Secretary of Interior to President, 28 October 1927," 104-Ch-1 Legajo 3, Obregón-Calles Papers.

78. Cervera, *La Gloria de la raza*, 127–29.

79. *Periodico Oficial del Estado de Colima*, November 27, 1926, 2.

80. Fallaw, "Seduction of Revolution."

81. *Periodico Oficial del Estado de Zacatecas*, July 23, 1927, 42; *Periodico Oficial . . . Zacatecas*, August 10, 1927, 7. Congressional debate in Zacatecas included calls for an investigation into how extensively the Chinese people had colonized the state. For that debate, see *Periodico Oficial . . . Zacatecas*, September 10, 1927, 14; "Point of Order from State of Guanajuato Legislature Communicated to Secretary of the Interior, 5 October 1927," 104-Ch-1 Legajo 3, Obregón-Calles Papers.

82. Ard, *Eternal Struggle*, 35–37.

83. *Periodico Oficial del Estado de Zacatecas*, July 23 1927, 42, and August 10, 1927, 7; *Periodico Oficial . . . Tlaxcala*, October 26, 1927, 5.

84. Buve, "Tlaxcala"; Ramirez Rancaño, "El socialismo."

85. Rockwell, *Hacer escuela, hacer estado*; Buve, "Tlaxcala."

86. *Periodico Oficial del Estado de Tlaxcala*, August 31, 1927, 1–4.

87. That year in Tlaxcala, the local agrarian commission was arbitrating a five-year backlog of petitions for ejido donations in what amounted to a massive reordering of the pueblos, ranches, and hamlets between Santa Cruz Tenancingo and Santa Catarina

Apatlacheo. The hearings of the commission decided who would receive the land near roads or in the mountains and their access to irrigation. *Periodico Oficial del Estado de Tlaxcala*, October 19, 1927, 1–6.

88. *Periódico Oficial del estado de Tlaxcala*, September 7, 1927, 1. See also Molina, "La educación socialista."

89. For an example, see "Letter from Comite Anti-Chino to President Calles. 21 Inero, 1926," 104-Ch-1 Legajo 2, Obregón-Calles Papers.

90. Mancilla and González Félix, *Viaje al corazón*.

91. A. Rodríguez, *Memoria administrativa*.

92. Reglamiento de la ley de colonization de 5 de April de 1926, *Diario Oficial*, May 11, 1926, http://biblio.juridicas.unam.mx/libros/3/1164/26.pdf.

93. The chief of the international waters committee of the foreign relations secretary wrote, "Without fear of over-exaggeration, I think that without a prompt and forceful assessment of the problem of Asian immigration in the international river basins not only jeopardizes the success of the negotiations that Mexico will have to undertake to defend and define their rights to international rivers, but also, over time, we may fear the loss of ownership and nationality of the vast and rich lands affected." Rodríguez, *Memoria administrativa*, 121.

94. Chang, "Racial Alterity."

95. Chang, "Outsider Crossings."

96. Camára de Diputados *DDCLEM*, June 20, 1926, http://cronica.diputados.gob.mx/DDebates/32/2do/CPerma/19280620.html.

97. Camára de Diputados *DDCLEM*, June 22, 1926, http://cronica.diputados.gob.mx/DDebates/32/2do/CPerma/19280622.html.

98. Pimentel, *Memoria sobre*, 237.

Chapter 5. Forging a Racial Contract

1. "Act No. 56," *Periodico Oficial de Estado de Tamaulipas*, May 1931, 5.

2. López Victoria, *La campaña nacionalista*.

3. Ibid., 21.

4. Loveman, "Modern State."

5. Wilkie, *Mexican Revolution*, 184.

6. Benjamin and Wasserman, *Provinces of the Revolution*.

7. Knight, "Cardenismo," and "Popular Culture."

8. Lazcano Armienta, *La política agraria*.

9. Rénique, "Race, Mestizaje, and Nationalism."

10. *Periodico Oficial del Estado de Tlaxcala*, January 30, 1929, 1; *Periodico Oficial . . . Tamaulipas*, June 5, 1929, 6; *Periodico Oficial . . . Zacatecas*, August 17, 1929, 11.

11. Vásquez, *Las locuras*, 83.

12. González Compeán and Lomelí, *El partido de la revolución*, 87.

13. "Notas Editoriales: Ecos de la Elecion Presidencial," *El Abogado Cristiano Ilustrado* (Mexico City), December 12, 1929, 3.

14. Barajas Durán, *La raíz NAZI*, 47–51; Savarino, "Sentinel of the Bravo," 104.

15. Gómez Izquierdo, *El movimiento antichino*, 134.

16. *Pro Patria*, November 1930, in Gardner, "Prensa obrera."

17. "Tapachula, Chiapas," Dirección General de Estadistica, *Censo de poblacion, 1930* (Mexico City: Direccion General de Estadistica, 1930), 3:38, 39, Benson Library, University of Texas, Austin.

18. Garrido, *El partido*, 133.

19. "Informe," *Periodico Oficial de Estado de Zacatecas*, October 17, 1931, 10; "Sesion Ordinaria," *Periodico Oficial . . . Chihuahua*, September 2, 1931, 3; "Circular No. 90," *Periodico Oficial . . . Morelos Nuevo*, August 16, 1931, 2; "La Elecion de las Variedades de Hortaliza," *Periodico Oficial . . . Tlaxcala*, July 1, 1931, 7; "Circular No. 34," *Periodico Oficial . . . Hidalgo*, March 24, 1932, 1; "Decreto No. 52," *Periodico Oficial . . . Durango*, July 24, 1932, 1; "Ramo de Gobernacion," *Periodico Oficial . . . Aguascalientes*, February 3, 1935, 2.

20. By 1933 the BNR was included in PNR's Comité Directivo Nacional. Comité Ejecutivo Nacional, *Proyectos*, 28.

21. For an example, see "Letter from Sub-Comité Anti-Chino to the Secretary of the Interior 9 August 1927," 104-Ch-1 Legajo 3, Obregón-Calles Papers.

22. Hernández Juárez, "Los extranjeros." Most of the Chinese people displaced from the state likely moved north to the city of Juarez or Torreón. More research like Juárez's is needed.

23. Dirección General de Estadistica, *Quinto censo de población*, 106, 162.

24. López Victoria, *La campaña nacionalista*.

25. Velázquez Andrade, *La educación sexual*.

26. "Comité Mexicano del Tercero Congreso Internacional de Higiene Escolar," *Periodico Oficial del Estado de San Luis Potosi*, August 19, 1909, 11–12.

27. Fidel Urbina, "Higiene Social: Eugenesia," *El Correo Español* (Madrid), August 20, 1912, 1.

28. Gabriel Malda, "Septimo Congreso Medico Latino-Americano," *Gaceta Médica de Mexico* (Mexico City), September 1, 1929, 61–65. By 1930 the Mexican census still only registered forty-eight Chinese residents for the entire state, yet marriage certificates specifically targeting marriage with Chinese men remained in practice. Dirección General de Estadistica, *Quinto censo de población*.

29. Manuel Escontria, "Eugenesia y la Limitacion de la Natalidad," *Gaceta Médica de Mexico* (Mexico City), July 1, 1930, 58–66.

30. Luz Suárez and Guazo, *Eugenesia y racismo*, 107–8.

31. "Decreto No. 2," *Periodico Oficial del Estado de Oaxaca*, December 31, 1932, 8.

32. Earlier censuses indexed the country's Indian people, mestizos (largely a category of detribalized Indians), and criollo colonists. After the revolution, these categories reflected inconvenient political realities, but more important, they were outdated categories of postrevolutionary racial rule. See González Navarro, "El mestizaje mexicano."

33. Augustine-Adams, "Making Mexico."

34. Chang, "Outsider Crossings."

35. Borah, "Race and Class in Mexico."

36. Manuel Rousseau, "Censos Mayo 1930: Poblacion Industrial, Agricola y Ganadero," *Periodico Oficial del Estado de Tlaxcala*, April 23, 1930, 3–4.

37. For the evaluation of the distribution of medical professionals, see Nigenda, "Regional Distribution." For schools, see Vaughan, *Cultural Politics in Revolution*, 16–17, 47–76.

38. Cámara de Diputados, *DDCLEM*, May 22, 1931, http://cronica.diputados.gob.mx/DDebates/34/1er/Extra/19310522.html.

39. Some of the most important changes made were the devolution of strike regulations to states, the application of contract law to strikes (article 9), and rules for organizing and carrying out agricultural labor, as well as the establishment of the eight-hour workday (article 21).

40. Jorge Robles, "Los Contratos de Protección: Un product de la Ley Federal de Trabajo," *Frente Auténtico del Trabajo*, November 26, 2010, https://fatmexico.wordpress.com/2010/11/26/los-contratos-de-proteccion-un-producto-de-la-ley-federal-de-trabajo/. See also Middlebrook, *Paradox of Revolution*.

41. Velásquez Morales, "Xenofobia y Racismo."

42. Lewis, *Iron Horse Imperialism*. In the railroad industry, the majority of those expelled were American workers, some Chinese workers were also railroad employees and were also forced out but not specifically on the grounds of being Chinese, like so many others.

43. Buchenau, "Small Numbers, Great Impact."

44. "Telegram from Secretary of the Interior to President Rodríguez, 4 July 1933," 327–41, Abelardo Rodríguez Papers, AGN, Mexico City.

45. Cámara de Diputados, *DDCLEM*, September 1, 1928, http://cronica.diputados.gob.mx/DDebates/33/1er/Ord/19280901.html, and September 1, 1931, http://cronica.diputados.gob.mx/DDebates/34/2do/Ord/19310901.html.

46. Julia Schiavone Camacho's groundbreaking study of the displacement remains the most authoritative account of this tragedy.

47. Schiavone Camacho, *Chinese Mexicans*.

48. Baitenmann, "Counting on State Subjects."

Conclusion

1. Becerra, *Historia de los Pantenoes*.

2. Municipal Cemetery No. 1, 3rd Class Registry, Municipal Cemetery of Mexicali, 1924–44.

3. Becerra, *Historia de los Pantenoes*.

4. Gaxiola, *El Presidente Rodríguez*; A. Rodríguez, *Memoria administrativa*.

5. "Rodríguez May Be Named," *Los Angeles Times*, September 10, 1928.

6. "Policy Voiced by Rodríguez," *Los Angeles Times*, September 7, 1932.

7. Ezequiel Padilla, Cámara de Diputados, *DDCLEM*, September 4, 1932, http://cronica.diputados.gob.mx/DDebates/35/1er/Ord/19320904.html.

8. Cámara de Diputados, *DDCLEM*, October 21, 1932, http://cronica.diputados.gob.mx/DDebates/35/1er/Ord/19321021.html.

9. Ibid., original emphasis.

10. Cámara de Diputados, *DDCLEM*, December 27, 1932, http://cronica.diputados.gob.mx/DDebates/35/1er/Ord/19321227.html.

11. More research is called for in this area to examine the different ways that state-sponsored identifications invented credentials for nationality in different ethnic regions.

12. Gojman de Backal, *Camisas, escudos, y desfiles militares*.

13. The Mexican State Department drove a campaign to demonize Japanese growers who employed migrant Mexican labor. U.S. Labor Department intervention on behalf of Mexican workers was deemed a victory over Asian tyrants. Chang, "Outsider Crossings." See also G. Gonzalez, "Company Unions."

14. A. Rodríguez, *Memoria administrativa*.

15. Alonso, "Conforming disconformity."

16. "Campaña Nacionalista Mexicana, Published in 1933 by the General Committee of the Nationalist Campaign and Dedicated to President Abelardo L. Rodríguez describing the Mesoamerican Symbols Painted alongside His Portrait on a Piece of Hide in the Style of Some Pre-Columbian Painted Manuscripts," pamphlet, folder 5, box 3, Papers of Rafael Melgar, Special Collections, Howard Tilton Memorial Library, Tulane University.

17. "From Styles to Secretary of State regarding Anti-Chinese Activity in the Chihuahua Consular District, 27 May 1933," RG 59, 312.93/265, and "From Daniels to Secretary of State Regarding Campaign against the Chinese in Mexico, 1 June 1933," RG 84, 312.93/237, Chinese Problem.

18. Chong, *Hijos de un país poderoso*, 121.

19. Departamento Agrario, *Diario Oficial*, July 10, 1937, 11.

20. "Oficio No. 82," *Periódico Oficial del Estado de Chihuahua*, November 12, 1938, 7.

21. "Mexican Chief States Policy," *Los Angeles Times*, September 2, 1933, 1.

22. *Periódico Oficial del Estado de Morelos Nuevo*, October 23, 1932, 7; Satow, 7 *Décadas*.

23. *Periódico Oficial del Estado de Tamaulipas*, November 5, 1932, 3.

24. In December 1932 Abelardo Rodríguez formed the Consejo Nacional de Cultura Física (National Council of Physical Culture). The new council organized local, state, and national athletic competitions, expanding sports instruction and athletic training. On July 22, 1933, President Rodríguez, sports delegates from every state of the republic, the National Council of Physical Culture, and the Mexican Olympic Committee inaugurated the Confederación Deportiva Mexicana (Confederation of Mexican Sports) (CDM). Sports and athletics were not simply a metaphor but a social and biopolitical mechanism of the national state. By "the will of athletes from the Mexican nation and the supreme integration of a strong race whose muscles attest to its force," the CDM would provide the institutional infrastructure to display the self-evident racial strength of the nation. Arenas Rosas, *60 aniversario*.

25. Partido Revolucionario Institucional, *Historia documental*, 92.

26. Vargas and Menéndez, "Memoria."

27. Ibid., 112, 110–11.

28. This lack of experience with the ramifications of credit led one U.S. analyst to conclude that "the great mass of Mexico's farming population—the Indians in the thousands of little villages scattered throughout the land—have to this day—remained in almost total ignorance of even the meaning of credit." "Calles and the Agrarian Problem," *Agricultural Studies* 1, no. 5 (1928): 18, Bancroft Library, University of California, Berkeley.

29. *Informes Presidenciales: Abelardo L. Rodríguez*, Centro de Documentación, Información y Análisis (Mexico City: Cámara de Diputados, 2006), 4, http://www.diputados.gob.mx/sedia/sia/re/RE-ISS-09-06-07.pdf.

30. Ibid., 75–81, 77. These schools represented a convergence of the Ministry of Education and the secretary of agricultural development.

31. Cámara de Diputados, *DDCLEM*, November 16, 1933, http://cronica.diputados
.gob.mx/DDebates/35/2do/Ord/19331116.html.

32. Siqueiros, "La Nacionalidad Mexicana."

33. Leonor Llach, "La Etica de la educación sexual," *El Nacional* (Mexico City), June
3, 1933, in Secretaria de Educación Pública, *Algunos datos*, 17–18.

34. Secretaria de Educación Pública, *Algunos datos*, 53–65.

35. "Academia Nacional Medicina," *Periódico Oficial del Estado de Baja California Norte*,
August 10, 1932, 15.

36. Lazcano Armienta, *La política agraria*.

37. Cámara de Diputados, *DDCLEM*, December 30, 1935, http://cronica.diputados
.gob.mx/DDebates/36/2do/Ord/19351230.html.

38. Cámara de Diputados, *DDCLEM*, December 31, 1935, http://cronica.diputados
.gob.mx/DDebates/36/2do/Ord/19351231.html.

39. Kurczyn and Arenas, *La Población en México*, 57–79. Also see Valdés, "XXV Aniversario."

40. Velázquez Morales, "Diferencias políticas."

41. Francisco Gaxiola, "Telegram from Gaxiola, Private Secretary to President Rodríguez to Edmundo Guajardo, Attorney for the Chinese, February 22, 1934," RG 85,
55855.380B, NARA, Washington, DC.

42. At the time, even Governor Lujo of the territory believed that the Chinese businesspeople helped bring Mexican jobs to the valley; he cited more than two thousand
Mexicans who worked for various Chinese businesses. "Letter from Augustin Olachea
and Antonio Banuet to the Secretary General, May 10, 1934," 2/73, Abelardo Rodríguez
Papers, Instituto de Investigaciones Históricos, Universidad Autónoma de Baja California, Tijuana; "Letter from Daniels, Mexico City, to Secretary of State, Washington,
D.C., February 10, 1934," RG 85, NARA, Washington, DC.

43. Papers of Abelardo Rodríguez, 181–17–1, 1934 AR, AGN, Mexico City. In Ensenada,
antichinistas issued an order for the town's Chinese people to leave the city. After
failed talks with the territorial government and resistance by the Chinese community,
the orders failed to produce evictions as in San Luis Potosi. See F. González, "Chinese
Dragon."

44. While Guajardo advocated for a direct appeal to President Rodríguez, many of
the Chinese residents remained less convinced that conditions would improve. See
"Letter from Perkins, Inspector in Charge, INS, San Ysidro, CA, to the District Director
at INS, Los Angeles, CA, February 26, 1934," RG 85, 55855.380B, NARA, Washington,
DC. Guajardo implored Rodríguez to replace the current governor with someone who
would be able to offer real protection to the Chinese community or else the overall
community would risk a possible exodus. "Letter from Guajardo, Attorney for the Chinese, to Mexican President Rodríguez, February 25, 1934," RG 85, 55855.380B, NARA,
Washington, DC.

45. "Letter from Hawks, Secretary of U.S. Embassy to Casauranc, Minister for Foreign
Affairs, April 22, 1934," RG 85, 55855.380B; "Memorandum of Conversation between
Hawks, Secretary of U.S. Embassy and Casauranc, Minister for Foreign Affairs, March
17, 1934," RG 85; "News Article: Chinese Migrating toward the Center (translated)," *El
Mundo*, RG 85, 55855.380B, all NARA, Washington, DC.

46. Mexico Executive Committee of the Federation of Syndicates and Labor Unions of the Northern District of the Territory of Lower California, "Notice to the Public Response to the National League (translated), March 13, 1934," RG 85, NARA, Washington, DC; "Newspaper, *El Nacionalista* (Mexico City), News Article: The First Anti-Chinese Movement (translated), April 15, 1934," RG 85, NARA, Washington, DC.

47. "Letter from Spurlock, Inspector in Charge, Calexico, CA, to the District Director, INS Calexico, October 24, 1934," Consulate at Mexicali, Mexico, RG 85, NARA, College Park; "Letter from Otto Matz, Immigrant Inspector, Calexico to Inspector in Charge, Calexico, October 22, 1934," Consulate at Mexicali, Mexico, RG 85, NARA, College Park.

48. Cárdenas, *El problema*.

49. "Report by Daniels on the Colonization of Lands near Mexicali, Lower California, by the Government of Mexico, August 24, 1936," Consulate at Mexicali, Mexico, NARA, College Park, Maryland.

50. "Letter from Daniels to the U.S. Consul in Mexicali, March 16, 1937," Consulate at Mexicali, Mexico, NARA, College Park, Maryland. The Mexican state would no longer tolerate their Chinese tenants.

51. Throughout the 1920s he headed the National Agrarian Confederation, a powerful lobby for land reform in the PNR. While the organization remained unsuccessful and mired in scandals, Magaña maintained the reputation of being a *gallo* of agrarian reform, true to Zapata's ideals. Hall, "Álvaro Obregón"; Solano, *Los hombres del poder*. A *gallo*, or rooster, is someone who is perceived as a strong masculine patriarch.

52. "Bowman Reports on Political Review for March 1936, March 31, 1936," Consulate at Mexicali, Mexico, NARA, College Park, Maryland.

53. "Report by Daniels on the Colonization."

54. "Bowman Reports on Agrarian Disorders at Mexicali," 1936, Consulate at Mexicali, Mexico, NARA, College Park, Maryland.

55. Adolfo Wilhelmy, "*La Opinion* news clipping, February 1, 1937," Consulate at Mexicali, Mexico NARA, College Park, Maryland.

56. "Bowman Reports on Agrarian Disorders."

57. Kerig, "Yankee Enclave."

58. "Bowman Reports on Present Status of the Agrarian Project at Mexicali, February 14, 1938," RG 85, 811.3–892.43, Consulate at Mexicali, Mexico, NARA, College Park, Maryland.

59. General Petition from the Union of Agrarian Communities of the Northern Territory of Lower California, November 12, 1937," RG 85, Consulate at Mexicali, Mexico, NARA, College Park, Maryland.

60. "Daniels Reports on the Agrarian Cases: Profiles of Affectations and Official Dotations, October 18, 1938," RG 85, Consulate at Mexicali, Mexico, NARA, College Park, Maryland.

61. The union had hoped to gain possession of key buildings and properties in the urban center left behind by the hoped-for Chinese exodus. "Bowman Reports on Political Review for April 1937, April 30, 1937," RG 85, Consulate at Mexicali, Mexico, NARA, College Park, Maryland.

62. "Moores Reports on the Political Review for February 1940, February 29, 1940," RG 85, Consulate at Mexicali, Mexico, NARA, College Park, Maryland.

63. "Myers Reports on the Proposed Expulsion of All Foreigners from the Northern Territory of Baja California, Mexico, October 5, 1937," RG 85, Consulate at Mexicali, Mexico, NARA, College Park, Maryland.

64. Hart, *Revolutionary Mexico*; Aguilar, Carmona, and Carrion, *Problemas del Capitalismo Mexicano*; Villegas, *American Extremes*.

65. Dwyer, *Agrarian Dispute*, 149.

66. Gamio, *Hacia un Mexico Nuevo*, 25.

67. Manuel Gamio, "Circular No. 45," *Periódico Oficial del Estado de Morelos Nuevo*, April 23, 1939, 1.

68. "Secretaria de Gobernacion," *Periódico Oficial del Estado de Baja California Norte*, June 30, 1934, 9.

69. "Ley de Secretaria de Gobernacion," *Periódico Oficial del Estado de Baja California Norte*, September 10, 1934, 14.

70. Gómez Izquierdo and Rozat Dupeyron, *Los caminos del racismo*.

Bibliography

Aguilar, Alonso, Fernando Carmona, and Jorge Carrion. *Problemas del Capitalismo Mexicano*. Mexico City: Editorial Tiempo, 1983.

Alacrón, Laura. *José Maria Maytorena: Una Biografia Politica*. Mexico City: Universidad Iberoamerica, 2008.

Albarran, Elena Jackson. *Seen and Heard in Mexico: Children and Revolutionary Cultural Nationalism*. Lincoln: University of Nebraska Press, 2015.

Alfaro-Velcamp, Theresa. *So Far from Allah, So Close to Mexico: Middle-Eastern Immigrants in Modern Mexico*. Austin: University of Texas Press, 2007.

Algunos datos y opiniones sobre la educación sexual en México. Mexico City: Secretaría de Educación Pública, 1934.

Alonso, Ana María. "Conforming Disconformity: 'Mestizaje,' Hybridity, and the Aesthetics of Mexican Nationalism." *Cultural Anthropology* 19 (2004): 459–90.

———. *Thread of Blood: Colonialism, Revolution, and Gender on Mexico's Northern Frontier*. Tucson: University of Arizona Press, 1995.

Anderson, Benedict. *Imagined Communities: Reflections on the Origin and Spread of Nationalism*. New York: Verso Press, 1991.

Annino, Antonio. "Ciudadanía 'versus' Gobernabilidad Republicana en México: Los Orígenes de un Dilema." In *Ciudadanía Política y Formación de las Naciones: Perspectivas Históricas de América Latina*, edited by Hilda Sabato, 62–93. Mexico City: El Colegio de México, 1999.

Appadurai, Arjun. *Modernity at Large: Cultural Dimensions of Globalization*. Minneapolis: University of Minnesota Press, 1996.

Appiah, Kwame Anthony, and Amy Gutmann. *Color Conscious: The Political Morality of Race*. Princeton: Princeton University Press, 1998.

Ard, Michael. *An Eternal Struggle: How the National Action Party Transformed Mexican Politics*. Santa Barbara, CA: Greenwood, 2003.

Arenas Rosas, Luis, coor. *60 aniversario: Confederación Deportiva Mexicana 1933–1993*. Mexico City: Confederación Deportiva Mexicana, Coordinación Nacional de Comunicación Social, 1993.

Augustine-Adams, Kif. "Making Mexico: Legal Nationality, Chinese Race, and the 1930 Population Census." *Law and History Review* 27 (2009): 113–44.

Azcárate y Lezama, Juán Francisco, and Orozco Luis Cháve. *Un Programa de Política Internacional: Junta Provisional Gubernativa, Comisión de Relaciones Exteriores, 1821–1822*. Archivo Histórico Diplomático Mexicano 37. Mexico City: Secretaria de Relaciones Exteriores, 1932.

Baitenmann, Helga. "Counting on State Subjects: State Formation and Citizenship in Twentieth-Century Mexico." In *State Formation: Anthropological Perspectives*, edited by Christian Krohn-Hansen and Knut Nustad, 292–363. London: Pluto, 2005.

Barajas Durán, Rafael. *La raíz NAZI del PAN*. Mexico City: El Chamuco Editorial, 2014.

Basch, Linda, Nina Glick-Schiller, and Cristina Szanton Blanc, eds. *Nations Unbound: Transnational Projects, Postcolonial Predicaments, and Deterritorialized Nation-States*. London: Routledge, 2005.

Becerra, Carmen. *Historia de los Pantenoes de Mexicali, Fondo de Pablo Martinez*. Mexicali, Mexico: Archivo Histórico del Estado de Baja California, 1990.

Benjamin, Thomas, and Mark Wasserman, eds. *Provinces of the Revolution: Essays on Regional Mexican History, 1910–1929*. Albuquerque: University of New Mexico Press, 1990.

Bennett, Herman Lee. *Colonial Blackness: A History of Afro-Mexico*. Bloomington: Indiana University Press, 2009.

Borah, Woodrow W. "Race and Class in Mexico." *Pacific Historical Review* 23, no. 4 (1954): 331–41.

Buchenau, Jürgen. "Small Numbers, Great Impact: Mexico and Its Immigrants, 1821–1973." *Journal of American Ethnic History* 20 (2001): 23–49.

Buchenau, Jürgen, and William Beezley. *State Governors in the Mexican Revolution, 1910–1952: Portraits in Conflict, Courage, and Corruption*. New York: Rowman, 2009.

Bulnes, Francisco. *Sobre el Hemisferio Norte, Once Mil Leguas: Impresiones de Viaje a Cuba, los Estados-Unidos, el Japón, China, Cochinchina, Egipto, y Europa*. Mexico City: Revista Universal, 1875.

———. "Las Tres Razas Humanas." In *El Porvenir de las Naciones Hispano Americanos ante las Conquistas Recientes de Europa y los Estados Unidos*, 5–31. Mexico City: Mariano Nava, 1899.

———. *The Whole Truth about Mexico: President Wilson's Responsibility*. Translated by Dora Scott. New York: M. Bulnes, 1916.

Buve, Raymond. *El Movimiento Revolucionario en Tlaxcala*. Mexico City: Universidad Iberoamericana, 1994.

———. "Tlaxcala: Consolidating a Cacicazgo." In Benjamin and Wasserman, *Provinces of the Revolution*, 185–217.

Canudas, Enrique. *Las Venas de Plata en la Historia de Mexico: Sintesis de Historia Economica, Siglo XIX*. 3 vols. Villahermosa, Mexico: Universidad Nacional Autónoma de Tabasco, 2005.

Cárdenas, Lazaro. *El problema de los territories federales: Un llamamiento al patriotismo y al sentido de responsibilidad del pueblo Mexicano.* Mexico City: Talleres Gráficos de la Nación, 1936.

Castellanos Guerrero, Alicia. *Imágenes del racismo en México.* Iztapalapa, Mexico: Plaza y Valdes, 2003.

Castellanos Guerrero, Alicia, and Juan Manuel Sandoval. *Nación, racismo, e identidad.* Mexico City: Nuestro Tiempo, 1998.

Castillo-Muñoz, Veronica. *Divided Communities: Agrarian Struggles, Transnational Migration, and Families in Northern Mexico, 1910–1952.* Berkeley: University of California Press, 2009.

Cervera, José Juan. *La Gloria de La Raza: Los Chinos en Yucatán.* Merida, Mexico: Grupo Impresor Unicornio, 2007.

Chan, Sucheng. *This Bittersweet Soil: The Chinese in California Agriculture, 1860–1910.* Berkeley: University of California Press, 1989.

Chang, Jason Oliver. "Outsider Crossings: History, Culture, and Geography of Mexicali's Chinese Community." PhD dissertation, Department of Ethnic Studies, University of California, Berkeley, 2010.

———. "Racial Alterity in the Mestizo Nation." *Journal of Asian American Studies* 14 (2011): 331–59.

Chang, Kornell. *Pacific Connections: The Making of the U.S.-Canadian Borderlands.* Berkeley: University of California, 2012.

Chong, José Luis. *Hijos de un país poderoso. La inmigración china a América (1850–1950).* Mexico City: Palabra Clio, 2008.

Chuh, Kandice. *Imagine Otherwise: On Asian Americanist Critique.* Durham: Duke University Press, 2003.

Comité Ejecutivo Nacional. *Proyectos de Estatutos.* December. Mexico City: Partido Nacional Revolucionario, 1933.

Cott, Kenneth. "Mexican Diplomacy and the Chinese Issue, 1876–1910." *Hispanic American Historical Review* 67 (1987): 63–85.

Covarrubias, José. "La Inmigracion China: Considerada Desde Los Puntos de Vista Intelectual y Moral." *Revista Positiva* 67 (1908): 153–70.

———. *La Trascendencia Politica de la Reforma Agraria.* Mexico City: Antigua imprenta de Murguía, 1922.

Craib, Raymond B., III. *Cartographic Mexico: A History of State Fixations and Fugitive Landscapes.* Durham: Duke University Press, 2004.

———. *Chinese Immigrants in Porfirian Mexico: A Preliminary Study of Settlement, Economic Activity and Anti-Chinese Sentiment.* Latin American Institute, University of New Mexico, Research Paper Series 28. Albuquerque: University of New Mexico, 1996.

Cuba Commission Report: A Hidden History of the Chinese in Cuba: The Original English-Language Text of 1876. Baltimore: Johns Hopkins University Press, 1993.

Cumberland, Charles C. *Mexican Revolution: Genesis under Madero.* Austin: University of Texas Press, 2014.

Dambourges, Leo Jacques. "The Anti-Chinese Campaigns in Sonora, Mexico, 1900–1931." PhD dissertation, Department of History, University of Arizona, 1974.

———. "The Chinese Massacre in Torréon (Coahuila) in 1911." *Arizona and the West* 16 (1974): 233–46.

Daniels, Roger. *The Politics of Prejudice: The Anti-Japanese Movement in California and the Struggle for Japanese Exclusion.* Berkeley: University of California Press, 1999.

Day, Iyko. "Lost in Transnation: Uncovering Asian Canada." *Amerasia* 33 (2007): 67–96.

de la Maza, Francisco F. *Código de Colonización y Terrenos Baldíos de la República, 1451–1892.* Mexico City: Oficina de la Secretaría de Fomento, 1893.

Delgado, Grace. *Making the Chinese Mexican: Global Migration, Localism, and Exclusion in the U.S.-Mexico Borderlands.* Palo Alto: Stanford University Press, 2012.

Dirección General de Biblioteca, Universidad Nacional Autónoma de Nuevo Leon. *Breve Reseñas de Las Obras del Desagüe del Valle de Mexico.* Mexico: Tipografia de Francicso Diaz de Leon, 1901.

Duntley, Joshua, and David Buss. "Homicide Adaptations." *Aggression and Violent Behavior* 16, no. 5 (2011): 399–410.

Dwyer, John. *The Agrarian Dispute: The Expropriation of American Owned Rural Land in Postrevolutionary Mexico.* Durham: Duke University Press, 2009.

Escobar, José U. *Las tribus de exploradores mexicanos.* Mexico City, 1929.

Espinoza, Jose Angel. *El Ejemplo de Sonora.* Mexico City, 1932.

———. *El Problema Chino en Mexico.* Sonora, Mexico, 1931.

Falcón, Romana. "Force and the Search for Consent: The Role of the Jefeturas Politicas of Coahuila in National State Formation." In *Everyday Forms of State Formation: Revolution and the Negotiation of Rule in Modern Mexico*, edited by Gil Joseph and Daniel Nugent, 107–35. Durham: Duke University Press, 1994.

Fallaw, Ben. "The Seduction of Revolution: Anticlerical Campaigns against Confession in Mexico, 1914–1935." *Journal of Latin American Studies* 45 (2013): 91–120.

Fanon, Frantz. *Black Skin, White Masks.* New York: Grove, 1967.

Felix, Maricela Gonzalez. *Viaje al corazón de la península: El testimonio de Manuel Lee Mancilla.* Mexicali, Mexico: Instituto de Cultura de Baja California, 2000.

Fitzgerald, David Scott, and David Cook-Martín. *Culling the Masses: The Democratic Origins of Racist Immigration Policy in the Americas.* Cambridge, MA: Harvard University Press, 2014.

Foucault, Michel, François Ewald, and Alessandro Fontana. *The Birth of Biopolitics: Lectures at the Collège de France, 1978–1979.* Edited by Michel Senellart. New York: Palgrave Macmillan, 2010.

Gamio, Manuel. *Forjando Patria: Pro-Nacionalismo.* Mexico City: Porrúa, 1916.

———. *Hacia un Mexico Nuevo: Problemas Sociales.* Mexico City: Instituto Nacional Indigenista, 1935.

Garcia, Jerry. *Looking like the Enemy: Japanese Mexicans, the Mexican State, and U.S. Hegemony, 1897–1945.* Tucson: University of Arizona Press, 2014.

Gardiner, Clinton Harvey. "Early Diplomatic Relations between Mexico and the Far East." *The Americas* 6 (1950): 401–14.

Gardner, David Allen. "Prensa obrera, crisis y nacionalismo: Pro Patria ante la Gran Depresión." *Historiadores de la Prensa* 282 (2007): 6–7.

Garrido, Luis Javier. *El partido de la revolución institucionalizada (medio siglo de poder político en Mexico): la formación del nuevo estado, 1928–1945*. Mexico City: Siglo Veintuno Editores, 1982.

Gaxiola, Francisco. *El Presidente Rodriguez*. Mexico City: Cultura, 1938.

Giddens, Anthony. *A Contemporary Critique of Historical Materialism: The Nation-State and Violence*. Berkeley: University of California Press, 1985.

Gojman de Backal, Alicia. *Camisas, escudos y desfiles militares: Los dorados y el anti-semitismo en Mexico, 1934–1940*. Mexico City: Universidad Nacional Autónoma de Mexico, 2000.

———. "Minorías, estado, y movimiento nacionalistas de la clase media en México: Liga anti China y anti-judia, siglo XX." In *Judaica latinoamericana: Estudios histórico-sociales*, 174–91. Jerusalem: Editorial Universitaria Manges, 1988.

Goldberg, David Theo. *The Racial State*. New York: Wiley, 2002.

Gómez Izquierdo, José Jorge. *El movimiento antichino en México (1871–1934): problemas del racismo y del nacionalismo durante la Revolución Mexicana*. Mexico City: Instituto de Antropología e Historia, 1991.

Gómez Izquierdo, José Jorge, and Guy Rozat Dupeyron. *Los caminos del racismo en México*. Mexico City: Plaza y Valdés, 2005.

González, Fredy. "Chinese Dragon and Eagle of Anáhuac: The Local, National, and International Implications of the Ensenada Anti-Chinese Campaign of 1934." *Western Historical Quarterly* 44 (2013): 48–68.

———. "'We won't be bullied anymore': Chinese-Mexican Relations and the Chinese Community in Mexico, 1931–1971." PhD dissertation, Department of History, Yale University, 2013.

Gonzalez, Gilbert. "Company Unions, the Mexican Consulate, and the Imperial Valley Agricultural Strikes, 1928–1934." *Western Historical Quarterly* 27, no. 1 (1996): 53–73.

González Compeán, Miguel, and Leonardo Lomelí. *El partido de la revolución: institución y conflicto, 1928–1999*. Mexico City: Fondo de Cultura Económica, 2000.

González Navarro, Moisés. *La Colonización en México, 1877–1910*. Mexico City: Talleres de Impresión de Estampillas y Valores, 1960.

———. "El mestizaje mexicano en el periodo nacional." *Revista Mexicana de Sociología* 30 (1968): 35–52.

———. *El Porfiriato: La vida social*. Edited by Daniel Cosío Villegas. 8 vols. Historia Moderna de Mexico 4. Buenos Aires: Editorial Hermes, 1957.

Granados, Marta. "Inmigración de una 'raza prohibida': Afro-Estadounidenses en Mexico, 1924–1940." *Aztlán: A Journal of Chicano Studies* 34 (2009): 169–92.

Guidotti-Hernández, Nicole. *Unspeakable Violence: Remapping U.S. and Mexican National Imaginaries*. Durham: Duke University Press, 2011.

Guzmán, Rosendo Romero. "Segregación racial en Sinaloa: la formación de los barrios chinos." *Clio* 2 (1994): 133–37.

Habermas, Jürgen, Sara Lennox, and Frank Lennox. "The Public Sphere: An Encyclopedia Article (1964)." *New German Critique* 3 (1974): 49–55.

Hale, Charles A. *The Transformation of Liberalism in Late Nineteenth-Century Mexico*. Princeton: Princeton University Press, 1989.

Hall, Linda. "Alvaro Obregon and the Politics of Mexican Land Reform, 1920–1924." *Hispanic American Historical Review* 60 (1980): 213–38.

Hart, John Mason. *Empire and Revolution: The Americans in Mexico since the Civil War.* Berkeley: University of California Press, 2002.

———. *Revolutionary Mexico: The Coming and Process of the Mexican Revolution.* Berkeley: University of California Press, 1989.

Hernández, José Angel. *Mexican American Colonization during the Nineteenth Century: A History of the U.S.-Mexico Borderlands.* Cambridge: Cambridge University Press, 2012.

Hernández Juárez, Saúl Iván. "Los extranjeros en San Luis Potosi, 1929–1932." Master's thesis, History Department, El Colegio de San Luis, 2012.

Hernández, Tanya Katerí. *Racial Subordination in Latin America: The Role of the State, Customary Law, and the New Civil Rights Response.* Cambridge: Cambridge University Press, 2012.

Herrera Barreda, Maria del Socorro. *Inmigrantes Hispanocubanos en Mexico durante el porfiriato.* Mexico City: Biblioteca de Signos, 2003.

Hing, Bill Ong. *Defining America through Immigration Policy.* Philadelphia: Temple University Press, 2004.

Holden, Robert. *Mexico and the Survey of Public Lands: The Management of Modernization, 1876–1911.* DeKalb: Northern Illinois University Press, 1994.

Hu-DeHart, Evelyn. "Immigrants to a Developing Society: The Chinese in Northern Mexico, 1875–1932." *Journal of Arizona History* (1980): 275–312.

———. *Yaqui Resistance and Survival: The Struggle for Land and Autonomy, 1821–1910.* Madison: University of Wisconsin Press, 1984.

Jamieson, Tulitas, and Evelyn Payne. *Tulitas of Torreón: Reminiscences of Life in Mexico.* El Paso: Texas Western Press, 1969.

Jenkins, John Edward. *The Coolie: His Rights and Wrongs.* London: Strahan, 1871.

Jones, Halbert. *The War Has Brought Peace to Mexico: World War II and the Consolidation of the Post-Revolutionary State.* Albuquerque: University of New Mexico Press, 2014.

Joseph, Gilbert Michael. *Revolution from Without: Yucatán, Mexico, and the United States, 1880–1924.* Durham: Duke University Press, 1988.

Jung, Moon-Ho. *Coolies and Cane: Race, Labor and Sugar in the Age of Emancipation.* Baltimore: Johns Hopkins University Press, 2006.

Kerig, Dorothy P. "Yankee Enclave: The Colorado River Land Company and Mexican Agrarian Reform in Baja California, 1902–1944." PhD dissertation, Department of History, University of California, Irvine, 1988.

Kerig, Dorothy Pierson, and Tomás Segovia. *El valle de Mexicali y la Colorado River Land Company, 1902–1946.* Mexicali, Mexico: Universidad Autónoma de Baja California, 2001.

Knight, Alan. "Cardenismo: Juggernaut or Jalopy?" *Journal of Latin American Studies* 26 (1994): 73–107.

———. *The Mexican Revolution: Counter-Revolution and Reconstruction,* Vol. 2. Lincoln: University of Nebraska Press, 1990.

———. "Popular Culture and the Revolutionary State in Mexico, 1910–1940." *Hispanic American Historical Review* (1994): 393–444.

Knowlton, Robert, and Lucrecia Orensanz. "El ejido mexicano en el siglo XIX." *Historia Mexicana* 48 (1998): 71–96.

Kourí, Emilio. "La invención del ejido." *Nexos*, January 2015. http://www.nexos.com.mx/?p=23778.

———. *A Pueblo Divided: Business, Property, and Community in Papantla, Mexico.* Stanford: Stanford University Press, 2004.

Kurczyn, Patricia, and César Arenas. *La Población en México, un enfoque desde la perspectiva del derecho social.* Instituto de Investigaciones Jurídicas. Mexico City: Universidad Nacional Autónoma de México, 2009.

Lafragua, José María. *Memoria Que en Cumplimiento del Precepto Constitucional Presentó al Septimo Congreso de la Union en el Primer Periodo de sus Sesiones.* Mexico City: Secretaría de Relaciones Exteriores, 1873.

Lazcano Armienta, Matías Hirám. *La política agraria del PNR durante el Maximato.* Culiacán Rosales, Mexico: Universidad Autónoma de Sinaloa, Facultad de Historia, 2007.

League of Nations. "China and the United States of Mexico: Exchange of Notes Embodying an Agreement for the Provisional Modification of the Sino-Mexican Treaty, Concluded at Washington, December 14, 1899, Mexico, September 26, 1933." In *League of Nations*, 201–10. Lausanne, Switzerland: League of Nations, 1922. http://www.worldlii.org/int/other/LNTSer/1922/154.pdf.

Lee, Erika. *At America's Gate.* Chapel Hill: University of North Carolina Press, 2003.

———. "Orientalisms in the Americas: A Hemispheric Approach to Asian American History." Journal of Asian American Studies 8, no. 3 (2005): 235–56.

Lee-Loy, Anne-Marie. "The Chinese Are Preferred over All Others: Nineteenth-Century Representations of the Chinese in Trinidad and British Guiana." *Asian Studies Review* 27 (2003): 205–25.

———. *Searching for Mr. Chin: Constructions of Nation and the Chinese in West Indian Literature.* Philadelphia: Temple University Press, 2010.

Lesser, Jeffery. *Negotiating National Identity: Immigrants, Minorities, and the Struggle for Ethnicity in Brazil.* Durham: Duke University Press, 1999.

Lewis, Daniel. *Iron Horse Imperialism: The Southern Pacific of Mexico, 1880–1951.* Tucson: University of Arizona Press, 2007.

Liceaga, Eduardo. "Bubonic Plague in the Port of Mazatlan, State of Sinaloa, Republic of Mexico." *Public Health Pap Rep* 30 (1905): 226–37.

Lipsitz, George. *The Possessive Investment in Whiteness: How White People Profit from Identity Politics.* Philadelphia: Temple University Press, 2006.

Lomnitz-Adler, Claudio. "Anti-Semitism and the Ideology of the Mexican Revolution." *Representations* 110 (2010): 1–28.

———. *El Antisemitismo y la Ideologia de la Revolución Mexicana.* Mexico City: Fondo de Cultura Económica, 2010.

———. *Deep Mexico, Silent Mexico: An Anthropology of Nationalism.* Minneapolis: University of Minnesota Press, 2001.

———. *Modernidad indiana: nueve ensayos sobre nación y mediación en Mexico.* Barcelona: Planeta, 1999.

López Victoria, José Manuel. *La campaña nacionalista.* Mexico City: Ediciones Botas, 1965.

Loveman, Mara. "The Modern State and the Primitive Accumulation of Symbolic Power." *American Journal of Sociology* (2005): 1651–83.

———. *National Colors: Racial Classification and the State in Latin America*. Oxford: Oxford University Press, 2014.

Lowe, Lisa. *Immigrant Acts: On Asian American Cultural Politics*. Durham: Duke University Press, 1996.

Luz Suárez, Laura, and López Guazo. *Eugenesia y racismo en Mexico*. Coyoacán, Mexico: Universidad Nacional Autónoma de Mexico, 2005.

Lye, Colleen. *America's Asia: Racial Form and American Literature, 1893–1945*. Princeton: Princeton University Press, 2005.

Mallon, Florencia. *Peasant and Nation: The Making of Postcolonial Mexico and Peru*. Berkeley: University of California Press, 1995.

Mancilla, Manuel Lee, and Maricela González Félix. *Viaje al corazón de la península: El Testimonio de Manuel Lee Mancilla*. Mexicali, Mexico: Instituto de Cultura de Baja California, 2000.

Mandujano-López, Ruth. "Transpacific Mexico: Encounters with China and Japan in the Age of Steam, 1867–1914." PhD dissertation, Department of History, University of British Columbia, Vancouver, 2012.

McBride, George. *The Land Systems of Mexico*. American Geographical Society Research Series 12. New York: American Geographical Society, 1923.

McKeown, Adam. "Conceptualizing Chinese Diasporas, 1842–1949." *Journal of Asian Studies* 58 (1999): 306–31.

Medina Peña, Luis. *Hacia el Nuevo Estado: Mexico, 1920–1994*. Mexico City: Fondo Cultura Económica, 2010.

Memoria Presentado al Congreso de la Union. Mexico City: Secretaria de Comunicaciones y Obras Publicas, 1907.

Meyers, William K. "Seasons of Rebellion: Nature, Organisation of Cotton Production, and the Dynamics of Revolution in La Laguna, Mexico, 1910–1916." *Journal of Latin American Studies* 30 (1998): 63–94.

Middlebrook, Kevin. *The Paradox of Revolution: Labor, the State, and Authoritarianism in Mexico*. Baltimore: Johns Hopkins University Press, 1995.

Mills, Charles W. *The Racial Contract*. Ithaca: Cornell University Press, 1997.

Molina, Daniel. "La educación socialista y un gobierno anti cardenista: El Caso de Tlaxcala, Mexico 1935–1936." *Huellas de la Historia* 4 (2012): 1–11.

Molina, Natalia. *Fit to Be Citizens: Public Health and Race in Los Angeles, 1879–1939*. Berkeley: University of California Press, 2001.

———. *How Race Is Made in America: Immigration, Citizenship, and the Historical Power of Racial Scripts*. Berkeley: University of California Press, 2013.

Molina, Olegario. *Mensaje leido por el C. Gobernador del estado de Yucatán*. Mérida, Mexico: Gamboa Guzman, 1904.

Molina Enríquez, Andrés, and Arnaldo Córdova. *Los Grandes Problemas Nacionales*. Mexico City: A. Carranza e hijos, 1909.

Moon-Ho, Jung. *Coolies and Cane: Race, Labor, and Sugar in the Age of Emancipation*. Baltimore: John Hopkins University Press, 2008.

Moreno Figueroa, Mónica G. "Distributed Intensities: Whiteness, Mestizaje, and the Logics of Mexican Racism." *Ethnicities* 10, no. 3 (2010): 387–401.

Ngai, Mae. *Impossible Subjects: Illegal Aliens and the Making of Modern America*. Princeton: Princeton University Press, 2004.

Nigenda, Gustavo. "The Regional Distribution of Doctors in Mexico, 1930–1990: A Policy Assessment." *Health Policy* 39 (1997): 107–22.

Northrup, David. *Indentured Labor in the Age of Imperialism, 1834–1922*. Cambridge: Cambridge University Press, 1995.

Omi, Michael, and Howard Winant. *Racial Formation in the United States*. New York: Routledge, 2014.

Partido Revolucionario Institucional. *Historia documental del Partido de la Revolución*. Vol. 2. PNR 1933. Mexico City: Instituto de Capacitación Política, 1981.

Patterson, Wayne. "The Early Years of Korean Immigration to Mexico: A View from Japanese and Korean Sources." *Seoul Journal of Korean Studies* 6 (1993): 87–103.

Peffer, George Anthony. *If They Don't Bring Their Women Here: Chinese Female Immigration before Exclusion*. Urbana: University of Illinois Press, 1999.

Pérez Jiménez, Marco Antonio. "Raza, nación y revolución: la mantanza de chinos en Torreón, Coahuila, mayo de 1911." Masters thesis, Departamento de Relaciones Internacionales y Ciencias Politicas, Escula de Ciencias Sociales, Artes, y Humanidades, Universidad de las Americas, Puebla, Mexico, 2006.

Pimentel, Francisco. *Memoria sobre las causas que han originado la situacion actual de la raza indígena de México, y medios de remediarla*. Mexico City: Imprente de Andrade y Escalante, 1864.

Piñera Ramírez, David. *Visión histórica de la frontera norte de México: De la revolución a la Segunda Guerra Mundial*. 6 vols. Instituto de Investigaciones Históricos. Mexicali, Mexico: Universidad Autónoma de Baja California, 1994.

Puig Casauranc, J. M. *La Cosheca y la Sembra: Exposición: Critica Social y Politica*. Mexico City, 1928.

Quijano, Aníbal. "Coloniality of Power and Eurocentrism in Latin America." *International Sociology* 5 (2000): 215–32.

Raigosa, Genaro. *Desagüe de la Ciudad Del Valle de Mexico*. Monterrey, Nuevo Leon: Imprenta de Jose Vicente Villada, 1882. Dirección General de Biblioteca, Universidad Nacional Autónoma de Nuevo Leon, Mexico. http://cdigital.dgb.uanl.mx/la/1080013971/1080013971.pdf.

Ramirez Rancaño, Mario. "El socialismo en Tlaxcala 1926–1933." *Secuencia* 5 (1986): 62–80.

Redfield, Robert. "The Indian in Mexico," *The Annals of the American Academy of Political and Social Science* (1940): 132–43.

Reed, John. *Insurgent Mexico*. New York: International, 1969.

Rénique, Gerardo. "Race, Mestizaje and Nationalism: Sonora's Anti-Chinese Movement and State Formation in Post-Revolutionary Mexico." *Political Power and Social Theory* 14 (2000): 91–140.

Rippy, J. Fred. "A Negro Colonization Project in Mexico, 1895." *Journal of Negro History* 6 (1921): 66–73.

Ristow, Colby Nolan. "From Repression to Incorporation in Revolutionary Mexico: Identity Politics, Cultural Mediation, and Popular Revolution in Juchitan, Oaxaca, 1910–1920." PhD dissertation, Department of History, University of Chicago, 2008. ProQuest, 2008.

Robins, Nicholas A. *Native Insurgencies and the Genocidal Impulse in the Americas.* Bloomington: Indiana University Press, 2005.

Rockwell, Elsie. *Hacer escuela, hacer estado: La educación posrevolucionaria vista desde Tlaxcala.* Zamora, Mexico: Colegio de Michoacán, 2007.

Rodríguez, Abelardo L. *Memoria administrativa del gobierno del districto Norte de la Baja California, 1924–1927.* Mexicali: Secretaria de Educacion Publica, 1928.

Rodríguez, Eduardo. *Manual de Física General y Aplicada a la Agricultura y a la Industria,* Vol. 401. Madrid: Eusebio Aguado, 1858.

Roediger, David R. *The Wages of Whiteness: Race and the Making of the American Working Class.* London: Verso, 1999.

Romero, José M. *Comisión de Inmigración: Dictamen del Vocal Ingeniero José María Romero, Encargado de Estudiar la Influencia Social y Económica de La Inmigración Asiática en México.* Mexico City: Imprenta de A. Carranza e Hijos, 1911.

Romero, Matias. *Geographical and Statistical Notes on Mexico.* New York: Putnam's Sons, 1898.

Romero, Robert Chao. *The Chinese in Mexico, 1882–1940.* Tucson: University of Arizona Press, 2010.

Root, Elihu. *Charges against Lebbeus R. Wilfley, Judge of the United States Court for China, and Petition for His Removal from Office.* Washington, DC: Government Printing Office, 1908.

Ruiz Medrano, Ethelia. *Mexico's Indigenous Communities: Their Lands and Histories, 1500–2010.* Translated by Russ Davidson. Boulder: University Press of Colorado, 2010.

Said, Edward. *Orientalism.* New York: Vintage, 1979.

Santiago, Mark. *The Jar of Severed Hands: Spanish Deportation of Apache Prisoners of War, 1770–1810.* Norman: University of Oklahoma Press, 2011.

Satow, Armando. *7 Décadas: Confederación Deportiva Mexicana A.C.* Mexico City: CODEME, 2003.

Savarino, Franco. "The Sentinel of the Bravo: Italian Fascism in Mexico." *Totalitarian Movements and Political Religions* 2 (2001): 97–120.

Saxton, Alexander. *The Indispensable Enemy: Labor and the Anti-Chinese Movement in California.* Berkeley: University of California Press, 1971.

Schiavone-Camacho, Julia María. *Chinese Mexicans: Transpacific Migration and the Search for a Homeland, 1910–1960.* Chapel Hill: University of North Carolina, 2012.

Schröder, Ingo W., and Bettina E. Schmidt. "Introduction: Violent Imaginaries and Violent Practices." In *Anthropology of Violence and Conflict,* edited by Schmidt and Schröder, 1–24. New York: Routledge, 2001.

Secretaría de Comunicaciones y Obras Públicas. *Memoria Presentado al Congreso de la Unión.* Mexico City: Secretaria de Comunicaciones y Obras Publicas, 1907.

Secretaría de Desarrollo Agrario, Territorial y Urbano (SEDATU). "Las transformaciones del cardenismo." Mexico City, June 29, 2015. *SEDATU*. http://www.sedatu.gob.mx/sraweb/conoce-la-secretaria/historia/lastransformaciones-del-cardenismo/.

Secretaría de Educación Pública. *Algunos Datos y Opiniones sobre la educación sexual en México*. Mexico City: Secretaria de Educación Publica, 1934.

Seijas, Tatiana. *Asian Slaves in Colonial Mexico: From Chinos to Indians*. New York: Cambridge University Press, 2014.

Shah, Nayan. *Contagious Divides: Epidemics and Race in San Francisco's Chinatown*. Berkeley: University of California Press, 2001.

Siqueiros, Jose Luis. "La Nacionalidad Mexicana." In *Síntesis del Derecho Internacional Privado*, 611–21. Mexico City: Universidad Nacional Autónoma de Mexico, 1971.

Skocpol, Theda. *States and Social Revolutions: A Comparative Analysis of France, Russia, and China*. Cambridge: Cambridge University Press, 1979.

Slack, Edward, Jr. "The Chino in New Spain: A Corrective Lens for a Distorted Image." *Journal of World History* 20 (2009): 35–67.

Smith, Anthony. *Nationalism*. Cambridge: Polity Press, 2010.

Solano, Veronica Oikion. *Los hombres del poder en Michoacán, 1924–1962*. Zamora, Mexico: El Colegio de Michoacán, 2004.

Stern, Alexandra Minna. "Mestizofilia, biotipología, y eugenesia en el México postrevolucionario: Hacia una historia de la ciencia y el Estado." *Relaciones* 21 (2008): 57–92.

———. "Responsible Mothers and Normal Children: Eugenics, Nationalism, and Welfare in Post-Revolutionary Mexico, 1920–1940." *Journal of Historical Sociology* 12 (1999): 369–97.

Sue, Christina A. *Land of the Cosmic Race: Race Mixture, Racism, and Blackness in Mexico*. Oxford: Oxford University Press, 2013.

Tejada, Roberto. *National Camera: Photography and Mexico's Image Environment*. Minneapolis: University of Minnesota Press, 2009.

Tilley, Virginia. *Seeing Indians: A Study of Race, Nation, and Power in El Salvador*. Albuquerque: University of New Mexico Press, 2005.

Tilly, Charles. "Does Modernization Breed Revolution?" *Comparative Politics* 5 (1973): 425–47.

Topik, Steven. "The Revolution, the State, and Economic Development in Mexico." *History Compass* 3 (2005): 1–36.

Turner, John Kenneth. *Barbarous Mexico*. New York: C. H. Kerr, 1910.

Utley, Robert Marshall. *Frontiersmen in Blue: The United States Army and the Indian, 1848–1865*. Lincoln: University of Nebraska Press, 1981.

Valdés, Luz María. "XXV Aniversario del Consejo Nacional de Población." *Este País* 104 (1999): 1–7.

Valdés Lakowsky, Vera. *Vinculaciones Sino-Mexicanas: Albores y Testimonios, 1874–1899*. Mexico City: Universidad Nacional Autónoma de Mexico, 1981.

Vance, John Thomas, and Helen Lord Clagett. *A Guide to the Law and Legal Literature of Mexico*. Latin America Series 6. Washington, DC: Library of Congress, 1945.

Van Hoy, Teresa M. *A Social History of Mexico's Railroads.* Lanham, MD: Rowman, 2008.

Vargas, Antonio M., and Miguel A. Menéndez. "Memoria de la segunda convension nacional ordinaria del Partido nacional revolucionario efectuada en la ciudad de Querétaro del 3 al 6 de diciembre de 1933." Partido Nacional Revolucionario. Mexico City: La Impresora, 1934.

Vasconcelos, José. *La Raza Cósmica.* Translated by Didier T. Jaén. 1925. Baltimore: Johns Hopkins University Press, 1997.

Vásquez, Samuel. *Las locuras de Vasconcelos.* Los Angeles: Vasquez, 1929.

Vaughan, Mary K. "Cultural Approaches to Peasant Politics in the Mexican Revolution." Special Issue: Mexico's New Cultural History: Una Lucha Libre. *Hispanic American Historical Review* 79, no. 2 (1999): 269–305.

———. *Cultural Politics in Revolution: Teachers, Peasants and Schools in Mexico, 1930–1940.* Tucson: University of Arizona Press, 1997.

Velázquez Andrade, Manuel. *La educación sexual: lo que en México se ha hecho a este respecto.* Mexico City: Tipografica Económica, 1913.

Velázquez Morales, Catalina. "Diferencias políticas entre los inmigrantes chinos del noroeste de México (1920–1930), El caso de Francisco L. Yuen." *Historia Mexicana* 55 (2012): 461–512.

———. "Xenofobia y Racismo: Los Comités Antichinos en Sonora y Baja California, 1924–1936." *Meyibó* 1 (2010): 43–79.

Villegas, Daniel Cosio. *American Extremes.* Translated by Américo Paredes. Austin: University of Texas Press, 1964.

Vincent, Ted. "The Blacks Who Freed Mexico." *Journal of Negro History* 79, no. 3 (1994): 257–76.

Vinson, Ben, III. "The Racial Profile of a Rural Mexican Province in the 'Costa Chica': Igualapa in 1791." *The Americas* 57, no. 2 (2000): 269–82.

Vinson, Ben, and Matthew Restall. *Black Mexico: Race and Society from Colonial to Modern Times.* Albuquerque: University of New Mexico Press, 2009.

Wilfley, L., and A. Bassett. *Memorandum on the Law and the Facts in the Matter of the Claim of China against Mexico for Losses of Life and Property Suffered by Chinese Subjects at Torreón on May 13, 14, and 15, 1911.* Mexico City: American, 1911.

Wilkie, James W., with the collaboration of Michael Hammond. "Primera Reforma Agraria en Mexico, 1853–1909, a través de la Estadística Nacional." *Mexico and the World* 3, no. 3 (summer 1998).

Williams, J. *The Isthmus of Tehuantepec.* New York: Appleton, 1852.

Womack, John. *Zapata and the Mexican Revolution.* New York: Vintage, 2011.

Wong Kin. *International Chinese Business Directory of the World: A Comprehensive List of Prominent Chinese Firms and Individuals.* San Francisco: Chinese Business Directory, 1913.

Wu, Frank. "Where Are You Really From? Asian Americans and the Perpetual Foreigner Syndrome." *Civil Rights Journal* 6 (2002): 14.

Yankelevich, Pablo. "Extranjeros indeseables en Mexico (1911–1940): Una aproximación cuantitativa a la aplicación del artículo 33 constitutional." *Historia Mexicana* 53 (2004): 693–744.

Young, Elliot. *Alien Nation*. Chapel Hill: University of North Carolina Press, 2014.

Yu, Henry. "Global Migrants and the New Pacific Canada." *International Journal* 64 (2009): 1011–26.

Yun, Lisa. *Chinese Indentured Laborers and African Slaves in Cuba*. Philadelphia: Temple University Press, 2008.

Zertuche Muñoz, Fernando. *Ricardo Flores Magón: El Sueño Alternativo*. Mexico City: Fondo de Cultura Económica, 1995.

Zuleta, María Cecilia. "La Secretaría de Fomento y el Fomento Agrícola en México, 1876–1910: La Invención de una Agricultura Próspera Que No Fue." *Mundo Agrario* 1 (2000). http://ref.scielo.org/463mzw.

Index

JASON OLIVER CHANG is an assistant professor of history and Asian American studies at the University of Connecticut.

The Asian American Experience

The University of Illinois Press
is a founding member of the
Association of American University Presses.

———————————————————————

Composed in 10.25/14 Chaparral Pro
with Archer display
by Kirsten Dennison
at the University of Illinois Press
Cover designed by Dustin J. Hubbart
Cover illustration: KwangHo Shin, 29 *Untitled* (charcoal on
canvas, 72.5 × 60 cm), 2013

University of Illinois Press
1325 South Oak Street
Champaign, IL 61820-6903
www.press.uillinois.edu